# The Uprising of Women in Philanthropy

*The Uprising of Women in Philanthropy* tells the inspiring, never-before-told, story of the Global Women's Funding Movement—considered the women's movement's greatest secret—and how it enabled women from all walks of life to harness the power of money to free themselves from oppression.

Brimming with feminist epiphanies, this social justice playbook is an urgent call for women's collective leadership to guide humanity through the gravest of challenges, overcoming patriarchy's multi-millennium reign through the uprising of women leaders and philanthropists. Founded during the second-wave women's movement of the early 1970s, small groups of women across the world, independent of each other, had the same epiphany: it will take a movement of women to raise the money needed to fund women's freedom. Since then, the Global Women's Funding Movement has grown into a global network of radically generous, risk-taking philanthropists who collectively wield financial might to win seismic gender equality victories. The authors document the "Women Effect" that results from gender equality and women's collective leadership, including improved public health and reproductive justice, expanded public education, stronger democracies, resilient economies, climate recovery and enduring peace. The Global Women's Funding Movement is guided by its Feminist Funding Principles and, through them, it has innovated the most effective philanthropic practices, including trust-based philanthropy.

*The Uprising of Women in Philanthropy* is for those interested in focusing the power of philanthropy on leveraging systemic social justice victories and gender equality gains. The long-practiced Feminist Funding Principles imparted by the authors is a recipe for the feminist alchemy needed to transform society for the betterment of all.

**The Uprising of Women in Philanthropy** is written in a collective voice and is also, we believe, an important human rights document. It offers a roadmap to achieve a thriving democracy. This book marks the first time that women's rights philanthropists have united, in book form and in one voice, to call for massive investments in women's rights for social justice change. *The Uprising of Women in Philanthropy* will be an important addition to the works of the few, but highly influential, feminist collective authorships.

"Everyone who cares about making the world a kinder and safer place should know that the women's funding movement is doing exactly that. Read this book, take heart, and pass it on!"

**Gloria Steinem,** *Writer, Activist, and Feminist Organizer*

"My work as Executive Director of UN Women and UN Under-Secretary-General taught me that activism without money falls short of implementation. Women's funds and women's funding movements knew this a long time ago and this book gives a glimpse of the power of women's ability to pay forward."

**Phumzile Mlambo-Ngcuka,** *Former United Nations Under-Secretary-General and Executive Director of UN Women*

"Every person involved in philanthropy should read this book to truly understand the partnership of philanthropists and activists around the world in making radical and upending change. Change that puts justice at the center of how communities survive and thrive."

**Lori Barra,** *Executive Director, The Isabel Allende Foundation*

"By capturing the stories of the women's funding movement over the past 50 years, this book invites us to think more expansively about what is possible when philanthropy gets serious about resourcing the movements working on issues that affect the lives of women and their communities. It is a historical reminder of what can be done for anyone seeking to boldly shift how to fund feminist movements so communities can thrive."

**Teresa C. Younger,** *President and CEO, Ms. Foundation for Women*

"Women have been philanthropic actors and activists in the truest sense of those words for generations—in every part of the globe. Yet such philanthropy continues to be under-acknowledged at best. This book tells the important stories of the activism and impact of women's funds across the world in support of feminist and justice movements. Shine that light!"

**Theo Sowa,** *Former CEO, African Women's Development Fund*

"Fascinating stories about gender, power, and philanthropy. This book gives you a behind the scenes look at how the Global Women's Funding Movement weaves its way around the globe to support activists on the ground and reimagine philanthropy."

**PeiYao Chen,** *President and CEO, Global Fund for Women*

"The Women's Funding Movement is a game changer in the world of philanthropy and gender justice around the globe. If you want to know what, why, when, where, and how, this is the book to read. This is a movement that invites all of us to participate regardless of resources. Read and be inspired."

**Pat Mitchell,** *Co-Founder of ConnectedWomenLeaders and Project Dandelion, and author of* Becoming a Dangerous Woman: Embracing Risk to Change the World

"Women's funds understood long ago that real change can happen when intersectional feminist movements are sustained, connected, and trusted to lead the way and define what success looks like. This is an urgent lesson for philanthropy at large that is explored in this book."

**Giselle Carino,** *Founding CEO of Fòs Feminista*

"I witnessed brave women catapult the Global Women's Funding Movement into a new era. This book, akin to a financial Wonder Woman, testifies to women's power to use money for equity and justice. It inspires boldness and bravery, deeply rooted in listening and co-creation. It's a call to action for those who believe in change and a better future. So, gear up and join the uprising!"

**Lisa Witter,** *CEO, Apolitical Foundation and Co-Founder, Apolitical*

"Finally, a book that covers, with great care, the history, impact, and stunning success of the Global Women's Funding Movement. Sharing stories of the amazing work of these changemakers is inspiring and will serve as a clarion call to keep the movement strong. Now more than ever we need to be reminded of all that has been done to secure economic, legislative, and reproductive justice for women and girls and gender-expansive folks. Read this book and then get to work!"

**Mary F. Morten,** *President, Morten Group, LLC*

"For anyone interested in learning about the global impact of women and how women continue to be intentional, allocating personal funding into Women's Foundations, this important book will inspire them."

**Laura Davis,** *Managing Director, Banker, J.P. Morgan*

"This is the untold story of how the women's funding movement, with its unexpected partnerships, has changed lives around the world. A must-read for change makers!"

**Elizabeth Seja Min,** *Strategist, Storyteller, & Facilitator*

"Women do lead differently, and the Global Women's Funding Movement is a wonderful illustration for us all. This book is a must-read for anyone committed to building a new philanthropy; a new way of connecting generosity to the opportunity to make a difference. At the center of re-imagining philanthropy must be a woman's wisdom that integrates intersectionality, collaboration, and transparency, and this is the blueprint."

**Dr. Wanjiru Kamau-Rutenberg,** *Founder &*
*Executive Director, Black Women in Executive Leadership (B-WEL)*

"Women and girls matter, and yet if you look at the philanthropic funding that goes to this half of the population, you would not know it. Achieving equality requires big funding and that is what the Women's Funding Movement is all about. Big Change."

**Jacki Zehner,** *Founder, SheMoney, Co-Founder*
*Women Moving Millions and former Partner, Goldman Sachs*

"Women's financial equity drives the growth of women's philanthropy. With increasing financial power, millions more women want to join the millions already part of the 'uprising' in philanthropy. Get this book on your reading list and get re-energized about equity!"

**Diana van Maasdijk,** *Co-Founder & CEO, Equileap*

"Shifting money and power—how women have been leading the charge and creating a philanthropic movement birthed in the intersectionality of women's rights and human rights. Every person involved in philanthropy should read this book to see 50 years of examples of centering justice and communities."

**Tuti Scott,** *Coach and Facilitator, Changemaker Strategies*

# The Uprising of Women in Philanthropy

NDANA BOFU-TAWAMBA, RUBY BRIGHT,
STEPHANIE CLOHESY, CHRISTINE GRUMM,
MUSIMBI KANYORO, HELEN LAKELLY HUNT,
ANA OLIVEIRA, LAURA RISIMINI, JANE SLOANE,
AND JESSICA TOMLIN

Routledge
Taylor & Francis Group

LONDON AND NEW YORK

Designed cover image: andipantz / Getty Images

First published 2025
by Routledge
4 Park Square, Milton Park, Abingdon, Oxon OX14 4RN

and by Routledge
605 Third Avenue, New York, NY 10158

*Routledge is an imprint of the Taylor & Francis Group, an informa business*

*British Library Cataloguing-in-Publication Data*
A catalogue record for this book is available from the British Library

ISBN: 9781032361468 (hbk)
ISBN: 9781032361475 (pbk)
ISBN: 9781003330455 (ebk)

DOI: 10.4324/9781003330455

Typeset in Dante and Avenir
by Apex CoVantage, LLC

# Contents

# Acknowledgements

As we have worked to bring the many voices of the Global Women's Funding Movement together, we want to thank our ghostwriter, **Cristina Page**, who worked hard to ensure that the manuscript was representative and written in one collective voice. We also want to acknowledge our editor, **Karen Wolny**, for her wise, calm guidance and enduring support. We also want to acknowledge **Kavita N. Ramdas** who authored the afterword, and also served as a member of our Reading Cluster.

The Co-Authors came together nearly five years ago to launch this project, with a shared desire to capture the rich history of 50 years of the Global Women's Funding Movement. Each one has a powerful voice based on their multiple roles as women's fund leaders, activists and donors, and they have extensive community and/or philanthropic leadership experience. These are women leaders who have innovated, built, rescued, and rebuilt the infrastructure of the Global Women's Funding Movement. Many of the book's stories are told by these leaders from across the globe, doing the work that changes the world every day, in every way.

This book could not have been written with authenticity and integrity without all of these voices.

## Co-Author Committee

- **Ndana Bofu-Tawamba,** CEO, Urgent Action Fund Africa
- **Ruby Bright,** Past President and CEO, Women's Foundation for a Greater Memphis

- **Stephanie Clohesy,** Independent Consultant, past Board Chair, Women's Funding Network
- **Christine Grumm**, Independent Consultant and Past President and CEO, Women's Funding Network
- **Dr. Musimbi Kanyoro**, Former President and CEO, Global Fund for Women
- **Dr. Helen LaKelly Hunt,** Founder and President, HLH Family Foundation
- **Ana Oliveira,** President and CEO, The New York Women's Foundation
- **Laura Risimini,** Independent Consultant
- **Jane Sloane,** Senior Director, Women's Empowerment and Gender Equality with The Asia Foundation
- **Jessica Tomlin,** Chief Executive Director, Equality Fund

We would also like to acknowledge our Reading Cluster, seasoned leaders of the Global Women's Funding Movement, who reviewed drafts of each chapter, and provided insight and direction on the manuscript. Each of you provided incredible and nuanced guidance, and the final manuscript is undoubtedly stronger because of your contributions.

## Reading Cluster

- **Katherine Acey,** Former Executive Director, Astraea Lesbian Foundation for Justice
- **Giselle Carino,** CEO, Fòs Feminista
- **Patti Chang,** CEO and Co-Founder, Feed the Hunger Fund
- **Sarah Haacke Byrd,** CEO, Women Moving Millions
- **Surina Khan,** CEO Emerita and Strategic Advisor, Women's Foundation California
- **Latanya Mapp Frett,** Immediate Past President and CEO, Global Fund for Women
- **Mary Morten,** President, Morten Group, LLC
- **Muadi Mukenge,** Senior Director of External Affairs, MADRE
- **Gloria Perez**, President and Chief Executive Officer, Women's Foundation of Minnesota
- **Kavita N. Ramdas**, Independent Feminist Advisor, KNR Sisters Consulting
- **Tuti Scott,** President, Changemaker Strategies
- **Rita Thapa,** Founder of Tewa

## Donor Collective

We want to give special thanks to the visionary donors to this book project, without whose support this book would not be possible. Through their financial gifts, they stood boldly side by side with the Co-Authors, editors, and readers in believing that the telling of this narrative at this time and place was critical for the current and future story of the Global Women's Funding Movement. We want to thank **Anne Delaney, HLH Foundation, Jacki Zehner, Katie Bouton, Kiersten Marek/Philanthropy Women, Ms. Foundation for Women, The New York Women's Foundation, and the Women's Foundation for a Greater Memphis**.

## Research Interns

We would also like to thank **Hadley Wilhoite**, our dedicated Research Intern, who provided countless hours of support to the development of the book and hand-selected many of the stories seen throughout. We would also like to thank our other research interns, **Mackenzie Barnes, Ximena Dilworth Velazquez**, and **Emily Roat** from Goucher College.

# About the Authors

The authors of *The Uprising of Women in Philanthropy* go by the title of the Co-Author Committee, and collaborated with a professional ghostwriter and editor to ensure that the manuscript had a cohesive and polished voice.

## Co-Author Biographies

(in alphabetical order)

**Ndanatsei Bofu-Tawamba** is the CEO of Urgent Action Fund Africa (UAF-Africa). She brings to the global human and womn's rights movements a wealth of international experience across a broad spectrum of equity-focused issues. For over two decades, Ndana has built bridges between civil society and social justice funders to address gender, racial, socio-political, economic, environmental and climate injustices. Ndana is a staunch feminist voice for enhanced womn's rights investments. She has leveraged over US$200 million towards strengthening African feminist and womn's rights movements. She is a published writer and public speaker on Pan-African and Feminist Philanthropies, African Womn's Leadership, and the Power of Social Movements in Africa.

**Ruby Bright** recently retired from the Women's Foundation for a Greater Memphis, as its President and CEO, after serving over 22 years of leadership. Under her tenure, the Women's Foundation invested over $35 million in 560 programs involving more than 182 local nonprofits, and Bright guided the organization's effort across the state in response to the COVID pandemic to distribute $12 million in funds to support local organizations. She currently serves on the board of ThinkTennessee, as the Honorary Co-Chair of the Ida B. Wells Memorial Committee in Memphis, and as an honorary co-chair for the Racial and Equity taskforce with Tennessee Nonprofit Network. Bright's awards include the 2015 Super Women in Business Award, the 2017 Girl Scouts One Smart Cookie Award, the 2017 Memphis Heritage Trail Trailblazers Award, Memphis Business Journal 100 Most Influential Memphians, 2021 Memphis Power Player, and 2022 Memphis Business Journal Power 100 consecutively for over a decade. She has also served as board chair of the Women's Funding Network. She has received the Ms. Foundation 2022 Woman of Vision Award and additional honors from Memphis Urban League and the U.S. Department of Housing and Urban Development. In 2023, she received the Shelby County Tennessee Alumnae Chapter Community Pioneer Economic Development Award.

**Stephanie Clohesy** is a lifelong activist for human rights and social justice, especially for women and girls. She has been a major force in the development and growth of Women's Funds throughout the U.S. and worldwide: She has founded, counseled, and/or governed more than 50 women's funds. She also supports mainstream funders to allocate more resources to social justice and benefiting women and girls and all those seeking equity. She led the NOW Legal Defense and Education Fund early in her career and worked for the W.K. Kellogg Foundation as a senior program director. A consultant since 1992, she has assisted social sector leaders, donors, and entrepreneurs in reaching their bold goals by accelerating their organizations toward high performance and momentous impact. As an author and co-author, she has reported on and created tools for gaining leverage from wide-ranging changes and trends in philanthropy. In the transition from the twentieth into the twenty-first century, her reports and articles cover, for example: the re-invention of philanthropy through the tech and financial booms; innovations in women's philanthropy participation; the acknowledgement of the importance of women's experiences at the edges and ultimately turning traditional philanthropic norms upside down. Stephanie has invented programs and tools to enable the nonprofit sector to grow stronger institutions for long-term change.

**Chris Grumm** was the CEO/President of the Women's Funding Network (WFN) from 2000–2011. During her tenure, the membership grew from 75 to over 160 funds with assets of over $500 million. She is the co-founder, with Helen LaKelly Hunt, of the first Women Moving Millions Campaign. In partnership with Women's Funds, the campaign raised over $200 million. Prior to WFN, Chris was the Executive Director of the Chicago Foundation for Women. She has served as the first Vice-President of the newly formed Evangelical Lutheran Church in America and as the Deputy General Secretary of the Lutheran World Federation in Geneva, Switzerland. She works with organizations in local, national, and global settings building agendas for gender/social justice. One of her passions is the investment in women, girls, and gender-expansive people and, through that investment, changing whole communities. She is an Alinsky-trained community organizer and health educator and throughout her career has worked on behalf of reproductive rights and justice. Currently, she is consulting through her company, Chris Grumm Consulting Group.

**Dr. Helen LaKelly Hunt**, Ph.D., is one in a small group of women who helped seed the Women's Funding Movement. She co-founded the Texas Women's Foundation, The New York Women's Foundation, Women's Funding Network, and Women Moving Millions. Helen is the author of *Faith and Feminism: A Holy Alliance* and *Sister Wisdom: Women of Faith, Fortitude, and Inspiration*. Her book *And the Spirit Moved Them: The Lost Radical History of America's First Feminists* shares the inspiring story of the abolitionist feminists. Helen was inducted into the National Women's Hall of Fame in 2001.

Helen and her husband of 30 years, Harville Hendrix, Ph.D., are internationally respected couple's therapists, educators, and speakers, and *New York Times* bestselling authors. Together, they have written over ten books with more than four million copies sold, including the timeless classic *Getting the Love You Want: A Guide for Couples*. Harville and Helen co-created Imago Relationship Therapy, which teaches Dialogue to promote connected relationships. They are the co-founders of Imago Relationships International, a nonprofit organization that has trained over 2,000 therapists and educators in 51 countries around the world. Eight years ago, Harville and Helen started Safe Conversations LLC to bring Dialogical skills to communities everywhere. The business is now called Quantum Connections LLC.

**Dr. Musimbi Kanyoro** is currently the Board Chair of United World Colleges and CARE International Supervisory Board. She is also a member of the Council of the London School of Economics and chairs its Ethics Committee. In addition, Musimbi is a Board Member of United

Nations Global Compact and also serves as a Senior Gender Advisor for its accelerator, Target Gender Equality.

Musimbi Kanyoro was President and CEO of the Global Fund for Women (2011–2019). Prior to that, she was the Director of Population and Reproductive Health at the David and Lucile Packard Foundation. Before moving to the USA in 2007, Musimbi spent 20 years in Geneva, Switzerland, where she worked for Lutheran World Federation for ten years as Executive Secretary for Women in Church and Society and, thereafter, was appointed as General Secretary of the World YWCA in 1998, a position she held for a decade.

Musimbi is a frequent public speaker and has written and published on women's human rights, gender, philanthropy, and theology. She facilitates many dialogues and mentorship programs for emerging leaders, including Circle of Concerned African Women Theologians, Homeward Bound, and WEAfrica.

**Ana Oliveira** is President and CEO of The New York Women's Foundation. Since 2006, Ana has increased in the Foundation's grantmaking from $1.7 million to $11 million annually. In its 36 years, The Foundation has distributed $125 million to over 350 organizations working to advance economic, gender, and racial justice. Ana sits on the Independent Commission to Study Criminal Justice Reform in NYC, and is a Board member of Sanctuary for Families and of Point Source Youth. She is part of Women of Color in Philanthropy Advisory Board and a member of Prospect Hill Foundation's Program Committee. She is a past board member of Philanthropy New York, and a past chair of WFN. She holds an MA in Medical Anthropology and a Ph.D. (Hon.) from the New School. She was born and raised in São Paulo, Brasil, and lives in New York City. Formerly, Ana was CEO of the Gay Men's Health Crisis.

**Laura Risimini** currently serves as the Director of Grants for the Amplify Her Foundation, a private grantmaking foundation supporting women and girls from underserved communities to become transformative changemakers. Her previous roles included serving as the Managing Director of the Purpose Foundation, a start-up organization serving as a fiscal sponsor for social impact campaigns and organizations; and Foundation Manager of the HLH Family Foundation, formerly known as The Sister Fund. Throughout her career, Laura has had the unique opportunity to support organizations in all areas of their lifecycle from start-up to sunset. She specializes in building nonprofit operating and programmatic structures and designing and implementing grant cycles aligned with feminist and trust-based funding principles.

**Jane Sloane** is Senior Director, Women's Empowerment and Gender Equality with The Asia Foundation based in San Francisco. Jane's previous roles include Vice President of Programs, Global Fund for Women, Vice President of Development, Women's World Banking, and Executive Director, International Women's Development Agency. Jane is a Trustee of Practical Action (UK) and is a Senior Atlantic Fellow with the Inequalities Institute at The London School of Economics and The Atlantic Institute, Oxford. She is a recipient of a Distinguished Alumni Award from the University of Adelaide, an Alumni Award for Service to Humanity from the University of Sydney, a Global Ambassadors Award from the Advance Foundation, a Woman of Distinction Award from the Asia Pacific Women's Business Council, a Churchill Fellowship, and a Human Rights Medal from the Vietnam Women's Union. Jane holds a bachelor's degree in history (Hons) from the University of Adelaide, a master's degree in Peace and Conflict Studies from the University of Sydney, and an Honorary Doctorate from the University of Adelaide.

**Jess Tomlin** is the CEO of the Equality Fund. In this role, Jess leads an effort to resource women's organizations around the world working to change systems, shift power, and dismantle barriers. Through feminist philanthropy, gender lens investing, storytelling, and advocacy, the Equality Fund backs the game-changing solutions to gender inequality at scale. Jess has worked in Sub-Saharan Africa, the Middle East, and Asia for a range of actors including the World Bank, the United Nations, and CARE Canada. Prior to her role with the Equality Fund, Jess led the re-creation of the MATCH International Women's Fund—Canada's only global fund for women— an organization that invested in women's rights movements in over 40 countries around the world. Jess was named by the Stevie Awards as 2017's Most Innovative Woman of the Year and is a recipient of the Women of Influence award in 2020. Jess has an undergraduate degree in Women's Studies in addition to a master's degree in Leadership.

The following individuals provided early thought leadership toward the development of the book, conceptualizing content, themes, and chapters. We are grateful for their early contributions to this project.

- **Emilienne De León Aulina,** immediate past Executive Director of Prospera, the International Network of Women's Funds
- **Cynthia Nimmo,** immediate past President and CEO of the Women's Funding Network
- **Gloria Steinem,** writer, political activist, and feminist organizer

# Contributors

We would like to acknowledge our dedicated writing team.

## Ghostwriter

**Cristina Page** has published two influential feminist books: *How the Pro-Choice Movement Saved America: Freedom, Politics and the War on Sex* (Basic Books), which was voted one of the 30 most important nonfiction feminist books of all time by readers of *Ms.*, and *The Smart Girl's Guide to College* (Farrar, Straus, and Giroux), the first in a genre of "smart girl" guides. Cristina's op-eds have appeared in *The New York Times*, *Time Magazine*, the *Chicago Tribune*, the *Baltimore Sun*, *Newsday*, *The Guardian, UK*, among many others.

## Editor

**Karen Wolny** is an editor with over three decades of book publishing experience. As the founder of Narrative Instincts, she provides editorial services for new and established authors of serious nonfiction. This includes everything from initial consults, writing book proposals, to developing and editing full manuscripts.

## Interviews

We would like to acknowledge the following individuals who provided an interview for this book.

**Hakima Abbas**
Founder, Black Feminist Fund

**Katherine Acey**
Former Executive Director, Astraea Lesbian Foundation for Justice

**Paige Andrew**
Chief of Programs Grantmaking and Operations, FRIDA

**Bettina Baldeschi**
CEO, International Women's Development Agency

**Elizabeth Barajas-Román**
President and CEO, Women's Funding Network

**Felicia Davis Blakley**
Former President and CEO, Chicago Foundation for Women

**Ndana Bofu-Tawamba**
CEO, Urgent Action Fund Africa

**Ise Bosch**
Founder, filia.die frauenstiftung

**Ruby Bright**
Immediate past President and CEO, Women's Foundation for a Greater Memphis

**Linda Calhoun**
Founder and Executive Producer, Career Girls, and Member of Women Moving Millions

**Giselle Carino**
CEO, Fòs Feminista

**Lauren Y. Casteel**
President and CEO, The Women's Foundation of Colorado

**Patti Chang**
CEO and Co-Founder, Feed The Hunger Fund

**Stephanie Clohesy**
Independent Consultant and past Board Chair, Women's Funding Network

**Michelle Coffey**
Executive Director, Lambent Foundation

**Paul-Gilbert Colletaz**
Former Coordinator, Red Umbrella Fund

**Meghan Cummings**
Former Executive Director, Women's Fund of Greater Cincinnati Foundation

**Anne Delaney**
Donor, The New York Women's Foundation, and Member of Women Moving Millions

**Abigail Disney**
Donor, The New York Women's Foundation, and Member of Women Moving Millions

**Jessyca Dudley**
Co-Founder, Queenmakers / South Side Giving Circle

**Amalia E. Fischer**
Founder of ELAS+ and Giving for Change

**Rose Flenorl**
Donor, Women's Foundation for a Greater Memphis

**Kerry Gardner**
Co-Chair of the Board of Directors, International Women's Development Agency

**Alexandra Garita**
Executive Director, Prospera International Network of Women's Funds

**Tracy Gary**
Philanthropic and Legacy Advisor

**Christian Giraldo**
Former Director of Programs, Third Wave Fund

**Sara Gould**
Former President and CEO, Ms. Foundation for Women, New York

**Christine Grumm**
Independent Consultant and Former President and CEO, Women's Funding Network

**Jessica Horn**
Regional Director—East Africa, Ford Foundation

**Jessica Houssian**
Former Co-Chief Executive Director, Equality Fund

**Helen LaKelly Hunt**
Founder and President, HLH Family Foundation

**Dena L. Jackson, Ph.D**.
Former Chief Strategy Officer, Texas Women's Foundation

**Coco Jervis**
Director of Programmes, Mama Cash

**Dr. Musimbi Kanyoro**
Former President and CEO, Global Fund for Women

**Surina Khan**
CEO Emerita and Strategic Advisor Women's Foundation California

**Carla López**
Executive Director of Fondo Centroamericano de Mujeres

**Latanya Mapp Frett**
Immediate past President and CEO, Global Fund for Women

**Mukami Marete**
Co-Executive Director, UHAI EASHRI

**Mary McDaniel**
Donor, Women's Foundation for a Greater Memphis

**Alicia Miller**
Executive Director, Women's Fund of Greater Cincinnati Foundation

**Françoise Moudouthe**
CEO, African Women's Development Fund

**Esther Mwaura Muiru**
Founder, GROOTS Kenya

**Muadi Mukenge**
Senior Director of External Affairs, MADRE

**Anne Firth Murray**
Founding President of the Global Fund for Women and Consulting Professor
at Stanford University

**Ana Oliveira**
President, The New York Women's Foundation

**Kenedy A. Owiti**
Knowledge, Evaluation and Learning Officer, UHAI EASHRI

**Gloria Perez**
President and Chief Executive Officer, Women's Foundation of Minnesota

**Kavita N. Ramdas**
Principal, KNR Sisters Consulting and former President and CEO, Global Fund for Women

**Michelle Reddy**
Co-Lead, Pacific Feminist Fund

**Vera Rodriguez**
Programme Associate, Red Umbrella Fund

**Caroline Sakina Brac de la Perrière**
Executive Director, Mediterranean Women's Fund

**Claudia Samcam**
Development and Program Coordinator, Fondo Centroamericano de Mujeres

**Tuti Scott**
President, Changemaker Strategies

**Mona Sinha**
Global Executive Director of Equality Now and former Board Chair, Women Moving Millions

**Jane Sloane**
Senior Director, Women's Empowerment and Gender Equality, The Asia Foundation

**Rita Thapa**
Founder of Tewa

**Jessica Tomlin**
Chief Executive Director, Equality Fund

**Tania Turner**
Former Executive Director, Fondo Semillas

**K.K. Verdade**
Former Executive Director of ELAS+ and Giving for Change

**Bia Vieira**
CEO, Women's Foundation California

**Dawn Oliver Wiand**
Former President & CEO, Iowa Women's Foundation

**Jacki Zehner**
Founder, SheMoney, Co-Founder Women Moving Millions, and former Partner, Goldman Sachs

# Preface

Books stop time for the reader.

In exchange for your attention, books animate a moment in time so that readers can get a sense of a complex landscape that is not otherwise visible or well known.

The challenge of this book—despite its static form—is to describe a historical movement that is alive and surging and still evolving. It aims to immerse readers in the past while also looking toward the near future to fully grasp the broader implications of a complex global movement whose influence spans multiple geographies comprised of diverse communities and cultures, all driven by myriad goals and purposes. By weaving together intersecting and shared journeys captured through a diverse ensemble of shared voices, this book breathes life into a world that might otherwise seem hidden from view. The world of women's philanthropy has many surprises and even more shocking truths that are revealed through acts of courage and defiance. *The Uprising of Women in Philanthropy* is a book that will elevate your appreciation of what has been and still needs to be accomplished.

It tells the story of the Global Women's Funding Movement as its own unique cause that parallels and supports women's movements all over the world which serve as social justice innovators for women, girls, and gender-expansive people. *The Uprising in Women's Philanthropy* has gathered many voices to tell the origin stories of how the Global Women's Funding Movement began over 50 years ago, embedded in the women's movement, and how it grew into its own distinctive movement. More importantly, it focuses on how women have amassed and currently use money to wield the necessary power to achieve equity and justice in the world. Although the Global Women's Funding Movement is about money and power, it is not about the financial power of the individual. Rather, it's the revelation of how collectively that money is applied to support the women, girls, and gender-expansive people doing the hard work across continents and communities, wherever justice is threatened in the lives of all people.

To truly understand the Global Women's Funding Movement, it would be ideal to hear and see what has been happening everywhere at once. *The Uprising of Women in Philanthropy* comes as close as possible to conveying the extensive human drama of building a funding movement. This movement has turned traditional philanthropic norms upside down while venturing into the challenging and often dangerous edges of women's lives where change is most needed and where few, if any other, philanthropists dare to tread!

To attempt to tell a story everywhere all at once, many voices have been included so that a diverse set of experiences and their collective wisdom could be highlighted here. A core group of women's funding activists / writers / observers gathered and grew into a group of nine Co-Authors who conceptualized and designed the overall story. They are:

- Ndana Bofu-Tawamba, CEO, Urgent Action Fund Africa
- Ruby Bright, Past President and CEO, Women's Foundation for a Greater Memphis
- Stephanie Clohesy, Independent Consultant, former Board Chair, Women's Funding Network
- Christine Grumm, Independent Consultant and Past President and CEO, Women's Funding Network
- Dr. Musimbi Kanyoro, Former President and CEO, Global Fund for Women
- Helen LaKelly Hunt, Founder and President, HLH Family Foundation
- Ana Oliveira, President and CEO, The New York Women's Foundation
- Laura Risimini, Independent Consultant
- Jane Sloane, Senior Director, Women's Empowerment and Gender Equality with The Asia Foundation
- Jessica Tomlin, Chief Executive Director, Equality Fund

Over the course of this project, they in turn reached out to other innovators and eyewitnesses with first-hand experience in the Global Women's Funding Movement; some are quoted in the book, some served as critical readers and advisors on early drafts, and all shaped and reshaped the stories to produce as robust and honest a narrative as possible.

The book chapters tangle with the same struggles and ethical knots faced by those building this movement every day. At all times, there are strains to resolve power dynamics and maintain close working relationships and clear communications. Power relationships define inclusion and exclusion, and can arbitrate who is at the center, who is at the periphery, and who decides who leads and who follows. In the very nature of the writing process, the Co-Authors, writers, and editors felt the burden of power in organizing the telling of the story: whether discussing whom to approach as readers, which stories were the best to include, and which concepts and whose exactly matter most—all these dilemmas mirror movement-based power struggles.

It is easy to fall into the "never-before-told" gap especially when narrating something as innovative as the Global Women's Funding Movement. But this movement has authenticity in its evolution, especially as every community, region, and culture has defined its own struggle for equity while holding to movement-wide ideals about equity and justice to build its women's foundation. The Co-Authors hope that this book will serve as a catalyst that opens and refreshes assumptions and questions. To do this, the process of reflection and refreshing our values needs to continue to happen with donors, with women's foundations, and with movements on the ground. Movement building is a constant process of reflection. It also encourages the willingness to embrace an open paradigm where searching for better solutions is more meaningful than relying on an authoritarian process or set of answers. Everyone in the Global Women's Funding Movement lives with the paradox of being egalitarian and participatory while also being strategic and coordinated in the search for implementing equity and justice.

The process of writing this book has been a mirror of how this movement struggles to find all the voices and then move things forward. The Global Women's Funding Movement has been innovating a new kind of philanthropy—one that has its roots throughout the ages—in how women come together to gather and share resources. The movement is guided by the voices of experience who have organized and formalized women's "share culture" by creating women's funds, foundations, giving circles, and giving networks around the world. The idea of sharing money, property, and other assets is new in comparison to the bureaucratic models of philanthropy common in our era. Moreover, it is shaped by egalitarian and participatory values, a belief that all people have gifts to share within flatter organizational models that help things to happen faster. To accomplish this, the women leading their own funding movement have normalized the practices of trust, transparency, shared power, intersectionality of racism, colonialism, sexism, sexual orientation, disability, classism, and casteism in ways that upend traditional philanthropy. The Global Women's Funding

Movement has done this work with limited financial resources, but explosive organizing, leadership, and authentic analysis of both problems and solutions from the ground up.

This movement has provided traditional philanthropy with many of its current ideas and organizing tactics for incorporating participatory philanthropy, though there usually has been no visible tie between mainstream and women's philanthropy. Practices proven by women's funds usually are described within a different lexicon, thereby enabling others to wave away the visibility of women's funds around the world. Recently, this trend has begun to change, with women's funds receiving overdue recognition as well as increased resources. This book of voices from everywhere lifts the veil on how things get done and how effective change occurs with women's philanthropic support. These are the stories from a quiet revolution created in the partnership between women at the source of a social injustice and women's foundations and donors. A sampling of stories to be found in the book includes:

- **Safetipin,** a social organization working with urban stakeholders including governments to make public spaces safer and more inclusive for women. Piloted in India, with seed funding from the Lotus Circle, supporting the Women's Empowerment Program of the Asia Foundation, the project can now be found in 18 countries.
- **The Dr. Beatriz María Solís Policy Institute at the Women's Foundation California,** which trains women community leaders in public policy and has worked to conceptualize and pass over 50 new pro-women laws or local policies in the state of California.
- **The Marea Verde, or "Green Wave" women's movement** that worked for years to legalize abortion across Latin America has been supported by women's funds such as the International Women's Health Coalition, Fòs Feminista.
- **Women's Foundation of Minnesota**'s funding support and leadership for the passage of the Safe Harbor Law and No Wrong Door, for sexually exploited youth.
- **Women of Liberia Mass Action for Peace**. In 2002, Leymah Gbowee negotiated a grant from the Global Fund for Women for the Women of Liberia's Mass Action for Peace. In Leymah's words, "We women, we are tired of war." Over time, the women organized collaborative efforts that led to reformers winning the war and electing the first woman President (Ellen Johnson Sirleaf) of Liberia.

All these stories and dozens more are told in exciting and graphic detail throughout the book. They are just a few illustrations of the vast quantity of past and present work going on in the hundreds of women's funds worldwide. By choice and deliberate strategy, women's funds have claimed roles at the forefront in bloody wars, face-to-face conflict with dangerous authoritarian leaders, and investigations in life-threatening zones where women are disappearing, while also attending to the everyday and pervasive barriers of jobs, food security, housing, childcare, healthcare, etc. that block women from full participation. Women's funds have trusted women to tell the truth about their own lives and then build the action strategies from those truths, whether that results in local change or an advancement in international law.

The bright threads throughout this book focus on the future of social justice work via the creation of successful and fast-paced change that benefits the people most affected by injustice and oppression. The success and speed of so much women's funding characterize how women's funds take action with their partners and how the mostly place-based organizing tactics, relationships, and leadership of women, girls, and gender-expansive people all come together as part of the action design. Women's funds believe that a community of women leaders more fully understands the depth and breadth of the problems and solutions than any single or small group of leaders. And they believe that, with adequate resources, they can solve the vast majority of the world's problems from the ground up.

Read this book with a vision in mind of a world with fewer problems, more diverse leadership, more equitable sharing of resources, and a willingness to get engaged with the entire ethos of the women's funding movement. We invite you to add your voice to this growing movement by **funding** your local women's fund/foundation, **acting** to advance gender justice activism globally, and/or **telling** the story of how women's funds changed philanthropy and the world. With an abundance of energy, the world needs you to do all three. If you are already involved, use your voice to tell new stories and share them with us.

Christine Grumm and Stephanie Clohesy, on behalf of the Co-Authors.

# Uprising

1

## The Global Women's Funding Movement Emerges

## Beginnings

We live in an era of inspiring women's movements. Today, women, girls, and gender-expansive people are uniting in unprecedented numbers, forming diverse coalitions that are dynamic, agile, and highly effective in addressing humanity's most pressing and deeply rooted problems. Today's women's movements, some well established and others newly forming, amount to the greatest force ever summoned against gender inequity, patriarchy, racial injustice, economic injustice, autocracy, violence, and climate collapse. Crucially, women's movements are modeling through their practices and building through their impact a vision for an equitable and just world. The emergence of so many women's movements today and their rapid spread across the globe is in response to the rising rates of catastrophe, growing inequality, especially gender inequality, and escalating threats to democracy. It also reflects a growing desire for female autonomy and voice, and a growing sense of self-worth that is manifesting across the planet.

Throughout millennia, women have united out of necessity and become the primary forces committed to undoing patriarchy's self-serving systems and forging a vision for a reimagined world. This was true of the first known women's movement, the Female Fury at the Forum, in 195 BC,[1] when single Roman women united to demand their financial freedom. It was true of the Women's March on Versailles in 1789, when women united to fight famine and ignited the French Revolution, triggering a global wave of democracy that continues today. It is true of the Nigerian women's movement against British colonial rule, which under the leadership of Funmilayo Ransome-Kuti challenged taxation and mobilized over 20,000 women as a formidable resistance that helped

DOI: 10.4324/9781003330455-1

bring an end to British rule.[2] It is true of the fierce modern-day women-led movements, including #MeToo, #BlackLivesMatter, #NiaUnaMenos, the Kandakas, and #MahsaAmini, that tackle oppressive social norms, making society more understanding to women's needs and rights.

History has proven that seismic women's rights victories—like voting rights, reproductive rights, pay equity, the right to live free of violence, and greater political representation—trigger additional social benefits that improve the population's health, spur economic prosperity, increase education levels, reduce violence, and save lives. Gender equality can be a steadying force in a world in crisis, leads to more robust democracies and more enduring peace among and within families, communities, and nations, and offers a strong mitigating factor for climate response.

## The Woman Effect

Dismantling patriarchy in all forms, including misogyny, white supremacy, other race-based supremacies, heteronormativity, imperialism, autocracy, and colonialism, is critical to achieving transformational social, gender, racial, and economic justice. Humanity's survival through the formidable challenges ahead depends on achieving wide-scale social stability and securing peace within and among nations. Gender equality is the social salve the world desperately needs.

The Global Women's Funding Movement coined a term to explain this phenomenon—the "Woman Effect." Today, it may be called the "Feminist Effect." It's the correlation of transformational social healing and democracy strengthening that happens with gender-inclusive feminist approaches to critical issues and opportunities. For example, national security is moored to women's rights. The more significant the gender gap between the treatment of men and women in a society, the more likely a country is to be involved in war.[3] Countries that oppress women are typically the ones to instigate conflicts and wage higher levels of violence when in them. Conversely, countries with protections from gender-based violence are vastly more secure in myriad ways, whether the issue is food security, risk of terrorism, or the peaceful resolution of disputes with other nations.[4]

Women's voting rights, reproductive and LGBTQIA+ rights, women's and girls' access to education, legal equity, freedom from violence, and widespread economic independence all took tenacious women's movements, some persisting for a century, to achieve progress. Massive gender justice victories have only ever been won by the insistence of women's and feminist movements as described in the next section of this chapter.

The World Economic Forum in its review of economic research spanning centuries 1500–1900, uncovered a relationship between women's independence and the strength of economies. In their article "Gender equality isn't just moral—it's also good economics," researchers Alexandra de Pleijt and Jörg Baten report: "The empirical results suggest that economies with more female autonomy became (or remained) superstars in economic development. Institutions that excluded women from developing human capital, such as early marriage, prevented many economies from being successful in human history."[5] In other words, gender equity is often linked to rapid economic growth. As an example, Botswana had the highest GDP growth rates of the most recent decades after reaching its highest rates of women's equity.[6]

Gender justice is a reliable indicator of the health of a democracy. Established in 2000, the Community of Democracies (CoD) is a global intergovernmental coalition comprised of the Governing Council Member States that support adherence to common democratic values.[7] CoD Member States work together to identify global priorities to advance and defend democracy. In 2017, they commissioned a detailed survey of the existing empirical literature and discovered that democracy and gender equity have a symbiotic, mutually reinforcing relationship. Researcher Ted Piccone writes:

> [H]igher levels of gender equality are strongly correlated with a nation's relative peace, a healthier domestic security environment, and lower levels of aggression toward other states. Strategies to strengthen democracy and human rights, therefore, should emphasize women's empowerment, accountability for violence against women and girls, and closing the political and economic gender gap.[7]

The link between democracy and domestic tranquility only holds if an increase in gender equity accompanies democracy. Peace, of course, matters to every culture in every country. Women, however, have an added interest in seeing peace prevail since they are increasingly the casualties of war.

## The Power of Autonomous Feminist Movements

There is also another influential factor that contributes to and is documented by researchers—the role of autonomous feminist movements. In their cross-national study of 70 countries across six continents and four decades, Htun and Weldon (2018) found that "a strong, autonomous feminist movement is both substantively and statistically significant as a predictor of government action to redress violence against women across all models." In fact, national autonomous feminist movements are a stronger predictor of legal and policy reform at the national level related to violence against women than the number of women in parliament, the presence/influence of leftist parties, or national wealth. The large number of countries and the time covered allows this study to draw robust conclusions about the impact of movements. Analyzing data from 1975 to 2005, Htun and Weldon further explain that "movements are critical catalysts for policy development in all years, though their efforts are supplemented by policy machinery, international norms, and other factors."[8] Regarding organized efforts to bring accountability for violence against women, [national] autonomous feminist movements ensure that institutional reforms live up to the potential imagined by activists who demanded them and ensure that "words become deeds."[9]

And yet patriarchy's power remains steadfast despite the massive advancements women have made over the last century. Men retain control of every social system: government, culture, business, finance, and religion. Yet women persevere. As women amass power, patriarchy's tactics to maintain control escalate, but the nature of these intensifying attacks is often highly predictable. For example, they almost always involve a salvo against reproductive rights—striking at the foundation of women's autonomy—which we are currently witnessing to an unprecedented degree. "Opposing women's right to control our own bodies is always the first step in every authoritarian regime," says Gloria Steinem.[10]

Throughout time, every significant advancement for women—including suffrage, women's legal rights, girls' access to education, protections from gender-based violence, and the invention and legalization of birth control—happened because of women's movements, which were funded by women philanthropists who invested their own money to drive those victories home.[11] One of the reasons the American feminist movements that began in the 1970s have thrived and grown into continuously stronger and larger waves of feminism ever since is because of the best-kept secret of the women's movement—the most powerful social justice tool of our time—a women-designed philanthropic innovation called the Global Women's Funding Movement.

The Global Women's Funding Movement is a worldwide network of women's funds that power gender equity and social justice movements with money and resources, focusing on the needs and concerns of women, girls, and gender-expansive people everywhere. Although most women's funds are public charities, they can also be private. Today, women's funds (sometimes they are called women's foundations) are typically public, non-profit funds that are led and governed by people who identify as ciswomen, transwomen, and non-binary people, whose primary purpose is to challenge dominant power structures by moving money, power, voice, and resources to efforts that are led by and advance the leadership and the empowerment of marginalized genders, including marginalized genders from Black, Indigenous, and communities of color.

By reconceptualizing philanthropy, redefining issues, and radically sharing power and learnings to leverage resources, amplify diverse voices, and fund movements for gender justice, women's funds are shifting power, norms, voice, policies, and resources and demonstrating that a transformed world is possible and, indeed, is underway.

The Global Women's Funding Movement has a feminist ethos as its guiding principle. As Srilatha Batliwala states, "Feminism stands for power to, not power over. We struggle to change the practice of power both within our own structures and movements as well as in the social, economic, and political institutions we engage."[12] In the words of bell hooks:

> Feminism is a *movement* to end sexism, sexist exploitation, and oppression. Feminism is not anti-men; rather, it's anti-discrimination (of all kinds); it's anti-patriarchy, it's anti-sexism[13] and with a positive focus on realizing a peaceful, just, creative and equitable world free of violence for all.[14]

Ndana Bofu-Tawamba, CEO of Urgent Action Fund Africa (UAF-Africa), reflects:

> When we're talking about feminism, it is an ideology. But within that ideology, it is driven and facilitated by values and principles. It is those values and principles that are seeking to bring about equity, transparency, accountability, and equality. Equity and equality, and above all, seeking to bring about justice in a world that is so highly unequal and marginalizing of the Other. It is *that* that I think has facilitated and informed most of what I see as feminist philanthropy.[15]

## The Global Women's Funding Movement Emerges

The Global Women's Funding Movement emerged during the second wave of the women's movement of the early 1970s. The origin story of the Global Women's Funding Movement is a feminist parable—a testament to the magnitude of what small groups of dedicated women can achieve together. Among the first women's funds were the Astraea Lesbian Foundation for Justice, a U.S. national lesbian action foundation which would later become global in reach, the Ms. Foundation for Women, the

Women's Sports Foundation (launched by sports legend Billie Jean King), the San Francisco Women's Foundation (now the Women's Foundation California), and Mama Cash, the first international women's fund. Each of these funds were founded by small, diverse groups[16] of four or five women, independent from each other, each having the same epiphany: it will take a movement of women to raise the money required to fund women's equality. These feminist philanthropic pioneers knew they needed to raise massive amounts of money to challenge patriarchal control. This money was needed to fund the formation of feminist funds, cover the money to rent or purchase gathering spaces that are essential for organizing, finance the budgets needed to amplify the call to equity, and pay for the essentials that sustain the feminist activists who show up for the fight, among other needs. Since that time, these feminist foundations built a worldwide philanthropic movement of women from scratch and, over the last half-century, raised the money needed to construct the strong women's movement infrastructure that exists throughout the world today. In the process, they established feminist funding practices as a counterpoint to the oppressive, hierarchical, patriarchal-styled power structures they sought to end.

Katherine Acey, Former Executive Director of Astraea Lesbian Foundation for Justice, says:

> Astraea started out in the 70s. It was started by a multi-racial, multi-ethnic class group of lesbians, but they were not all out. They started a women's foundation to fund grassroots women's organizations and cultural groups. They funded lesbians, but they didn't only. It was regional, and then it became national, and put lesbian in the name, and then it went global. So, it evolved. It was always feminist and always had a focus on lesbian and always had intersectional analysis around power and justice.[17]

From their inception, women's funds have focused on dismantling oppressive, sexist systems and quickly building democratic, justice-based ones in their place—beginning with their own systems. This work is ongoing in seeking to avoid replicating patriarchal structures, addressing the priorities of non-white communities, and making women's funds boards and institutions even more diverse and inclusive.

As the activist and founder of the Women's Environmental Development Organization (WEDO), Bella Abzug said, "Women will not simply be mainstreamed into the polluted stream. Women are changing the stream, making it clean and green and safe for all—every gender, race, creed, sexual orientation, age, and ability."[18] In the pages of this book, hundreds of years' worth of collective wisdom is distilled, earned from first-hand experience of leaders in the Global Women's Funding Movement by cultivating, resourcing, partnering, and supporting women's movements to unleash seismic and lasting social change. As Tracy Gary, Philanthropic and Legacy Advisor and founder of several women's funds, has observed, "The Women's Funding Movement is no small event. It is the counterbalance to a world that has diminished the light of its caring heart."[19]

When the Global Women's Funding Movement was born, it was unclear how much, if any, philanthropic money was being directed toward women's liberation. To better determine the situation, in 1975, a small group of foundation program officers surveyed the level of foundation giving for women and girls. The results were shared in a publication titled *Who's Funding the Women's Movement* by Mary Jean Tully and published by NOW Legal Defense and Education Fund in 1975. Key data points included that of the 30,000 foundations registered at that time, only 20 foundations identified women's organizations as grantees. A total of $12 million of the $7 billion distributed could be identified as having gone to women's organizations and projects and only $2 million for women's movement and feminist projects such as addressing gender-based violence.[20] That amounted to less than 5 percent of the total pool.[21] Only 12 corporations were identified as donors to women's organizations and projects, and most of these gifts were $5,000 or less. The research revealed that while generations of people were united and on the streets, demanding gender equity and equal opportunity, philanthropy—like society—was plagued with sexist and discriminatory practices, which resulted in it completely ignoring the systemic oppression of women and girls and gender-expansive people. When the second wave of the feminist movement emerged in the 1970s, the concept of gender lens philanthropy—a feminist funding practice of considering the influence of gender, its impacts on people of all genders, and funding organizations that work for gender equity—did not exist in any form in philanthropy. Indeed, the foundation survey revealed that donors to charity and foundation directors hadn't thought about how their philanthropic investments impacted women and girls and gender-expansive people.

Once the results of this survey were shared, feminist activists and philanthropic-minded women began organizing. Within five years of the survey, a dozen "women's funds" had been established as nonprofit funds created and run by women to support women and associated populations. After the first funds were founded, women's funds rapidly multiplied across the world and flourished—as did the women's movements and women's empowerment initiatives they funded.

In sharing the formation of Mama Cash, Coco Jervis, Director of Programmes, says:

> Mama Cash was started in 1983. It was started by a group of lesbians sitting around at the table, one of whom lost their parent. Unexpectedly, their parents died and left them with a huge trust fund that they did know about ... The decisions about whom to fund were made in communications with the community, but essentially by these women sitting around the table. As Mama Cash has professionalized over the last 40 years, they have grown in scope, and they brought in activists such as me into the work. We're also now giving grants to individuals, which is something I find to be interesting and exciting because it's a recognition of the movements. We can fund group initiatives and networks. Now, we are also supporting the work of individuals ... supporting them with the work they've already done. We're trying to figure out ways for us to continuously get funding to those who need it most and not letting the political or economic or safety-related challenges of funding human rights defenders prevent us from going to wherever we are around the world.

Gloria Steinem and the founders of *Ms.* wanted to do more than publish a magazine. They wanted to change women's lives by supporting organizations and programs that helped women with employment, domestic abuse, reproductive health, and other issues. To achieve that goal, in 1972, *Ms.* magazine established the nonprofit Ms. Foundation, which quickly established a reputation for fearless action. In 1976, they became the first national foundation to give money to shelters for women suffering domestic violence. The following year, they funded a project to defend lesbian mothers threatened with losing custody of their children.[22]

One of the other great catalyzers of the creation of women's funds were the UN World Conferences on Women in Nairobi in 1985, and more recently the 1995 World Conference on Women in Beijing. This conference was attended by 17,000 representatives from 189 countries and territories. In conjunction with the Fourth World Conference on Women, the Non-Governmental Women's Forum was held in Beijing between August 31 and September 8. This forum was attended by 31,549 people, including 26,549 overseas participants and 5,000 Chinese participants.[23]

The power of women's movements was so evident that women realized they needed to mobilize funding for the causes they cared about. The Urgent Action Fund in the U.S., the International Women's Development Agency in Australia, and the Victorian Women's Trust in Australia were all created by founders inspired by their experience at the UN women's conference in Beijing.

As a case study, Kavita Ramdas, who served as the second CEO of the Global Fund for Women, tells the story of the creation of the Global Fund for Women in 1987:

> A number of the founders had been at the Nairobi Conference for Women. This was the second UN conference for women, which was held in 1985. There was a formal UN conference, but for the first time, nonprofit organizations and women's associations held a parallel conference, what was known as the NGO Conference, on the streets of Nairobi. The three founders of the Global Fund for Women—Frances Kissling, Anne Firth Murray, and Laura Lederer—were watching all these women's rights organizations, and all of them were saying, "Oh, we just came here, we pieced together the money. We didn't have money to come." They came back from the conference, and Frances said, "Isn't it crazy that there are these amazing groups doing all this amazing work, and they can't get funding from all these big foundations?" At a Council on Foundations meeting in 1986 or 1987, Frances asked, "Wouldn't you give money to something like this? Wouldn't you feel proud to give money to a fund run by women for women for these amazing groups?" And Anne said, "Yeah, I would." And other people said, "Yeah, I would." That's how the Global Fund for Women was started in 1987. These three women each put in $500 of their own money. They asked other people. The founding donors gave $5,000 each of their own money.[24]

The following year, the Global Fund for Women awarded the fund's first grants to eight grantees totaling $27,000. By September 2005, the Global Fund for Women had created the Legacy Fund, which is now among the largest endowments in the world dedicated exclusively to women's rights and donates over $8.5 million annually to women-led funds.[25]

Kavita Ramdas says:

> The connection between women's movements and women's funding movements is very deep because women realized that we could put all our hearts and souls and unpaid labor, our care work into supporting these movements. For our movements to have staying power and resilience and a bigger reach and impact, we had to have financial resources at our disposal. That was true whether we were talking about a woman getting an education, whether it was about women fighting rape in their own countries, or whether we were fighting for the right to vote in our own country.[26]

## Building the Global Women's Funding Movement

In the immediate aftermath of the birth of the Global Women's Funding Movement, between 1975 and 1985, the number of women's movements worldwide more than doubled. This triggered a virtuous cycle: as gender justice movements grew and multiplied, women united to form new, powerful women's funds, which funded more women's movements. By 1985, approximately 35 women's funds were in some stage of development. The Global Fund for Women supported the emergence of other women's funds, such as the African Women's Development Fund, now a strong regional fund that made $11 million in grants in 2022 and which also brings an influential voice to philanthropic discussions in Africa and globally.

The early funding provided by women's funds were grants determined by what was needed immediately or as seed funding to pilot initiatives. Today, women's funds work through diverse strategies that enable them to seed new ideas, fund pilots, collaborate on funding projects, invest in programs that can be adapted and scaled in different contexts and settings, and mobilize hundreds of millions of dollars in funds for gender justice from larger, mainstream funders. The Global Women's Funding Movement is a revolutionary philanthropic movement that gives women, girls, and gender-expansive people a way to collectively wield their money as a source of great power for themselves and each other. Nearly every great social advancement for women over the last half-century has been powered by women's movements, many supported by this global women's philanthropic force. This includes laws expanding women's access to their own financial accounts, laws supporting women's inheritance rights (which is associated with greater agricultural landholding), and laws protecting women against sexual harassment.

A strong women's movement led to the UN's world-changing 1979 Convention on the Elimination of All Forms of Discrimination against Women (CEDAW). In the U.S., it has been feminist activism that has had the most profound effect on advancing policies that have improved women's lives and economic status, including more equal opportunities in the workplace and in education.[27] The movements that women's funds have funded have begun not only to close the gap in gender inequity, but to strengthen democratic practices and improve women's economic options and power.

## Democratizing Philanthropy

Women of all levels of means must be literally invested financially in gender equity movements for the movements to fully succeed. To ensure this, women's funds have incorporated and created new philanthropic vehicles that democratize philanthropy and allow them to partner with women, girls, and gender-expansive philanthropists at all giving levels. Women's funds also educate and engage men, family foundations, and other donors, including governments, about the importance of applying a gender lens to grantmaking and programming decisions to build a strong and expansive philanthropic movement for women's rights and gender justice. Women's funds believe that philanthropy deserves to be a part of everyone's life, regardless of one's level of wealth. For there to be broad societal investment in gender and racial equity, there must be a broad societal financial investment in gender and racial equity, and this will not happen by just engaging the wealthiest people. Philanthropy in Black communities and for Black transnational causes has a very long history but has usually been in parallel to majority-white institutions. Mainstream funds need to better address and fund the lived realities of women of color and people of color more broadly to achieve the level of systemic change required.

By creating philanthropic vehicles that enable all women and girls and gender-expansive people to be philanthropists, women's funds ensure that everyone can be an influential feminist funder. As Dr. Musimbi Kanyoro, former President and CEO of the Global Fund for Women, observes:

> These funds, these movements that handle money, are providing a service to the women's movement. They are providing a service to feminist issues. They are not the owners of the money in the sense of the ones who say, I'm going to be giving all this money, but they gather money together. Then, they enable that money, with the participation of the people who receive it, to do the most to improve the lives of women and girls.[28]

With the flourishing of women's funds came the opportunity to build collaboration, learning, and networks between the funds. In 1990, more than 70 women from 20 established women's funds, including representatives from the Netherlands and France, met outside of Washington, DC, to discuss values, goals, and concerns regarding the founding of an umbrella fund. As a result of the convening, the Women's Funding Network (WFN), initially called the National Network of Women's Funds, was established as a membership-based fund that could act as a collaborative network for women's funds throughout the United States and globally.

A decade after the founding of WFN, in 2000, another powerful fund network was formed—the International Network of Women's Funds (now called Prospera)—to be a global fund network with leadership, presence, and voice in the southern hemisphere. Prospera has always focused more on supporting women's funds and feminist funds in the Global South, and WFN has had a much greater focus on supporting women's funds and feminist funds in the U.S. However, WFN does have women's funds from other countries as members, as well as U.S. funds that focus on funding internationally. Prospera went on to sustain the work of funds from around the world whose early development and growth were funded and supported by Mama Cash and the Global Fund for Women.

During these 25 years, between 1985 and 2010, after the creation of these two strong collaborative networks, the number of women's funds surged worldwide: 71 percent of women's funds operating today were formed during this time. Over 150 women's funds are represented in these two strong networks, spanning up to 100 countries representing every continent.

Since its inception, the Global Women's Funding Movement has functioned as a dedicated and highly focused operating system within the decentralized women's movement, rapidly gathering and channeling to women's movements the resources they need to succeed in the form of money, guidance, and connections. Over the last half-century, the Global Women's Funding Movement has become a collective support system for global grassroots women's movements and a convening force for its collective efforts. Led by a diverse and influential network of highly skilled CEOs, philanthropists, and women's rights activists drawn from throughout the world, Women's Funds work as a highly communicative team to fund fierce and effective women's movements across the world. Women's funds have significantly influenced paradigm shifts in the global philanthropic landscape for the last 20 years. This has included demanding more and better resources for the Global South and advocating for a shift in power to the Global South and East. This includes establishing coalitions of northern and southern philanthropic funders.[29]

To date, women's funds have invested over a billion dollars[30] in gender equity efforts and women's movements. Beyond that, they have catalyzed hundreds of millions more in funding from mainstream philanthropy and the public sector to fuel gender equity worldwide. The growing success of the Global Women's Funding Movement has led to a virtuous cycle: by creating stronger, more independent women with more wealth and cultivating them to invest back into women's rights and women's movements, we have created the next generation of even stronger, more independent women with even greater wealth. These women inherit the power to invest in women's rights and women's movements so that the virtuous cycle continues.[31]

As Chris Grumm, CEO of the Women's Funding Movement (2000–2011), explained:

> Our vision propels us to raise enough capital to fund the kind of social change that can be passed from generation to generation. Our dreams must be big and bold. We must be willing to have visions so vivid and real that we can see an end to the violence against women or the eradication of poverty across the globe.[32]

## Feminist Principles

Women's funds have actively shared learnings and best practices with each other across generations and geographies, making for a richer community of funds that evolve as they learn and strengthen. One key tool the feminist funding movement has prioritized is the formation of feminist principles. For instance, on May 17, 2019, Astraea Lesbian Foundation for Justice released its top ten Feminist Funding Principles. The principles share what Astraea has learned over the last four decades about supporting activists on the front lines to make enduring social change. When combined, these feminist strategic precepts have the potential to unleash transformative and enduring social justice victories. Funds such as FRIDA, the Global Fund for Women, and Fondo Semillas use similar principles of grantmaking. These principles are: (1) Fund those most impacted by gendered oppression; (2) Fund at the intersection of women's rights and LGBTQI liberation movements; (3) Apply an intersectional lens to break down funding silos; (4) Provide flexible and sustained core funding to activists; (5) Fund efforts to make social and cultural change alongside and as part of legal and policy change; (6) Support cross-issue and cross-regional movement building; (7) Go beyond grantmaking: accompany activists with capacity building and leadership support; (8) Invest in holistic security and healing justice; (9) Support work at the crossroads of feminist activism, digital rights, and internet freedom; (10) Partner with women's and other activist-led funds to ensure that funding reaches the grass roots.[33]

Women's funds continue to flip the traditional philanthropic script by promoting and enabling frontline and marginalized communities to lead. This has made women's funds more agile, effective, cutting-edge, and open to innovation than traditional philanthropic practices. Unlike traditional philanthropy, women's funds provide unrestricted grants and trust that grantees know best how to deploy resources. This is the essence of the Feminist Funding Principle of trust-based philanthropy that women's funds practice.

## Trust-based Philanthropy

The overarching goal of trust-based philanthropy is to change the usual power dynamic between a funder and the social justice change agent to one of true partnership. Trust-based philanthropy is the antithesis of evidence-based philanthropy, a prominent practice in mainstream philanthropy. Rather, trust-based philanthropy is oriented to "trust" organizations and leaders to do the work more than requiring evidence of a project's impact in unrealistic timeframes and rigid reporting formats. Trust-based philanthropy also intersects with another feminist funding principle and power-shifting practice, and that is participatory grantmaking.

Participatory grantmaking is demonstrated when women's funds incorporate grantee partners into decision making to select new grantee partners. Women's funds have incorporated this practice, recognizing that those who receive grants from women's funds are on the frontlines in their communities and are the subject matter experts on the issues they confront. For this reason, women's funds often ask their grantee partners to serve on their advisory or grantmaking boards.

With trust-based philanthropy, there is an emphasis on relationship building and the belief that the grantee partner is the change agent best suited to lead the way. In practice, trust-based philanthropy gives multiyear, unrestricted funding, empowering women leaders to implement their strategies and solutions. This allows activist leaders to make critical strategic changes in real time, removing onerous paperwork that detracts from the most critical work and offering support beyond the check.

Dr. Musimbi Kanyoro tells a story she heard from an older woman from Brazil:

> This woman wrote a handwritten letter in Portuguese to Anne Firth Murray (one of the founders of the Global Fund for Women) and asked for a very limited amount of funding because she had an idea that she wanted to build, and she got that money. Anne Firth Murray introduced the idea that women should not have any barriers to their asking for money. They could apply to the Global Fund in any language, all the time, and in any format they could write— handwritten, et cetera. Anyway, the letter got there, they got help from volunteers, who translated, and the amount of money she asked for was given to them. The organization that this woman created is now found in every part of Brazil. When we visited with donors, we found that the movement had grown so much that it had branches in every part of Brazil. It draws from that small

idea being funded. I looked at several of the groups who had received grants. I think the biggest difference was the funding of ideas so that those ideas developed into something bigger, and the women who had those ideas, once they had organized and mobilized larger groups, they were able to invent and find different ways of fundraising.[34]

Trusting women's solutions and giving them the flexibility and freedom to convey this funding pitch for solutions in the language and form they choose is a hallmark of women's funds. With this commitment to trust-based giving, women's funds operate within a spectrum of social, cultural, political, economic, and historical contexts, with varying organizational structures, leadership styles, and origin stories.[35] Just like the first women's funds, each women's fund today is unique[36] and has its focus—usually by region of the world, such as the Texas Women's Foundation, the Women's Foundation of Alabama, the African Women's Development Fund, the New York Women's Foundation, and the HER Fund of Hong Kong. Some women's funds are centered on the needs and innovations of communities across multiple locations—for instance, FRIDA, an international feminist fund run by young feminists who believe in the collective power of young feminists to lead and transform their communities, and the Black Feminist Fund, which is focused explicitly on supporting Black feminist movements.[37] Other women's funds, like the Urgent Action Fund, were founded to meet emergency needs—whether on a local or international scale. When a crisis or opportunity strikes, many women's funds engage with the Women's Funding Network or with Prospera to quickly convene and direct resources to the best-situated women's fund, which, in turn, equips the local frontline communities with the resources they need for that situation.

## Flexible Funding and Rapid Response

The Global Women's Funding Movement is like a prism to look through to find new developments in feminism and gender equality and a portal to the frontlines of women's movements worldwide.

Over the course of time, women's funds and the movements they support routinely face fresh political and philanthropic challenges and possibilities. This requires nimbleness, flexibility, and responsiveness from grantmakers and activists alike. This reality is often at odds with traditional philanthropic practices, which can be based on fixed plans, top-down governance, and little flexibility with the resources offered. No other realm of philanthropy works as the Global Women's Funding Movements does—a decentralized, justice-centered, self-perpetuating movement of feminist funders investing in women's and feminist networks and movements.

Women's organizations can mobilize and reach the most isolated women, girls, and gender-expansive populations while working to sustain important gains made. Because of their rapid response and funding prowess, women's funds have been critical first responders in numerous wars and disasters, including Hurricanes Katrina and Sandy in the U.S., the 2015 earthquake in Nepal, the Taliban takeover in Afghanistan, the military coup in Myanmar, and the wars in the former Yugoslavia and Rwanda. Women's funds have become some of the most rapid responders in the philanthropic world, transforming first responder practices from the ground up with women-led, women-focused solutions.

Women's funds have deep relationships, networks, and knowledge that can be tapped during a crisis to get funds quickly to where they are most needed. For instance, upon the kidnapping of 276 primarily Christian female students aged from 16 to 18 on the night of April 14, 2014, by the Islamic terrorist group Boko Haram from the Government Girls Secondary School in the town of Chibok in Borno State, Nigeria, women's funds swung into action. Many donors were keen to provide funds to support the girls' recovery and strengthen women's organizing. Three funds—the Urgent Action Fund, the African Women's Development Fund, and the Global Fund for Women—liaised to get funds to where they were most needed, using their respective networks to rapidly send funds for women-led organizing and response. What is crucial about how women's funds work is they fund women's movements to pivot in a time of emergency while also sustaining funds to women's groups and movements to hold ground on significant gains made through continued organizing. This example shows that the women's funds recognize that women's organizing requires different forms of support at different times. There is value in urgent response, phased support, as well as flexible general support to implement long-term strategic priorities.

In their 2022 joint op-ed, "Ukraine Donations Go Further and Faster with Women's Funds," the CEOs of Prospera Network and the Women's Funding Network, Alexandra Garita and Elizabeth Barajas-Román, explain how these two strong networks of women's funds enable them to excel in rapid response and as first responders:

> Women's funds move money six times faster than traditional philanthropic channels, and we get it where it's needed the most since we often fund at the margins, reaching nascent, small, or underfunded but critical funds on the ground that are *led* by women.[38]

Today, the Global Women's Funding Movement is a strong, vibrant global feminist circuitry that keeps the decentralized women's movement interconnected and thriving. It girds many gender justice efforts across the globe, building on the self-organizing that has a strong tradition among local women's mutual efforts. Women's funds recognize that women's financial power is essential for their wellbeing and that of their families and society. By funding women's groups that work directly with women, the Global Women's Funding Movement has revolutionized women's relationship with money, increasing women's earning power, economic security, and financial influence. Strengthening the economic lives of women and all marginalized genders, creating systems in which women and their children thrive financially, and establishing paths to intergenerational wealth for those who have historically been economically vulnerable are a common mission of women's funds.

## Holding Ground, Gaining Ground

Experience has shown that it is crucial to practice constant vigilance to support women's rights movements to gain ground and to hold ground if political circumstances, climate impact, pandemics, or conflict make gaining ground impossible. The World Economic Forum's 2022 Global Gender Gap Report stated that:

> [A]mid multi-layered and compounding crises including the rising cost of living, the ongoing [Covid-19] pandemic, the climate emergency and large-scale conflict and displacement, the progress towards gender parity is stalling. As leaders tackle a growing series of economic and political shocks, the risk of reversal is intensifying. Not only are millions of women and girls losing out on access and opportunity at present, this halt in progress toward parity is a catastrophe for the future of our economies, societies, and communities. Accelerating parity must be a core part of the public and private agenda. While more women have been moving into paid work over the last decades and, increasingly, into leadership positions in industry, there have been continued headwinds: societal expectations, employer policies, the legal environment, and the availability of care infrastructure. This has continued to limit the educational opportunities women access and the career possibilities they can pursue. The economic and social consequences of the pandemic and geopolitical conflict have paused progress and worsened outcomes for women and girls around the world—and

risk creating permanent scarring in the labor market. Conversely, the increasing representation of women in leadership in many industries, engagement in tertiary education overall, and rebound in professional and technical roles are encouraging and may provide a basis for future efforts. Collective, coordinated, and comprehensive action will be needed to create sustained improvements and halt the risks of reversals.[39]

Crucially, this report observed that reaching full parity will take 132 years. Before the Covid-19 pandemic, the gender gap was set to close within 100 years. In response, women's funds are doubling down on their efforts to fund women's and feminist movements for justice. In times of crisis, supporting these movements to continue to function and organize through and beyond the crisis is critical. For instance, during the 2015 Nepal earthquake, the Global Fund for Women worked with TEWA, the Nepal Women's Fund, to get funds to a range of local women's networks and movements in Nepal to respond to the emergency and reach the most vulnerable and isolated while also working to sustain momentum in women's organizing by ensuring women had a voice in the new Constitution that was forming. To only focus on the emergency without representation in the new Constitution would have meant women's rights would suffer a significant setback, with ramifications over decades.

In 2022, threats to women's rights were manifest by a rollback on reproductive rights legislation in the United States, a cut in funding for women's rights following far-right elections in Europe, a resurgence in violence against women globally, and the emergence of populist governments that demonstrate lack of respect for democratic institutions and rights-based principles. This context presents a challenge for women's funds to face collectively and thoughtfully to protect the feminist gains of the past decades.

As examples, over the last decade, we have witnessed autocracy replace democracy throughout the world, including in countries such as Turkey, the Philippines, Hungary, Poland, Brazil, and Egypt. Gender equity and gender equality are the antidote to autocracy because they strengthen democracy. This is why women leaders, feminism, women's movements, and women's rights are under attack when autocrats seize control. Harvard political scientists Erica Chenoweth and Zoe Marks explain in their 2022 Foreign Affairs article entitled "Revenge of the Patriarchs: Why Autocrats Fear Women":

> It is not a coincidence that women's equity is being rolled back at the same time that authoritarianism is on the rise. Political scientists have

long noted that women's civil rights and democracy go hand in hand, but they have been slower to recognize that the former is a precondition for the latter.[40]

## Funding Women Leaders and Movements at the Frontlines

A key strategy of patriarchal power is creating conditions and cultures permissive to violence against women and gender-expansive people that impose strict gender roles. Over the last few years, a global surge in right-wing, authoritarian movements and "strong men" governments have contributed to a monumental rollback of women's rights and have aggressively attacked protections against gender-based violence. In 2017, Vladimir Putin signed into law legislation that decriminalized much of what was previously defined as domestic violence. Unless the abuse results in broken bones and occurs more than once a year, it is no longer punishable by long prison sentences.[41] Spain's surging far-right Vox party proposed that the country repeal a landmark law to protect women from violence, citing its unfairness toward men, claiming that men would be the victims by being unfairly accused.[42] The Trump administration diluted the definition of domestic violence in reauthorizing the Violence Against Women Act. No longer does it classify as domestic violence if a woman's partner isolates her from her family and friends, monitors her every move, belittles and berates her, or denies her access to money to support herself and her children, which are the core strategies of control used by domestic abusers.

In 2020, *The New York Times* best summarized the trend in their headline "Across the Globe, a 'Serious Backlash Against Women's Rights': The rise of authoritarianism has catalyzed a rollback of gender violence protections and support systems." The article quotes Kalliopi Mingeirou, who leads the UN division focused on ending violence against women and girls. She states, "In general, we see a very serious backlash against women's rights," and the article explains that this "has helped normalize violence and harassment, either by dismantling legal protections or by hollowing out support systems."[43] Far-right politicians and groups campaign on platforms and messaging designed to encourage violence against women to keep women "in their place." In the lead-up to their presidential elections, Brazilian President Jair Bolsonaro campaigned on his opposition to a law imposing penalties for gender-motivated killing and advised women to stop "whining" about femicide.[44] Philippine President Rodrigo Duterte ordered soldiers to shoot female communist guerrillas in their vaginas[45] to discourage them from joining the New People's Army.[46] This communist rebel force has been waging an insurgency since 1969, with autocrats seeding threats of violence against women to create a culture of fear and to chill resistance.

Feminist activism is the greatest threat to autocracy, and therefore feminism and women's autonomy are vilified by autocrats. A culture that promotes patriarchal power is the culture in which autocracy can thrive. It is why feminist author Carol Gilligan, in her 2018 book *Darkness Now Visible: Patriarchy's Resurgence and Feminist Resistance* (co-authored with David A.J. Richards), defines feminism as "the movement to free democracy from patriarchy" and the "key ethical movement of our age."[47]

Women deploy their own stealth strategies to respond to patriarchal laws that erode women's rights. When the legendary Dame Carol Kidu, who was the only woman in the Papua New Guinean parliament for most of her time in office, tried to introduce a law banning marital rape, the male politicians all cried, "Interference in the bedroom!" and there was uproar in parliament resulting in the bill being howled down in protest. But wily Dame Carol got it through in the end.

She bided her time until the last session of parliament in 2002 and bundled it in with a series of amendments to a Child Sex Exploitation and Rape Bill. So, the law banning marital rape finally did pass, and it was months later before all her all-male parliamentary colleagues found out they'd been asleep at the wheel. The legislation had passed when only a few members were in parliament, impatient and ready to go on a holiday. Such is the balance of diplomacy, strategic planning, and timing that defines a stellar politician.[48] What's crucial, then, is the role of women's funds in sustaining an ecosystem of support to women's organizations and leaders around such wins. This reality is true of women's political organizing around the world.

Yifat Susskind, Executive Director of the international feminist fund MADRE (founded in 1983), explained how women's movements are essential for democracy in a *Los Angeles Times* op-ed "Women are behind the most successful uprisings of 2019. Here's why." She writes:

> In over a dozen countries on five continents, people have risen up to confront economic inequity and even the most repressive governments. These mobilizations are answering the question of how to tackle ascendant right-wing authoritarianism—and women have been at the heart of it all. In part, that's because women know well the consequences of living under these draconian governments. Right-wing forces promote a toxic brand of masculinity that defines manhood through violence and aggression, promising men a slice of patriarchal power in exchange for backing authoritarian rule. They relegate women to silence and submission and force LGBTIQ people into hiding. They

have targeted female human rights activists who defy patriarchal norms with harassment, criminalization, and even murder.[49]

One of the reasons women-led, feminist organizing is an effective strategy to confront authoritarian power is that women's movements are nonviolent, inclusive movements, which means more people can join them and more do. According to a 2008 study of more than 320 uprisings from 1900 to 2006, nonviolent movements are twice as effective at achieving their goals as violent uprisings, succeeding more than 50 percent of the time.[50] When women are at the forefront, leading the mass mobilizations, they are more likely to be peaceful, another study found.[51]

More than 60 percent of nonviolent movements featured women's groups that formally called for peace. Of movements that turned violent, women's groups were a minority of organizing groups, comprising only 35 percent.[52] Susskind notes also, from her perspective as a women's fund leader, that feminist movements are a strong antidote to authoritarianism because they have the infrastructure, built over a half-century, needed to sustain peaceful grassroots organizing.[53]

Muadi Mukenge, Senior Director with MADRE, was formerly director of the sub-Saharan Africa program at the Global Fund for Women. In a report from 2010, she discussed the Global Fund for Women's partnership with the women's movement in Congo:

> As the country emerges from a ten-year war that claimed over five million lives and violated the dignity of up to half a million women and girls through organized rapes, one has to ask how best to support community efforts at rebuilding. I am Congolese. I direct the Sub-Saharan African program at the Global Fund for Women. I am often asked what can be done to help the Congo, especially women … Since 2004, the Global Fund for Women's support to women's groups in the Congo has quadrupled, and we've seen that grantmaking to women's groups, despite the closed political space and weak infrastructure, can make a difference in the lives of women and their communities in the aftermath of conflict … The Global Fund for Women's support has helped women's groups to promote peace, justice, women's leadership, and respect for human rights. Over five years, the Global Fund for Women supported 70 groups (in the Congo) with almost $1 million in grants.[54,55]

In a world of increasing military aggression and might, women's representation in peace-keeping measures is critical to achieving peace. A consensus is emerging that women's participation in peace negotiations contributes to the success of lasting peace. For example, women's participation increases the probability of a peace agreement lasting at least two years by 20 percent and a peace agreement lasting 15 years by 35 percent.[56]

The Global Women's Funding Movement is a strong pipeline for sharing information, trends, strategies, and resources. It is also the vehicle for women's funds to collaborate with each other to support, strengthen, and help defend women's movements and the women human rights defenders that lead them. In 2009, a decade before it would hit researchers' radars[57] two women leaders, Marusia López Cruz and Lydia Alpizar Durán, began detecting a pattern of violence against women leaders, in particular Indigenous women, in their networks across Mesoamerica—the historical region and cultural area in the southern part of North America and Central America. Women leaders throughout the region were being targeted for violence, and, ultimately, a number were murdered. They were being arrested and exiled systematically as they resisted threats to their freedom and their community's wellbeing.

This detection work was compiled through a mapping process supported by JASS (formerly Just Associates) led by Lisa VeneKlasen, their founding Executive Director. Two women's funds funded these women leaders at the time: Global Fund for Women and Fondo Semillas. Mama Cash later provided additional funding through the Dutch Lottery and managed through the Fondo Centroamericano de Mujeres (Central American Women's Fund). This mapping also unearthed the continuing discrimination by human rights movements against women leaders in this region. Indeed, there was also a lack of knowledge regarding this dire situation in the women's movement. As the information emerged, Marusia López Cruz and Lydia Alpizar Durán co-led a political alliance named the Mesoamerican Initiative of Women's Human Rights Defenders, also known as IM-Defensoras. At the same time, leaders in women's funds convened a donor gathering in 2014, where information was shared regarding the mapping project, and additional women's funds joined in the "building of a movement of protection."

This protection movement focused on the countries of Guatemala, Honduras, Mexico, and Nicaragua. The most vulnerable to violence were those in rural areas and Indigenous women defending land rights and fighting environmental justice, lesbian and transgender activists, and feminists advocating for an end to violence against women. Based on this mapping, the initiative prioritized a combination of plans: urgent action, social media activism, human rights advocacy, research, training, and self-care. They began to raise awareness about the critically important, increasingly more dangerous, but often invisible leadership role played by women defenders in advancing human rights. To date, the initiative has helped over 100 female human rights defenders who were at risk of violence and needed services, including relocation for them and their families. In 2013, the work of IM-Defensoras led to a UN Resolution on the Protection of Women Human Rights Defenders. Today, IM-Defensoras has expanded to five national Defensoras networks in El Salvador, Guatemala, Honduras, Mexico, and Nicaragua.

In 2018, Nicaragua's IM-Defensoras network began sounding the alarm that their nation's women's movement infrastructure was under a new method of attack by the government of the despotic ruler, Daniel Ortega. The women's movement in Nicaragua has been his steady opponent since he took power in 2007. According to IM-Defensoras, Ortega's regime has a new approach to speed up attacks on Nicaraguan women's movement infrastructure using a 2020 law that requires any group receiving funds from international donors to register as a "foreign agent." The wave of massive cancellations of feminist groups led to an average of 47 feminist and women's rights groups being illegally and arbitrarily shut down each month.[58]

This crackdown has been accompanied by the forced removal of prominent women human rights defenders from the country with at least 16 women defenders banished from Nicaragua since 2018.[59] IM-Defensoras defends the Nicaraguan women's movement infrastructure by relying on the movement-sustaining circuitry of the global women's movement. Reproductive healthcare services, shelters for survivors of gender violence, and loans and training for peasant women—to cite just a few activities run by feminist groups—are vanishing because of the government ban. As Ortega's actions chillingly demonstrate, erasing feminism is autocracy's and patriarchy's primary strategy. In response, the strength and solidarity of feminist movements and the sustained support of the Global Women's Funding Movement are crucial. In an interview with Mallika Dutt (now with the Hewlett Foundation), Lydia Alpizar Durán said:

> The nature of capitalism is to create fragmentation, to break the wholeness. And I think feminists want very deep transformations for the whole of society, including for Mother Earth. Part of my effort to bring us together—different issues, different actors—it's because I think we really need to work on the fragmentation and there's so much we need to learn from each other. Building the collective project is crucial and there's so much learning from movements on the ground.[60]

Women's funds are philanthropic vehicles to help sustain movements for transformative change. They are critical in rapidly identifying the nature of attacks against national feminist infrastructure and activists, and helping to convene the emergency response required. Challenging patriarchal forces effectively, as women's movements do, can be extremely dangerous. It takes very little for patriarchal operatives to resort to violence. Indeed, it appears to be the preferred tactic. Research indicates that violence against women in politics is soaring. "Women in politics" refers to women directly or indirectly engaging in political processes: women candidates for office, politicians, political party supporters, voters, government officials, and activists/human rights defenders/social leaders.[61] Worldwide, women are facing unprecedented levels of targeted political violence, according to the Armed Conflict Location & Event Data Project (ACLED)—in partnership with the Robert Strauss Center for International Security and Law at the University of Texas at Austin. The Project began compiling data on political violence targeting women in 2018 and detected an immediate spike in political violence targeting women across the world.

According to a 2019 article by Rebecca Ratcliffe in *The Guardian* entitled "Political violence against women tracked for the first time as attacks soar", analysis suggests "a recent spike in violence, with twice as many cases reported during the first quarter of 2019 (261 events) as during the first quarter of 2018 (125 events)" based on reports collected across Africa, Southeast Asia, South Asia, the Middle East, South-Eastern and Eastern Europe and the Balkans.[62] The data traces the spike in violence against women in politics directly to women's level of political involvement. The ACLED researchers report: "Unprecedented numbers of women have engaged in elections in recent years, both by seeking office and by voting, setting new records in countries around the world. With these accomplishments, however, they have faced heightened risks of violence." The analysis finds that political violence targeting women has increased dramatically in nearly all regions, including Africa, Central Asia, Europe, Latin America, the Middle East, South Asia, and Southeast Asia. Since 2020, some of the most violent countries for women in politics include Mexico, Colombia, China, India, Brazil, Burundi, Myanmar, Afghanistan, the Philippines, and Cuba.[63] Women-led protests—such as demonstrations by mothers of prisoners or women campaigning for reproductive rights—were more likely to be peaceful than other demonstrations. However, the researchers found such events were disproportionately met with violent crackdowns, involving weapons, arrests, and teargas, usually by state forces.

Women, of course, are not backing down. They are, instead, uniting into the most powerful political forces ever known, in the greatest numbers ever seen, and using that collective power to forge paths to democracy, to women's rights, to climate repair, to gender equity, to non-violence, to racial justice, to Indigenous people's rights, to economic justice, to public health and more education and enduring peace.

> Aspiring autocrats and patriarchal authoritarians have good reason to fear women's political participation: when women participate in mass movements, those movements are both more likely to succeed and lead to a more egalitarian democracy. In other words, fully free, politically active women threaten authoritarian and authoritarian-leaning leaders, so those leaders have a strategic reason to be sexist. Understanding the relationship between sexism and democratic backsliding is vital for those who wish to fight against both. Established autocrats and right-wing nationalist leaders in contested democracies are united in using hierarchical gender relations to shore up nationalist, top-down, male-dominated rule. That is why countries that pretend to embrace increased female representation in their parliaments employ multiple tactics to prevent elected women from passing transformative policies in favor of women and girls. Having long fought against social hierarchies that consolidate power in the hands of the few, feminist movements are a powerful weapon against authoritarianism. Those who wish to reverse the global democratic decline cannot afford to ignore them.[64]

## Gender Justice Is Crucial for Climate Justice

Gender equity and gender equality are increasingly crucial to humanity's survival. In fact, they are one of the only fast tracks and most critical steps needed to address climate collapse. Women's funds paid attention to the impact of climate change on women's gendered roles long before climate change became a major concern on the global stage. And they funded women creating solutions to drought, flooding, and innovations in climate adaptation. More recently, in 2013, environmental activist and author Paul Hawken recruited a large team to assess and model practical solutions to climate change based on available data and research from numerous sources. The results are summarized in *Drawdown*,[65] a book edited by Hawken that identifies 100 substantive ways for people, governments, and companies to reduce the pace of global warming over the next 30 years. "Drawdown" refers to the desired point at which the current buildup of atmospheric carbon is halted.

Hawken's team ranked solutions by their estimated capacity to stanch the carbon buildup through 2050. And here's the big news: increasing girls' education and increasing access to family planning ranked six and seven, respectively, on the list (number one is most impactful). The authors noted that these two solutions are so closely linked in a practical sense that they should be considered together, yielding a combined impact that would top the *Drawdown* climate solution rankings by a wide margin.[66]

Also making a strong case that gender equity is necessary to address climate change successfully are the six authors of the 2022 book *Earth for All: A Survival Guide for Humanity*.[67] In the book, these illustrious authors—all leading climatologists and economists—contend that climate collapse is still avoidable and that it is possible to stabilize temperatures below 2°C, but reaching gender equity by 2050 is vital. Their model shows that to achieve what they termed "The Giant Leap," we must achieve full gender equity in the next 30 years. The authors posit that without full gender equity, rising gender, racial, and economic inequity in the next three decades will "lead to increasingly dysfunctional societies, making cooperation to deal with existential threats like climate change more difficult."[68]

The climate field is an example of where the women's movement has contributed an intersectional analysis that elevates new learning for the wider public and for decision makers. Applying a gender lens to climate change analysis allows us to appreciate that women and children are 14 times more likely to die in a disaster than men.[69] The girls and women who don't die are at far greater risk than men of suffering ill-health effects, face unemployment, lose assets, slip into poverty, and experience forced marriage or sexual violence following a disaster. Eighty percent of people displaced by climate change are women and children.[70]

In 1991, during the cyclone disasters in Bangladesh, of the 140,000 people who died, 90 percent were women. After the 2004 tsunami in the Indian Ocean, in the villages in Sri Lanka, Indonesia, and India surveyed by Oxfam, surviving men outnumbered women by almost 3:1.[71] During the emergency caused by Hurricane Katrina in the United States in 2007, 80 percent of the victims trapped in New Orleans were women[72] and most were Afro-American mothers with their children[73]—the poorest demographic group in that part of the country. Because of droughts, women in some parts of Kenya burn up to 85 percent of their daily calorie intake just by fetching water.[74] On average, women and girls in developing countries walk approximately 3.5 miles a day and carry over 40 pounds of water during these trips.[75] In Guatemala, drought conditions have dramatically increased the distance some women and girls, traditionally the water carriers for their families, needed to travel to get enough supply. This added exposure has made the girls more vulnerable and doubled their risk of kidnapping—an increasingly common and brutal way for men in rural regions to secure "wives."[76] Another study of 4,605 natural disasters occurring in 141 countries discovered that the effects on women were most severe in countries with very low social and economic rights for women.[77] Where patriarchy is most potent, the impact of climate disaster is most devastating on women.[78]

Disaster is not a singular experience; it unfolds. Domestic and family violence soars in the months and years following natural disasters. It usually involves physical and psychological violence perpetrated by men against women and children, but it can also include an array of other violence, including sexual, financial, and emotional abuse.[79] Studies in the U.S. documented a devastating 98 percent increase in physical violence against women after Hurricane Katrina, which remained elevated for two years.[80,81]

Following the 2009 Victorian Black Saturday bushfires in Australia, more than half of women in one study reported experiencing domestic violence. Many had never experienced it before.[82] Another study of the same disaster found that the closer they lived to the worst affected areas of the bushfires, the more domestic violence the women experienced.[83]

Disaster perpetuates patriarchy, and patriarchy perpetuates disaster. While natural disasters have become drastically more common, autocracy has, too, and this is no coincidence. Women's funds have been able to contribute a gendered analysis to the climate justice discussions which have taken a front seat in sustainable development platforms. Women's funds have resourced activists and their movements to be heard at critical tables, and to craft solutions around food production and natural resource management in their communities. This flexibility is an example of how the global women's movement has evolved as the lived realities of our global population evolve. This work will only grow and remain on the agenda as a critical human rights and development concern. Thankfully, the predictions around rising women's wealth and propensity to give are encouraging and give hope for mobilizing more funds for women's organizing and gender justice in the time ahead.

## The Great Wealth Transfer

Women's unprecedented financial power today is, in large part, the result of feminism's victories. In 2015, women bypassed the halfway mark for controlled personal wealth in the U.S. Women now own 51 percent of all personal wealth in the nation. By 2030, it is estimated that women in the U.S. will control two-thirds of the nation's wealth, which means women's philanthropic impact will increase substantially, given their propensity for giving. This is because as much as $68 trillion is expected to be passed on from U.S. baby boomers, a phenomenon that financial experts have coined the "Great Wealth Transfer." It is considered a monumental occurrence, not because of the wealth itself, but because women who typically outlive men will inherit most of it.

Moreover, many women will inherit twice—once from their parents and once from their spouses or partners. According to the Social Security actuarial life expectancy tables, women outlive men by three to five years on average. Therefore, it can be presumed that single or married women or women with partners in the boomer generation will have custody of the Great Wealth Transfer before it is ever transferred to the millennial generation.

This historic occurrence is linked directly to both the victories in women's property law reform by the first-wave feminist movement in the 1800s and due to women living longer and having better education, greater financial autonomy, and near equal participation in the workforce—all resulting from the work of the second and third waves of women's movements. Other countries are on a similar trajectory. As a result of the successes of the first three waves of feminism, we are about to experience a female financial phenomenon that has never occurred in recorded history.

Women, far more than men, believe that gender equity is critically important. As more and more women are coming into financial power, what's also critically important is that they wield it very differently than men historically have. Women give more of their wealth to philanthropy than their male counterparts: in single-headed households, researchers consistently find that women are more likely than men to give to charity. Today, the gathering threats against women are counterbalanced by an unprecedented opportunity to rapidly advance women's rights. If channeled properly, women's newfound collective financial power and unique philanthropic instincts will propel gender equity efforts forward faster, more formidably, and more fully.

Reflecting on this trend, Angel Investor and former Women's Funding Network Board member Jacki Zehner says:

> Finance is the new frontier of feminism. There will never be gender equity without financial equity. We don't have to wait for men. We just need to mobilize women. My whole thing is getting more money in the hands of women.

Mona Sinha, Former Board Chair of Women Moving Millions and Global Executive Director of Equality Now, agrees: "Unless women are economically secure, they're never going to be equal."

As the primary funders of women's rights efforts for the last five decades, and by being deeply embedded in nearly every gender justice effort underway on the planet, the Global Women's Funding Movement has acquired a deep intelligence, the ability to detect threats to women as well as opportunities for equity that are invisible to most others. Dismantling patriarchal systems is dangerous. When women strike effectively at the root of oppressive systems, those benefiting from them strike back with full force. As women gain and exert their power in the most basic ways, like voting, uniting to confront oppression, or when they run for office, they are increasingly targeted, intimidated, and attacked. Currently, we are witnessing a patriarchal backlash at an unprecedented scale globally. Violence against women in politics is now so pervasive throughout the world that it's considered its own category of gender-based violence. Also, the stronger and more autonomous women become, the more threatened and violent patriarchal forces grow. Patriarchal and anti-gender attacks today are profuse, both brazen and insidious, and extremely well-funded. These attacks, as always, seek to strike at every source of women's power—their political power, their reproductive power, their financial power, and their collective power. In addition to being guided by the moral compass of the Feminist Funding Principles, the Global Women's Funding Movement is hawk-eyed to patriarchy's sinister strategies, which women's funds' grantee partners are on the frontlines of resisting these forces on a daily basis, in the U.S. as well as globally.

## A Force More Powerful

While women's funds around the globe were organizing and developing, so were women's funds in the U.S. Sarah Gould, former President of the Ms. Foundation, recalls her experience:

> I came to the foundation in 1986. That was a time, then moving into the 1990s, when philanthropy was actually growing by leaps and bounds. When I got to the foundation, it was extremely small. I was the fifth employee. When I arrived at Ms., we were probably giving $200,000 a year. There was only one way to go, and that was up. And then Marie Wilson (former President of the Ms. Foundation) came. Literally, I think of it as she took the foundation world by storm. What was unique about it was it was making grants at the intersection of race, class, and gender. Astraea was doing that. The Women's Foundation of California also had that analysis; we were leading that analysis that it's not just gender; it's race, class, and gender at an intersection. It's at that intersection that

you can make a real impact, and it's at that intersection that you can attract people into the women's movement, so to speak.

What was also unique is we began experimenting with different ways to grant money. I arrived in 1986, and by 1989 or 1990, Marie and I were trying to develop a collaborative fund for women's economic development, which was, believe it or not, one of the first, if not the first, collaborative funds in philanthropy bringing institutions and individuals around the table to learn to make grant decisions together and to be able to make multiyear grants. That first collaborative fund made its first grants in 1991. We had 13 funders. They were all institutions, including Ford, Levi Strauss, the Charles Stewart Mott Foundation, and Hitachi. There were 13 of them. We had about $2.3 million that we gave away over three years. For the first time, the Ms. Foundation could make multiyear grants of $50,000 a year. And this was in 1991. That was a lot of money. That was revolutionary for the foundation. We had a whole piece of the collaborative fund that was about learning, so we were trying to learn in the field, and certainly, we were trying to influence the funders around the table. We specifically said if you come to this table of the collaborative fund, it doesn't mean that you don't fund in this area on your own. It means that if you come to this table, you'll learn more. We'll learn together.

People in philanthropy institutions and philanthropy began to hear about what the collaborative fund was doing. At that time, we mainly focused on women's micro-enterprise development and cooperative development, meaning home healthcare cooperatives, daycare cooperatives, etc. And we made 13 grants of $150,000 over three years. We brought those grantees together to learn from each other and help each other in their various projects. Then we had a second round of that collaborative fund. This time, I think we pooled nearly $4 million, and we had many more funders. We were then experimenting with bringing funders and donors, like program officers and individual donors, together to the same table. They were, of course, fascinated by each other. It's one of the reasons that people came to that table because they really wanted to learn about the field. They wanted to learn about each other. They wanted to work together.

One of the things, as I was coming up in leadership, and then when I began to lead the foundation in 2004, I wanted the foundation to be squarely positioned in the larger progressive movement. So another thing that was unique was we started … one of the very first donor circles. We started the Fight the Right, or what was later called the Democracy Funding Circle, and had 12 to 15 donors a year who would be part of the Democracy Funding Circle, and they would be doing funding in the area of really fighting the growth of the right wing.

Ms. Foundation was a trailblazer. We were a beacon in many ways; we were also looking outward, and we were deeply in relationship. We were inclusive of everyone because we were also trying to build a movement. Our experience at Ms. Foundation was a complete joy to work with donors at different monetary levels. We were not just trying to give money away to organizations that build movements. That's a big thing we do. But in our own practice, we were trying to build a larger movement.[84]

This vision was the momentum driving the Global Women's Funding Movement. It was a rising force, powerfully intent on shifting power, norms, voice, policies, and resources to support a transformed world, one that is possible and underway. The following chapters demonstrate how.

## Notes

1 "Female Fury in The Forum, Ancient Rome, 195 & 42 B.C." PRIMARY SOURCE ACTIVITY, Women in World History Curriculum, Classroom Lesson Series, accessed November 25, 2023, www.womeninworldhistory.com/lesson10.html.

2 Oyindamola Depo Oyedokun, "Meet Funmilayo Ransome-Kuti, the Formidable Nigerian Activist Who Simultaneously Fought for Women's Rights and Her Nation's Freedom," AfricaRebirth.com, January 29, 2024, accessed May 24, 2024, www.africarebirth.com/meet-funmilayo-ransome-kuti-the-formidable-nigerian-activist-who-simultaneously-fought-for-womens-rights-and-her-nations-freedom.

3 Catalina Crespo-Sancho, "Can gender equality prevent violent conflict?" World Bank Blog, March 28, 2018, accessed November 25, 2023, https://blogs.worldbank.org/dev4peace/can-gender-equality-prevent-violent-conflict#:~:text=The%20larger%20the%20gender%20gap,response%20in%20a%20conflict%20setting.

4 Catalina Crespo-Sancho, "Can gender equality prevent violent conflict?" World Bank Blog, March 28, 2018, accessed November 25, 2023, https://blogs.worldbank.org/dev4peace/can-gender-equality-prevent-violent-conflict#:~:text=The%20larger%20the%20gender%20gap,response%20in%20a%20conflict%20setting.

5 Jörg Baten and Alexandra de Pleijt, "Gender equality isn't just moral—it's also good economics," World Economic Forum, June 4, 2019, accessed

November 25, 2023, www.weforum.org/agenda/2019/06/history-shows-that-women-s-autonomy-leads-to-long-term-development.

6   Jörg Baten and Alexandra de Pleijt, "History shows that women's autonomy leads to long-term development," *LSE Business Review*, May 29, 2019, accessed November 25, 2023, https://blogs.lse.ac.uk/businessreview/2019/05/29/history-shows-that-womens-autonomy-leads-to-long-term-development.

7   Ted Piccone, "Democracy, gender equality, and gender security," The Brookings Institute, September 2017, accessed November 25, 2023, www.brookings.edu/wp-content/uploads/2017/08/fp_20170905_democracy_gender_security.pdf.

8   *Feminist activism works! A review of select literature on the impact of feminist activism in achieving women's rights* (Amsterdam: Mama Cash, 2020) accessed May 14, 2024, www.mamacash.org/wp-content/uploads/2020/10/feminist__activism_works_mama_cash.pdf.

9   *Feminist activism works! A review of select literature on the impact of feminist activism in achieving women's rights* (Amsterdam: Mama Cash, 2020) accessed May 14, 2024, www.mamacash.org/wp-content/uploads/2020/10/feminist__activism_works_mama_cash.pdf.

10   Stacey Tisdale, "Gloria Steinem on patriarchy, abortion and economic independence," *Al Jazeera*, July 12, 2019, accessed November 25, 2023, www.aljazeera.com/economy/2019/7/12/gloria-steinem-on-patriarchy-abortion-and-economic-independence.

11   Joan Marie Johnson, *Funding Feminism: Monied Women, Philanthropy, and the Women's Movement, 1870–1967* (The University of North Carolina Press, 2020).

12   Srilatha, Batliwala, *Feminist Leadership for Social Transformation: Clearing the Conceptual Cloud for CREA (Creating Resources for Empowerment in Action)*, May 2010, accessed November 25, 2023, https://creaworld.org/wp-content/uploads/2020/11/feminist-leadership-clearing-conceptual-cloud-srilatha-batliwala.pdf.

13   "Feminist Glossary," Centre for Social Research, Delhi, India, accessed November 25, 2023, www.csrindia.org/feminist-glossary.

14   hooks, bell, *Feminism is for Everybody: Passionate Politics* (Pluto Press, 2000).

15   Ndana Bofu-Tawamba, interview by Laura Risimini, August 31, 2022.

16   *Investment, Influence, Impact, 2009 Annual Report* (San Francisco: Women's Funding Network, 2009), accessed November 25, www.womensfundingnetwork.org/wp-content/uploads/2014/02/AnnualReport-2009.pdf.

17   Katherine Acey, interview by Christine Grumm, October 31, 2022.

18   "Bella Abzug (1920-1998)," The Emily Fund for a Better World, Do One Thing: Be a Hero for a Better World, accessed November 25, 2003, www.doonething.org/heroes/pages-a/abzug-quotes.htm.

19   Tracy Gary, personal email correspondence with Helen LaKelly Hunt, January 24, 2023.

20  Mary Jean Tully, *Who's Funding the Women's Movement* (NOW Legal Defense and Education Fund, 1975) rediscovered by Mary Jean Collins and Stephanie Clohesy.

21  Mary Jean Tully, *Who's Funding the Women's Movement* (NOW Legal Defense and Education Fund, 1975) rediscovered by Mary Jean Collins and Stephanie Clohesy.

22  Winifred Conkling, *Ms. Gloria Steinem: A Life* (New York: A Feiwel and Friends Book, an Imprint of Macmillan Publishing Group, 2020), 273.

23  "The Fourth World Conference on Women met in Beijing in September, 1995," Ministry of Foreign Affairs, People's Republic of China, accessed November 25, 2023, www.fmprc.gov.cn/eng/ziliao_665539/3602_665543/3604_665547/200011/t20001117_697845.html.

24  Kavita Ramdas, interview by Laura Risimini, September 15, 2022.

25  "Global Fund for Women," Wikipedia, last modified on November 12, 2023, accessed November 25, 2023, https://en.wikipedia.org/wiki/Global_Fund_for_Women.

26  Kavita Ramdas, interview by Laura Risimini, September 15, 2022.

27  Victoria M. Massie, "White women benefit most from affirmative action—and are among its fiercest opponents," Vox, May 25, 2016, accessed November 25, 2023, www.vox.com/2016/5/25/11682950/fisher-supreme-court-white-women-affirmative-action.

28  Musimbi Kanyoro, interview by Laura Risimini, August 18, 2022.

29  Leila Hessini, "Financing for gender equality and women's rights: the role of feminist funds," *Gender & Development*, Vol. 28, No. 2 (2020), 357–376, accessed November 25, 2023, https://doi.org/10.1080/13552074.2020.1766830.

30  Muhungi, W., and Edwards, E., "Supporting Women's Rights in Troubled Times." *Stanford Social Innovation Review*, Vol. 16, No. 1 (2018), A9, accessed November 25, 2023, https://doi.org/10.48558/0TJ0-BH77.

31  Bonnie Chiu, "Women And Millennials Among Strongest Donors On Giving Tuesday," *Forbes*, November 29, 2022, accessed November 25, 2023, www.forbes.com/sites/bonniechiu/2022/11/29/women-give-more-than-men-on-giving-tuesdayhow-about-generally/?sh=5680b6fd65c4.

32  Christine Grumm, interview by Laura Risimini, August 22, 2022.

33  "Feminist Funding Principles," Astraea Lesbian Foundation for Justice, accessed November 25, 2023, https://astraeafoundation.org/microsites/feminist-funding-principles.

34  Musimbi Kanyoro, interview by Laura Risimini, August 18, 2022.

35  *In It Together: Reflections and Recommendations on Global Fund for Women and Mama Cash's Engagement with Women's Funds 2018*, Global Fund for Women and Mama Cash, April 25, 2019, accessed November 25, 2023, www.globalfundforwomen.org/latest/article/in-it-together.

36 Today, there are 157 "women's funds" under our two network umbrellas. The Women's Funding Network has 127 member women's funds across 32 states in the U.S. and six continents. The Prospera Network currently gathers 47 women's and feminist funds, who collectively provide grants in over 172 countries.

37 "We are the Black Feminist Fund," Black Feminist Fund, accessed November 25, 2023, https://blackfeministfund.org.

38 Alexandra Garita and Elizabeth Barajas-Román, "Ukraine Donations Go Further and Faster with Women's Funds," *Ms. Magazine*, March 30, 2022, accessed November 25, 2023, https://msmagazine.com/2022/03/30/donate-ukraine-women/#:~:text=In%20addition%2C%20Urgent%20Action%20Fund,care%20and%20increasing%20shelter%20capacity.

39 *Global Gender Gap Report 2022* (Geneva: World Economic Forum, 2022), accessed November 25, 2023, www3.weforum.org/docs/WEF_GGGR_2022.pdf.

40 Erica Chenoweth and Zoe Marks, "Revenge of the Patriarchs: Why Autocrats Fear Women," *Foreign Affairs*, February 8, 2022, accessed May 24, 2024, www.foreignaffairs.com/articles/china/2022-02-08/women-rights-revenge-patriarchs?check_logged_in=1&utm_medium=promo_email&utm_source=lo_flows&utm_campaign=registered_user_welcome&utm_term=email_1&utm_content=20240524.

41 Amie Ferris-Rotman, "Putin's War on Women: Why #MeToo Skipped Russia," *Foreign Policy*, April 9, 2018, accessed November 25, 2023, https://foreignpolicy.com/2018/04/09/putins-war-on-women.

42 Raphael Minder, "On Day to End Violence Against Women, Spain's Far Right Champions Men," *The New York Times*, November, 25, 2019, accessed November 25, 2023, www.nytimes.com/2019/11/25/world/europe/spain-vox-ortega-smith-violence-women.html.

43 Alisha Haridasani Gupta, "Across the Globe, a 'Serious Backlash Against Women's Rights,'" *The New York Times*, December 4, 2019, accessed November 25, 2023, www.nytimes.com/2019/12/04/us/domestic-violence-international.html.

44 Adriana Carranca, "The Women-Led Opposition to Brazil's Far-Right Leader," *The Atlantic*, November 2, 2018, accessed November 25, 2023, www.theatlantic.com/international/archive/2018/11/brazil-women-bolsonaro-haddad-election/574792.

45 Felipe Villamor, "Duterte Draws Fire for Crude Threat to Female Rebels in Philippines," *The New York Times*, February 12, 2018, accessed November 25, 2023, www.nytimes.com/2018/02/12/world/asia/philippines-duterte-vagina.html.

46 Felipe Villamor, "Duterte Jokes About Rape, Again. Philippine Women Aren't Laughing," *The New York Times*, August 31, 2018, accessed November 25, 2023, www.nytimes.com/2018/08/31/world/asia/philippines-rodrigo-duterte-rape-joke.html.

47  "Why Feminism Now? Carol Gilligan and David Richards argue that feminist resistance to patriarchy is the key to saving democracy," *NYU Law News*, January 15, 2019, accessed November 25, 2023, www.law.nyu.edu/news/ideas/darkness-now-visible-why-does-patriarchy-persist-carol-gilligan-david-richards-resisting-injustice.

48  Jane Sloane, *Citizen Jane: Transformative Citizenship in a Globalized World* (Amazon Create Space, 2014).

49  Yifat Susskind, "Opinion: Women are behind the most successful uprisings of 2019. Here's why," *Los Angeles Times*, December 26, 2019, accessed November 25, 2023, www.latimes.com/opinion/story/2019-12-26/women-lead-uprisings-2019.

50  Maria J. Stephan and Erica Chenoweth, "Why Civil Resistance Works: The Strategic Logic of Nonviolent Conflict," *International Security*, Vol. 33, No. 1 (Summer 2008), 7–44, accessed November 25, 2023, www.belfercenter.org/sites/default/files/legacy/files/IS3301_pp007-044_Stephan_Chenoweth.pdf.

51  Yifat Susskind, "Opinion: Women are behind the most successful uprisings of 2019. Here's why," *Los Angeles Times*, December 26, 2019, accessed November 25, 2023, www.latimes.com/opinion/story/2019-12-26/women-lead-uprisings-2019.

52  Erica Chenoweth, "Women's Participation and the Fate of Nonviolent Campaigns: A Report on the Women in Resistance (WiRe) Data Set," One Earth Future Foundation, accessed November 25, 2023, https://oneearthfuture.org/sites/default/files/documents/publications/Policy_Brief_Womens_Participation_Nonviolent_Campaigns_Digital_0.pdf.

53  Yifat Susskind, "Opinion: Women are behind the most successful uprisings of 2019. Here's why," *Los Angeles Times*, December 26, 2019, accessed November 25, 2023, www.latimes.com/opinion/story/2019-12-26/women-lead-uprisings-2019.

54  Global Fund for Women, "Funding a Women's Movement Against Sexual Violence in the Congo," YouTube, July 13, 2010, 3:49, www.youtube.com/watch?v=2dSH1iMAoGI#t=34.

55  Aili Mari Tripp, Isabel Casimiro, Joy Kwesiga, and Alice Mungwa, *African Women's Movements: Transforming Political Landscapes* (Cambridge University Press, 2008).

56  "Women's Participation in Peace Processes," Council on Foreign Relations, accessed November 25, 2023, www.cfr.org/womens-participation-in-peace-processes.

57  Rebecca Ratcliffe, "Political violence against women tracked for first time as attacks soar," *The Guardian*, June 10, 2019, accessed November 25, 2023, www.theguardian.com/global-development/2019/jun/10/political-attacks-women-tracked-first-time-surge-violence.

58  "Nicaragua / During the month of August, 42 more feminist and women's rights organizations lost their legal status, with a total of 147 illegally canceled by Daniel Ortega since 2018." WHRD Alert, Mesoamerican Initiative of Women Human Rights Defenders, September 6, 2022,

accessed November 25, 2023, https://im-defensoras.org/en/2022/09/whrd-alert-nicaragua-during-the-month-of-august-42-more-feminist-and-womens-rights-organizations-lost-their-legal-status-with-a-total-of-147-illegally-canceled-by-daniel-ortega-since-20.

59  "NICARAGUA / Miskita defender Anexa Alfred Cunningham denied entry into her own country, Nicaragua." WHRD Alert, Mesoamerican Initiative of Women Human Rights Defenders, October 4, 2022, accessed November 25, 2023, https://im-defensoras.org/en/2022/09/whrd-alert-nicaragua-during-the-month-of-august-42-more-feminist-and-womens-rights-organizations-lost-their-legal-status-with-a-total-of-147-illegally-canceled-by-daniel-ortega-since-20.

60  Lydia Alpízar Durán, "Focusing on Diversity, Care, and Sustainability in Building Collective Capacity to Respond to Oppression," interview by Mallika Dutt, *Leadership Moves*, 2022, accessed November 25, 2023, https://mallikadutt.com/podcast/collective-capacity-oppression.

61  "FAQs: Political Violence Targeting Women (PVTW), Demonstrations Featuring Women (DFW), and Political Violence Targeting Women in Politics (PVTWIP)," Armed Conflict Location & Event Data Project (ACLED), 2022, accessed November 25, 2023, https://acleddata.com/acleddatanew//wp-content/uploads/dlm_uploads/2022/08/ACLED_Political-Violence-Targeting-Women_FAQs_8.2022.pdf.

62  Rebecca Ratcliffe, "Political violence against women tracked for first time as attacks soar," *The Guardian*, June 10, 2019, accessed November 25, 2023, www.theguardian.com/global-development/2019/jun/10/political-attacks-women-tracked-first-time-surge-violence.

63  "FAQs: Political Violence Targeting Women (PVTW), Demonstrations Featuring Women (DFW), and Political Violence Targeting Women in Politics (PVTWIP)" Armed Conflict Location & Event Data Project (ACLED), 2022, accessed November 25, 2023, https://acleddata.com/acleddatanew//wp-content/uploads/dlm_uploads/2022/08/ACLED_Political-Violence-Targeting-Women_FAQs_8.2022.pdf.

64  Erica Chenoweth and Zoe Marks, "Revenge of the Patriarchs: Why Autocrats Fear Women," *Foreign Affairs*, March/April 2022, accessed November 25, 2023, www.foreignaffairs.com/articles/china/2022-02-08/women-rights-revenge-patriarchs?check_logged%20_in=1&utm_medium=promo_email&utm_source=lo_flows&utm_campaign=registered_user_welcome&ut%20m_term=email_1&utm_content=20220907.

65  Paul Hawken, *Drawdown: The Most Comprehensive Plan Ever Proposed to Reverse Global Warming* (New York: Penguin Books, 2017).

66  "Family Planning and Girls' Education: Antidotes to Climate Change," PRB, accessed November 25, 2023, www.prb.org/resources/family-planning-and-girls-education-antidotes-to-climate-change.

67  Sandrine Dixson-Declève, Owen Gaffney, Jayati Ghosh, Jørgen Randers, Johan Rockström, and Per Espen Stokne, *Earth for All: A Survival Guide for Humanity* (New Society Publishers, 2022).

68  Sandrine Dixson-Declève, Owen Gaffney, Jayati Ghosh, Jørgen Randers, Johan Rockström, and Per Espen Stokne, *Earth for All: A Survival Guide for Humanity* (New Society Publishers, 2022).

69  *Why Is Climate Change A Gender Issue?* UN Women, accessed November 25, 2023, www.uncclearn.org/wp-content/uploads/library/unwomen704.pdf.

70  Mary Halton, "Climate change 'impacts women more than men,'" BBC News, March 8, 2018, accessed November 25, 2023, www.bbc.com/news/science-environment-43294221.

71  "The tsunami's impact on women," Oxfam Briefing Note (March 2005), accessed November 25, 2023, https://oxfamilibrary.openrepository.com/bitstream/handle/10546/115038/bn-tsunami-impact-on-women-25%200305-en.pdf?sequence=1&isAllowed=y

72  L. Butterbaugh, "Why Did Hurricane Katrina Hit Women So Hard?" *Off Our Backs*, Vol. 35, No. 9/10 (September/October 2005), 17–19, accessed November 25, 2023, www.jstor.org/stable/20838463.

73  "Disaster and gender statistics," Fact Sheet, International Union for Conservation of Nature, accessed November 25, 2023, www.unisdr.org/files/48152_disasterandgenderstatistics.pdf.

74  "Disaster and gender statistics," Fact Sheet, International Union for Conservation of Nature, accessed November 25, 2023, www.unisdr.org/files/48152_disasterandgenderstatistics.pdf.

75  Maria Otero, "Six Kilometers a Day," USAID website, accessed November 25, 2023, www.usaid.gov/six-kilometers-day.

76  Stella Paul, "From rape to disasters, climate change a threat to women—funders," Thomas Reuters Foundation, May 21, 2016, accessed November 25, 2023, https://news.trust.org/item/20160520144607-yi719.

77  Elizabeth Ferris, "When disaster strikes: women's particular vulnerabilities and amazing strengths," Brookings Institution Keynote presentation, Women's Leadership Lunch, National Council of Churches Assembly, November 10, 2010, New Orleans, Louisiana, accessed November 25, 2023, www.refworld.org/pdfid/4d0771202.pdf.

78  "Disaster and gender statistics," Fact Sheet, International Union for Conservation of Nature, accessed November 25, 2023, www.unisdr.org/files/48152_disasterandgenderstatistics.pdf.

79  Julie A. Schumacher, Scott F. Coffey, Fran H. Norris, Melissa Tracy, Kahni Clements, and Sandro Galea, "Intimate Partner Violence and Hurricane Katrina: Predictors and Associated Mental Health Outcomes," *Violence and Victims*, Vol. 25, No. 5 (October 2010), accessed on November 25, 2023, https://connect.springerpub.com/content/sgrvv/25/5/588.

80  Nidhi Sahni, Debby Bielak, and Sonali Madia Patel, "If You Care About Climate Change, Fund Feminist Movements," *Inside Philanthropy*, July 20, 2022, accessed on November 25, 2023, www.insidephilanthropy.com/home/2022/7/20/if-you-care-about-climate-change-fund-feminist-movements#:~:text=While%20 climate%20events%20exacerbate%20existing,drive%20to%20realize%20 those%20changes.

81  Michael Anastario, Nadine Shehab, and Lynn Lawry, "Increased Gender-based Violence Among Women Internally Displaced in Mississippi 2 Years Post–Hurricane Katrina," *Disaster Medicine and Public Health Preparedness*, Vol. 3, No. 1 (2013), 18–26, accessed on November 25, 2023, www.cambridge.org/ core/journals/disaster-medicine-and-public-health-preparedness/article/abs/ inc%20reased-genderbased-violence-among-women-internally-displaced-in-mississippi-2-years-posthurricane-ka%20trina/D576CBEB73639E69823A1391 B5BF160B.

82  Debra Parkinson and Claire Zara, "The hidden disaster: domestic violence in the aftermath of natural disaster," *Australian Journal of Emergency Management*, Vol. 28, No. 2 (2013), accessed May 14, 2024, www.preventionweb.net/ publication/hidden-disaster-violence-aftermath-natural-disaster.

83  Debra Parkinson and Claire Zara, "The hidden disaster: domestic violence in the aftermath of natural disaster," *Australian Journal of Emergency Management*, Vol. 28, No. 2 (2013), accessed May 14, 2024, www.preventionweb.net/ publication/hidden-disaster-violence-aftermath-natural-disaster.

84  Sara Gould, interview ssby Laura Risimini, October 11, 2022.

# And Still We Rise! Building a Global Women's Funding Movement

**2**

## Funding Women and Girls and Gender-Expansive People Who Are Changing History

This focus on supporting women's movements and leaders in their organizing for human rights and democracy has been a through-line for the Global Women's Funding Movement. One of the greatest milestones for a women's movement occurred in 2003 in Liberia. For the first time in known history, a women's movement deposed a regime and installed a leader of its own into power. One of the women who had received a grant from the African Women's Development Fund and the Global Fund for Women was Leymah Gbowee. In 2002, as the unpaid leader of the Women of Liberia Mass Action for Peace, and following a prophetic dream, Leymah Gbowee applied for a small grant to support women in the refugee camps to engage in sits-in and picketing in Monrovia and to influence the men who were responsible for sustaining the Liberian Civil War and who were meeting in Accra, Ghana.

Jessica Horn, Former Director of Programmes at the African Women's Development Fund and now Regional Director for East Africa for the Ford Foundation, recalls that time.

> In the context of the Liberian Civil War, women were really active in creating broad-based social movements for peace. They were women who were organizing through the churches. There were women organizing through different mechanisms. And they became the Women's Mass Action Movement. They would sit every day on the

DOI: 10.4324/9781003330455-2

airstrip and sing songs, and it would be the route that Charles Taylor would go in his motorcade, and he would see them every day. They managed to use access from one of Charles Taylor's wives to get to him and basically plead for an end to the war. They were instrumental in that transformation. But when there was a formal peace process established, women were not invited at all to the table. This group of women decided on a delegation that would go to the peace talks that were going on in Accra.[1]

The African Women's Development Fund and the Global Fund for Women helped the women attend the peace talks in Accra, organizing them with Liberian women in the refugee camps in Accra and helping to sustain the funding for women's organizing.

In Accra, Leymah asked the women to surround the compound where the men were meeting, and then she addressed the men inside:

We women, we are tired of war. We are tired of running. We are tired of begging for bulgur wheat. We are tired of our children being raped. We are now taking this stand, to secure the future of our children. Because we believe, as custodians of society, tomorrow our children will ask us, "Mama, what was your role during the crisis?"

In an interview with Amy Goodman on Democracy Now (April 25, 2015), Leymah Gbowee said:

One of the things that we were able to accomplish in Liberia was bringing together groups that would not necessarily come together to build peace: Christian and Muslim … [W]e knew that … to build peace, we needed to bring not just the women together, but women from diverse background. We have 16 ethnic groups and two major religious groups in Liberia, Christians and Muslims. So we were able to bring those women together to work together. And I would say one of the strategies we used was reconceptualizing religious spaces. A lot of the time, people use religion as a means of disempowering women. And if you go into the Qur'anic text and even in the Bible, you'll find there were some great women. So we use the examples of those very great women to talk about how they helped to change their time. As a Christian and working with Christian women, we used Deborah, Esther. They were engaged in political issues in biblical times. Once the narrative of those women had been kind of reconceptualized, the women were able to resonate with it and were able to bring them together, but also not just bringing the groups together, but to protest nonviolently.

Fourteen years of violent uprising. We started with two groups, the government and the warring faction, the rebel group. By 2003, we had gone through almost 12 or 13 different armed groups. And so, everyone's response to the war was bringing in more violence or bringing in more guns. And we realized that if there were changes that should happen in Liberia, it had to be nonviolent. So we protested. We did sit-ins. We were just like invading spaces that women would not necessarily be in.

A Muslim woman, my colleague, well, very good friend of mine, Asatu Bah Kenneth. She's like, "We're going to do a sex strike." And it was like, "Whoa!" for me because usually, the stereotypes we have about Muslim women is that they are quiet, obedient and that they do not have those kinds of, you know, mind. But she was the one who came up with the idea.

And once we put it out there, it became a huge issue, first not in our—in our community, it wasn't because sex is exotic, even though it is, but people wanted to know who were these women to even dare their husbands or the men, who are supposed to be in power, to say they won't give sex because of the war. One day, we got tired, and we seized the entire hall, locked the men in, and said they would not come out until we had a peace agreement signed. We were going to almost a third month of a peace process that should have lasted three weeks. After we did our locking in of the men and giving our own position to them that this is what we want, two weeks later, we got a peace agreement signed.[2]

After successfully working to end the civil war, Leymah Gbowee and the other women turned their attention to securing full implementation of the peace agreement, which included disarmament, demobilization, civic education, and inclusion of women. With this momentum, and with a woman on the ballot for President, there was excitement to vote for her, and that woman was Ellen Johnson Sirleaf, who became the twenty-fourth President of Liberia.

Abby Disney, grandniece of Walt Disney and a feisty, fabulous, proudly feminist filmmaker, heard about Leymah Gbowee's story because Abby was on the board of the Global Fund for Women.

Abby Disney was stunned that she hadn't heard the story about what Leymah Gbowee and these women had done to end the civil war in Liberia and get Ellen Johnson Sirleaf elected. Abby asked, "Why didn't I know about this story? Why didn't the media cover this stunning achievement by these women?" Her producer asked the male photojournalists who covered the civil war this question, and they said they thought the women on the streets agitating for peace looked straggly and pathetic, so they trained their cameras on the militiamen clutching guns.[3]

Abby felt compelled to make a film of Leymah's story, which became *Pray the Devil Back to Hell*. Through the film, news of Leymah Gbowee's story spread quickly and came to the attention of the Nobel Peace Prize committee. In 2011, Leymah Gbowee, together with Ellen Johnson Sirleaf—and activist Tawakkul Karman from Yemen—was awarded the Nobel Peace Prize. Without the film being made, it's doubtful that the judges would have known Leymah Gbowee's story.

In the prologue to her book *Mighty Be Our Powers*, Leymah Gbowee writes:

> Once, a foreign journalist asked me, "Were you raped during the Liberian war?" When I said no, I was no longer of any interest. During the war in Liberia, almost no one reported the other reality of women's lives. How we hid our husbands and sons from soldiers looking to recruit or kill them. How, in the midst of chaos, we walked miles to find food and water for our families—how we kept life going so that there would be something left to build on when peace returned. And how we created strength in sisterhood and spoke out for peace on behalf of all Liberians.
>
> This is not a traditional war story. It is about an army of women in white standing up when no one else would—unafraid because the worst things imaginable had already happened to us. It is about how we found the moral clarity, persistence, and bravery to raise our voices against war and restore sanity to our land.
>
> You have not heard it before because it is an African woman's story, and our stories rarely are told.
>
> I want you to hear mine.[4]

Making women's lives visible is a political act. Bringing a female lens and feminist perspective to the way films are created and how issues are viewed is a political act. "What would happen if one woman told the truth about her life?" poet Muriel Rukeyser asked. "The whole world would split open."[5]

Women's leadership is getting stronger with each generation. Not only are women rising, but girls are also taking the lead on some of the most critical issues of our time, including climate action. At age 16, Greta Thunberg, through sheer force of will, emerged onto the world stage to castigate leaders for flouting the people's will by failing to forestall the worst effects of climate change. Her campaign for climate action mushroomed into a global movement, with four million people materializing for her climate strike in 2019. In one year, Greta went from being a teenager taking a lone stand to one of the most recognized and influential people on the planet. Her single, sustained, brave action catalyzed a phenomenal movement for climate justice led by young people.

By her own account, Greta had no other option but to lead. "Learning about climate change triggered my depression in the first place," she says. "But it was also what got me out of my depression because there were things I could do to improve the situation. I don't have time to be depressed anymore."[6] After she became an activist, her father reported, she "came back to life."[7] For Greta, becoming a global icon was more doable than living an existence with no agency over the most critical issue of our time.

## Funding the Feminist Wave for Rights and Justice

Harnessing the transcendent organizing power of social media, new and rising girl-led and women-led movements quickly gained traction to spread justice across borders and cultures. The fierce Ni Una Menos (Not One Less) movement, which began in Argentina in 2015, has swiftly spread throughout Latin America, raging against the culture of machismo it considers the source of spiking femicides. Marcela Ojeda, an Argentinian radio journalist sparked the movement with a single tweet, "They're killing us. Aren't we going to do anything?"[8] Her daily beat covering the surging numbers of femicides had become unbearable. Marcela was usually the first civilian to meet with the families of women and girls murdered by husbands, boyfriends, and exes. Femicides were an epidemic, spiking in number yet going unchecked and unpunished. Law enforcement had turned a blind eye, not even bothering to compile the numbers. Outraged, Marcela united with several other women journalists to call for a march, enlisting influencers and celebrities to help in promotion and getting the word out.

Within three weeks of her tweet, Argentinian women were mobilized, and hundreds of thousands gathered in cities across the nation to demand an end to the killing.[9] The very next day, the Supreme Court and the Human Rights Secretariat in Argentina moved to create expert task forces and began collecting data on violence against women.[10] Since then, the Argentine Secretariat for Human Rights established the Centre for the Registration, Systematization, and Monitoring of Femicides to gather data as a guide to finding solutions. By the year's end, in November 2015, another demand of the Ni Una Menos movement was met with the creation of the Lawyers Bureau for Victims of Gender Violence, through which victims of domestic violence or sexual abuse can receive free comprehensive legal advice from women's rights lawyers. The legislature passed a law requiring mandatory training for all who work in the civil service on gender issues and violence against women, and established the Ministry of Women to address inequalities in public policies as they related to women, LGBTQI+, and other marginalized groups. The Ni Una Menos movement united with the Green Wave abortion rights movement in Argentina which had been building for decades and made abortion rights a demand of the Ni Una Menos movement.[11] In 2020, the Argentine legislature delivered on that demand too, legalizing abortion. "We have been riding this feminist wave, this collective construction that has changed our lives, for six years," the Ni Una Menos movement posted to its Instagram page. "The feminist struggle brings us together; it funds us, and it sustains us. We all want to be freer, more alive, and more independent."[12]

## Investing in Changing Gender Norms

In the U.S., women's funds grew rapidly across states and communities as they responded to diverse needs and opportunities. One of the best-known initiatives started by the Ms. Foundation was Take Our Daughters to Work Day, which began in 1992. The goal of the project was to introduce girls to a broad range of job opportunities.

Recalling this initiative, Marie C. Wilson, former President of the Ms. Foundation, said:

> [It came from] Carol Gilligan's research looking at how adolescent girls started to lose their sense of who they were—thinking, talking and saying what they felt. You weren't supposed to question boys. You weren't supposed to know anything, so to speak. [The Ms. Foundation] hired a great consultant, Nell Merlino, who told us a story that she had heard about a girl who was at a school and made arrangements for her to have an internship at a wonderful place in downtown New York. The girl went to the building, and she couldn't go in. She was really intimidated, and she went home. They sent her a second time, and she got there, got a little further [inside the building], but she just couldn't [go upstairs]. Finally, the person who had been working with her at the school just came with her and took her up to see the woman, and she got a great internship and lived happily ever after. Gilligan knew that

it was important for women's voices to support girls in keeping their sense of self in adolescence. So, we thought, how could they do this at work? What if we got people, on one day, to pay attention to girls in this way? ... We thought it would just be a little day in New York [until] Gloria [Steinem] stopped by the foundation on her way to talk to *Parade* magazine, and we told her about "Take Our Daughters to Work Day," and then she told *Parade*, and that's how [the idea] got out into the world ahead of schedule.[13]

In sharing some of the early experiences by girls taken to work for the day, Marie C. Wilson said:

There were the girls who went and overheard their fathers talking about investing in tobacco companies. These girls went home and told them, "You don't want me to smoke, and yet you are making a living investing in tobacco companies?!" At a newsroom, one girl asked, "Why are there only white men here making the news?"

Recalling that time, Sarah Gould, who later went on to become President and CEO of Ms. Foundation, said, "Take Our Daughters to Work Day is a program that really reached the general public. It was a complete home run."[14]

## Investing in Economic Equity

Reflecting on her experience with the Global Women's Funding Movement, Patti Chang, Former President and CEO of the Women's Foundation California and CEO and co-founder of Feed the Hunger Fund, said, "The women's movement was about establishing equality, and I think the Global Women's Funding Movement on its best day was about funding equity. How do we want to raise all the boats, so to speak?"[15]

One of the women's funds that contributed to raising all boats was the Iowa Women's Foundation, with its focus on economic equity. Dawn Oliver Wiand, former President & CEO of the Iowa Women's Foundation, tells the story:

Several years ago, the Foundation began a community-based and participatory research project to help to define the best points for intervention—programs and services that would make a difference on economic equity. The starting point was discovering the barriers to economic equity for Iowa women. We looked at the poverty numbers in Iowa and the communities where it was worst, and we decided to visit 18 communities to ask questions. We designed a research methodology for a community process. We asked consistent questions using a consistent methodology in each community while also listening to how people expressed their own ideas. The result was a research report on the barriers identified through the process. As we prepared the report, we saw the consistency of the top five barriers across all communities: employment, mentoring, education and training, childcare, and transportation.

With the completed report, we went back to the 18 communities, presented the data, and asked them what would be most influential to work on first. More than half identified childcare. We took that information to our board and advisory committees and designed an approach to use our leadership resources, our willingness to collaborate, and our grantmaking. We identified partners in every community to co-design a local strategy and work plan.[16]

The Iowa Women's Foundation then established a Child Care Collaborative Fund to focus on strategies to increase the economic security of women in communities across Iowa by expanding access to quality, affordable childcare. Its first grant was to Linking Families and Communities in Fort Dodge to fund pre-design work by an architect for an expansion to the Community Early Learning Center, as well as a new childcare center to create 200 additional childcare spaces in that community. "The lack of affordable, accessible childcare is a major barrier to women's economic self-sufficiency in all of Iowa's 99 counties, and the Iowa Women's Foundation will increase our focus on finding solutions to the childcare crisis," said Dawn Oliver Wiand.[17]

In reflecting on the power of an equity lens, Lauren Y. Casteel, President and CEO, Women's Foundation of Colorado, says:

> I think the context of justice changes when we add the word equity. When one begins to talk about equity, justice takes on a slightly different meaning because it can be the redistribution of resources. It takes into context the history of where investments have not been distributed equally and where wrong may have, in fact, been done.[18]

## Funding Collective Action

One of the early projects supported by women's funds in California was a Migrant Farmworkers Rights Project which dealt with life and death issues in the fields of California. Speaking about the project, one of the women coordinators said:

> Many of these women don't have the language or the confidence in being able to talk to anyone, and so they really feel that they are isolated. They work alongside their husbands in the fields, but they are still not allowed to express themselves. They want to know this information (about their rights), and it's a triple effect—they can organize other women while also increasing their own power and that of their community. These women have been promised so many things, and no one has really followed through, and so that's one of the commitments I have … even if we only put one program here … [voice breaking] …we will.[19]

In a 1988 video describing the rise of women's funds, Philanthropic advisor Tracy Gary says:

> We're trying to create democracy in society. And there's a table that people come to, to make decisions. Many tables. And that women and minorities, particularly people of color, disabled people, lesbians, and people who have the least access to resources, are not being represented at that table. And if change is really going to happen, that kind of representation has to happen.[20]

Tracy Gary also shares the momentum that became the Women's Funding Network:

> I'd been on the board as a young 29-year-old in 1980–1985 of Women and Foundations, Corporate Philanthropy. It was through Joanne Hayes, the ED of Women and Foundations, that I asked to meet Helen (La Kelly) Hunt. We needed more wealthy women to partner with to grow the movement. We had six women's funds only in 1982, and I said to Joanne Hayes, "I'd like to get us, with your help, to grow to 100 by the year 2000." Joanne introduced me to Helen, and Helen to many others, and with 12 women's funds, we organized the 1985 convening. The Women's Funding Network was thereafter founded, naming Carol Mollner as interim Director. By the year 2000, Chris Grumm had taken the helm of the Women's Funding Network, accelerated our efforts, and dynamically grew foundation support for WFN and its tools and funds. There were 102 funds by the year 2000. And now there are over 180, including 45 globally.[21]

In a conversation with Chris Grumm and Laura Risimini, Anne Delaney, co-founder of the Lambent Foundation, and Michelle Coffey, Executive Director of the Lambent Foundation, share their experience of discovering and practicing feminist philanthropy.

Recalls Anne:

> I was a member of WDN [Women Donors Network] and the New York Women's Foundation and learning participatory grantmaking also. And WDN always did it globally. You could join donor circles to do that. I was also in the Ms. Foundation, and we did donor circles there. It was Tracy Gary who introduced me to the idea of women's funds. And Quinn, my sister. It was really like [Tracy] took you by the hand and invited you in, to talk and consider that your values are not reflected in mainstream philanthropy. And it was one of my many "aha" moments, especially being in a strong patriarchal family. It was a door opened, one of many in philanthropy. Michelle [Coffey] did for me, and Ana Oliveira did it for me, and so many people have this way of showing you that we can live our values, that we can operate in a way that grantmaking reflects our values, and we can model the values we want to see. The system of patriarchy is not the way the world has to be; it is not written in stone, and there are and have been alternative economic and political systems. All that, to a young woman especially, is pretty, earth-shattering.[22]

Michelle Coffey:

> I love, Anne, how you were speaking about who pulled you in and offered a grounding and a relationship for that shared caring, and it reminded me of the WFN [Women's Funding Network] conferences and convenings. For me, to see a larger community of aligned radical, feminist thought. It not only held me as I was learning, but also showed me how radical we can be. And it wasn't a choice. It began to feel like a mandate. So, thank you, Chris, for posting and holding all of those at a really important time within progressive philanthropy, so that we could see each other, learn alongside donors and activists and administrators. It really trained me on a feminist, practice, a feminist philanthropic practice.

Chris Grumm:

> As I listen to you, I am hearing an understanding of how the women's funding movement is based in the women's movement. Because all those pieces that you put out there—about the importance of

relationships and being in community and learning from each other and becoming wise women—all of that came out of the women's funding movement via the women's movement. And the importance of the global aspect of the women's funding movement.

Michelle Coffey:

I would add one more element, and that's the intergenerational element. When you think about second-wave feminism, third-wave feminism, how we can hold our elders and the younger individuals coming in simultaneously, and value the full life cycle of women comes out of the women's movement and is applicable in our funding strategies now. In recognizing everybody's place or season, the value of what is emerging, and the value of what is here, and transitioning and paying attention to the full cycles of a career, of a community, of movements is just another connective tissue.

Anne Delaney:

Women's funds' gift to mainstream philanthropy has been the practice of listening to and supporting women activists who may have been overlooked as people who hold solutions to problems in their communities and who should be included in wider policy discussions on state and federal levels.[23]

Chris Grumm:

I remember your Starry Night Fund (which Anne founded and where Michelle was director). You all had long-term relationships with your grantee partners, up to ten years, as I recall.[24]

Michelle Coffey:

Well, it's the work of a lifetime. When we talk about progressive movement building, it does not get checked off and done. And we've also seen underneath all our watches that the work that we've done over the last 25 years continues to have significant threats.[25]

Anne Delaney:

There has to be a big learning curve on our part. We're still learning about how to be racially equitable; we're still learning how to include

Indigenous practice and all these new ways of thinking around gender. We're still trying to be supportive of movements. That's what Starry Night Fund always was about, supporting movements.[26]

Michelle Coffey:

In the end, it really is about changing hearts and minds. So, while we are in the relationships with grantee partners, we are also recognizing that our philanthropic practice is important. To have trust, there must be some intimacy and vulnerability. It's usually through these dark, turbulent times that you don't know where the next step is; it's just remembering each other's humanity in it. And that we, as a funder, don't know either. But can we figure this out together? Are you stuck? Are there other needs that we might be able to offer that have nothing to do with a grant but those are our assets that we could also share. And so, we found ourselves doing that a lot in these past years, and it's going to have to continue.[27]

Anne Delaney:

Philanthropy, by way of giving time, talent, and treasure, offers us a way to practice a collective coming together in the service of others and reminds us to hold each other with respect and dignity.[28]

It is this commitment to trusting the collective wisdom of the women's movement to know what is needed in response to issues and situations on the ground. This in turn allows for the rapid mobilization of resources to support the work being done on the ground by activist/women leaders for the implementation of local solutions.

In the United States, women-led movements are more pervasive than ever in organizing around issues of culture and politics. The day after the inauguration of President Trump, the Women's March formed to protest the installation of an egregiously misogynistic president. It is considered by political scientists to be the largest day of protests in U.S. history.[29] Immediately afterward, rather than stew under the viral sexism of the new president, American women channeled their collective rage into the #MeToo movement, originated by activist Tarana Burke. This movement had a visceral effect, triggering legions of women worldwide to come forward with their experiences of sexual assault and harassment. In 2018, female actors in Hollywood launched the #TimesUp movement and bravely came forward and named their perpetrators, which culminated in the dramatic career implosions of well-known, powerful men who had sexually preyed on women for decades. These women's movements provoked immediate and tangible change. Harvard researchers noted that within two years of the #MeToo movement taking off, sexual coercion in the workplace had decreased by 36 percent, and unwanted sexual attention declined by 63 percent. Women's collective action stormed through the 2018 midterm elections, propelling more U.S. women into elected office than ever before.[30]

The New York Women's Foundation's (NYWF) The Fund for the #MeToo Movement and Allies ("The Fund") was launched in 2018 based on the work of Tarana Burke. The first round of funding was distributed to support eight organizations working with communities of color in late 2018/early 2019, and a second round of grantmaking in 2020 continued to support these organizations to sustain and advance existing work. The Fund also expanded in year two by awarding grants to five women's funds to enable them to strengthen their anti-violence grantmaking to local organizations.

While many of them had been part of cohorts together previously, being deliberately brought together by a peer organization felt especially motivating. As a representative from the Women's Foundation for a Greater Memphis (WFGM) said:

> I learned so much from other women's funds … they're very strategic in their thought and their delivery … Just having that teamwork and shared vision and comradery of the team and just the passion. To me, that really fed into us and our strategy and really helped us to have the confidence that we could do more, and we could be more intentional.[31]

In addition to building connections with one another, support from the NYWF enabled other women's funds to gain credibility with their boards to support Black, Indigenous, People of Color (BIPOC) anti-violence work. The matching grant format encouraged women's funds to raise additional monies. For example, the WFGM found the matching grant format to be motivating and not too burdensome. The Women's Foundation California "talked to an amazing major donor of ours, and they significantly increased their giving, and that was how we got the match from New York Women's Foundation's Me Too Fund."[32]

## Investing in Women of Color Leading Movements and Change

The Fund also played an important role in enabling significant work for women of color-led organizations providing services with political analysis and an orientation towards healing and restorative justice. This was especially true given the uptick in demand for such services resulting from Covid-19. Women's funds spoke about how the funds helped them to prioritize support for women of color and their leadership and to maintain a focus on anti-violence in their funding.

In Asia, emboldened by the #MeToo Movement, women led important social media campaigns to challenge patriarchy and misogyny. The Asian Pacific Institute on Gender-Based Violence documented the most impactful campaigns. This included a campaign in the Philippines that translates as "I Am Woman." The social media campaign began in May after President Duterte declared that the next Chief Justice of the Philippines could not be a woman. In Japan, facing unsympathetic employees, women created the #WithYou hashtag in solidarity with women experiencing sexual harassment in the workforce. In India, women released a crowdsourced list of known sexual harassers in journalism, Bollywood, and other prominent roles to call out men whose status had once protected them. And in Pakistan, #GirlsAtDhabas post pictures of themselves sitting at dhabas (roadside restaurants) to reclaim public spaces—traditionally dominated by men—for Pakistani women. [33]

In the United States, the powerful #BlackLivesMatter (BLM) movement was founded in 2013 by three young Black women, Alicia Garza, Opal Tometi, and Patrisse Khan-Cullors. With the continual killings of African Americans going unpunished, the three envisioned and built an "inclusive and spacious" movement to address anti-Black, state-sanctioned violence and all oppression of Black people. As one of the BLM founders, Opal Tometti, explained to *Ms.* Magazine:

> It should be no real surprise to people that Black Lives Matter was founded by three women. However, I find that oftentimes people are surprised to learn that. And the fact is that Black women and women, period, are oftentimes key architects of social movements, of community organizations. And far too often we get erased from the books and our names don't get shared and so on. But the fact of the matter is, and especially in this case, that, yes, three Black women helped to found Black Lives Matter. And I love that we're three women who started this. I think it's brilliant. I think the fact that my sisters are queer, myself with a background of having immigrant parents, just the diversity even within who it is that we are allows us to have a necessary perspective and organizing framework that is really inclusive and that demands that we support, protect and defend all Black people, period.[34]

By 2020, #BlackLivesMatter had rocketed into one of the most prominent and effective civil rights movements in U.S. history, innovating new, powerfully effective strategies and public responses to state violence against Black people. BLM focused the public's attention on the unchecked problem in real time, using undeniable footage of case after case to reveal how ever-present and deadly systemic racial injustice is in the U.S. According to the Brookings Institute:

> Black Lives Matter normalized the filming of Black pain at the hands of individuals sworn to treat everyone equally. Without personal video and the efforts of citizen journalists, we may not collectively know about George Floyd, Freddie Gray, Eric Garner, Sandra Bland, or Korryn Gaines. Black Lives Matter shifted public opinion. For example, a 2017 Pew study found that 54% of white people viewed officer-involved shootings involving Black people to be signs of a broader problem. The fact that over 50% of white people think that policing has racial issues is a huge achievement. This attitudinal shift created a policy window for local, state, and federal changes to policing and the criminal justice system.[35]

#BlackLivesMatter also transformed into a global movement with the Black Lives Matter Global Network, with chapters to support grassroots organizing globally. This has included protests against police brutality in countries including Israel, Kenya, Colombia, and France. In Nairobi, Kenya, hundreds marched against police brutality, which was particularly acute during the country's coronavirus lockdown. "Black Lives Matter slogans became famous internationally and created a vast network of grass-roots organizations and a moral collective for activists and supporters' social justice and equality."[36]

Today, while massive movements like BLM effect dramatic change, most movements that are highly effective don't number in the millions of followers and most typically have a smaller and core group of highly dedicated frontline activists. Contrary to common perceptions, many effective movements aren't massive. A social movement is defined as "an organized set of people vested in making a change in their situation ['constituents'] pursuing a common political agenda through collective action."[37] Successful movements can be big or small, and they typically share one thing in common: a vigorous base of passionate, energetic, and well-organized grassroots support for a political and social vision.[38] Under the most challenging circumstances—including reduced funding for women's rights organizations in recent years and an extremely well-funded conservative opposition on a mission to stop women's advancements, moving the needle toward gender justice requires sustained commitment. Throughout the world, many activists supported by women's funds work amidst sustained patriarchal backlash, with constant attacks on reproductive rights, the reversal of protections from gender-based violence, unrelenting attacks on women human rights defenders, and rising fundamentalisms. Despite powerful opposition and constraints, women's movements are proving to be resilient and tenacious because of their holistic strategies and the growing collective monetary power of the Global Women's Funding Movement backing them. Often, the focus has been on holding ground on rights won when gaining ground isn't possible due to conflict, humanitarian or climate emergencies, or political repression. To respond to the level of transformation needed, women's funds are also mobilizing phenomenal funding, as evidenced by the Equality Fund which was formed with a $300 million (Canadian) investment by the Canadian government. Jessica Houssian, Former Co-CEO says, "The Equality Fund is an innovative model that brings together bold government funding, feminist philanthropy, and gender lens impact investing, as well as policy advocacy work to shift power and resources to global feminist movement sustainably and at scale."[39]

Women's and feminist funds are also constantly innovating in response to shared learning. Paige Andrew, Programs Co-Manager Participatory Grantmaking & Operations, of FRIDA The Young Feminist Fund, says:

> Next year, for the first time, we're going to be implementing a special grant called a safety net grant. That grant comes from just us understanding that there are so many emergencies that young feminists constantly have to respond to. It's important for us to fund them to be able to respond to emergencies within their contexts. We've been playing around in the last two years with giving urgent response funding, but also realizing our capacities to do that may not be 100 percent. We feel like it's easier for us to give the groups a safety net funding and they can use that at the emergency, or they can use it as a risk reserve, maybe put it away for a rainy day when things come up. It's again up to the group, centering their needs and trusting them to use the money however they need to. I think that's really political, and it's really important for us when we say that we care about groups to give them that flexibility.[40]

## Building Sustainable Community Capital

Emerging organically, women's movements are typically led by those most affected by a particular injustice and whose personal experiences turn them into subject matter experts. Women's funds also often include activist staff, advisors, and board members who are part of the global women's movement, which keeps the approach real. As Ana Oliveira, CEO of the New York Women's Foundation, says, "Radical generosity is the type of philanthropy we practice at The New York Women's Foundation. It's a philanthropy that knows problems and solutions live in the same place. That people living the issues know the answers."[41]

## Propelled by Passion and A Drive for Justice

In speaking of what is unique about being a women's fund donor, Stephanie Clohesy, founder of the Iowa Women's Foundation and with deep experience working with many women's foundations, shared the importance of personal transformation in driving a commitment:

> [Women donors] came with super passion, and many had been hurt in some ways by the system. And that hurt pulled them into action. It's like, how dare you block me? How dare the system treat me like this? How do I take something that's been hurtful and turn it around into change? This interplay of extraordinarily personal transformation is just an engine, a nonstop engine for the desire to make change. It's so profound, really. I watched it over and over and over again, especially in the last 20 or 30 years, as I did so much more work with women donors. So, to me, that's feminist philanthropy. That inseparability of personal empowerment with wanting more for the world, and as women, how we work in a more egalitarian way. The whole idea of participatory grantmaking emerged from the consciousness-raising discussions that if you want equality, you have to do equality. You can't want equality and run a hierarchy where only a few people have a voice.

Chris Grumm, former President and CEO of the Women's Funding Network, shares this analogy about how women's funds operate:

> In the world of development there is a wonderful saying that if you give a person a fish, they will eat for the day, but if you teach a person

to fish, they will eat for a lifetime. In the world of women's funds this is how we want to be thinking: if you give a woman a fish, she will feed her family first and might possibly go hungry, if you teach a woman to fish, she will feed her family first until the lake becomes polluted or they take away her fishing rights. However, if you give women the resources and access to community capital, they will buy the lake, feed their families, keep the lake environmentally clean and have something to pass on for generations to come. As a movement, we are about building sustainable community capital to support women and girls who are ready to buy the lake and/or steward it responsibly.[42]

And that resourcing goes beyond money. As Claudia Samcam, Development Coordinator for Institutional Donors, Fondo Centroamericano de Mujeres (FCAM) or Central American Women's Fund, says:

We understand that movements need resources to do the critical work they are doing, but we also understand that not only funding is needed, so there are whole different conditions that organizations need in order to even continue to do their work. We have a capacity-strengthening program that focuses on providing organization knowledge, contacts, relationships, etc. Also, we always believe in the relevance of bringing organizations together. It's not FCAM telling them how to do their work in a better way, but it's how in the collective they can learn from the experience of others and create this sense of community across issues, across populations, and also across countries.[43]

Emilienne De León, former Executive Director, Prospera (formerly International Network of Women's Funds), shares the diversity of support that women's funds provide, and their exponential rise over the last decade:

Women's funds, members of Prospera, follow the agenda of the feminist movements and support women's rights organizations worldwide, especially in the Global South. They have grown significantly in the past 10 years, mobilizing 6 times more than they did in 2010, when I arrived as Executive Director. In 2010, they mobilized 30 million USD annually; in 2020, 200 million dollars was achieved. The way women's funds put money into the hands of women's rights organizations and feminist networks and movements is flexible, giving multiyear and core support grants. They also do accompaniment and support capacity-building processes, including the advocacy and joint efforts made by national, regional, and global networks. Because they come from the feminist movements, they build very close and trustworthy relationships with their grantee partners. The fact is that no matter how difficult the context, women's funds, grassroots women's rights organizations, and feminist movements will always stand by their principles and will look for the advancement of equality and justice.[44]

## Connecting Feminist Leaders to Seed New Funds

Women's funds have also benefited from great leadership. Another example of a women's movement leader who has played a seminal role in the Global Women's Funding Movement is Hope Chigudu. For ten years, Hope was Chair of the board of the Zimbabwe Women's Resource Centre. Around the same time that the Centre was formed, the Global Fund for Women was also being birthed by Anne Murray in 1987. Anne visited Zimbabwe to talk about the importance of this new women's fund, the result being that Hope joined the board and eventually took on the position of Chair of the Fund. Hope also sat on the board of the Urgent Action Fund (UAF), founded in 1997 following the Fourth World Conference on Women in Beijing. The co-founders had identified a severe gap between activists' needs in the face of crises or unexpected opportunities and the resources available to them, especially in areas experiencing armed conflict or escalating violence. Most donors required several months to process a grant request, but many interventions had only a small window of opportunity in which they could be effective. By 2001, a significant portion of UAF's Rapid Response Grants were going to women's rights groups in conflict-affected areas of Africa. UAF consulted with activists from countries throughout Africa, and the board decided to establish a local presence in Nairobi to provide more strategic and informed support to women activists throughout the continent. Eventually, UAF-Africa became semi-autonomous, and Hope was its first Chair.

The Global Fund for Women encouraged and supported the formation of regional funds and that is how the African Women's Development Fund was born. The fund used the Zimbabwe Women's Resource Centre as a fiscal sponsor and, later, when it was well established, Hope was asked to be its technical organizational development advisor. This is a role that she still plays.

## Deploying Rapid Funds for Feminist Resistance and Revolution

The revolution led by women in Sudan in 2019 is a stunning example of the unique relationship between women's funds and the women's movement. It was at this time that women rose to take down one of history's most merciless patriarchal monsters.

Founded in 2001, Urgent Action Fund-Africa (UAF-Africa) is a pan-African and feminist fund that uses a rapid-response grantmaking model to support unanticipated, time-sensitive, innovative, and bold initiatives across the continent. With staff in Kenya, Uganda, Burundi, Egypt, Ethiopia, Nigeria, Cameroon, and Zimbabwe, UAF-Africa provides grants and resources that enable African women's rights and gender justice activists, organizations, and movements to seize the opportunities within crises. UAF-Africa seeks to break patriarchal patterns and systems, and raise women's voices and visibility so they can significantly influence politics and laws on the continent. The fund's activist character, strengthened through its network of over 120 activist advisers across Africa, centers movement building at the core of their work. Their proximity to the frontlines gives women's funds, like UAF-Africa, the vision and agility to respond with flexible funds to the urgent and ever-shifting needs of grassroots women's groups.[45]

In 2019, a huge mandate arose for UAF-Africa to provide wellbeing, security, and support to women human rights defenders who were faced with threats and attacks as a direct result of their activism during the Sudanese women-led revolution. President Omar al-Bashir had waged terror on the nation for 30 years. He presided over the murders of more than 300,000 Sudanese and used his military to hone rape as a weapon of genocidal war.[46] Wanted by the International Criminal Court for crimes against humanity, by 2019 al-Bashir's brutality was in full force in quashing unrest among the people, particularly the women and girls who were rising up most fiercely and in the greatest numbers. Women had taken over the streets of Sudan's capital, Khartoum, for four months, creating a "street movement." It is estimated that 70 percent of the thousands of protesters were women.[47] Some Sudanese, in solidarity, called them "Kandakas," a reference to the earliest known, independently ruling African queen of ancient Nubia.[48]

These women human rights defenders had established a "Revolutionary Area" of Khartoum, setting up and staffing food stations, feeding thousands of protesters, keeping them vital and able to stay on the scene. The women were united in protest against worsening social conditions, including escalating food and medicine prices, and the "public order" laws which regulate their every action, from how they dress, to how they cover their hair, to how they travel in public. Many women accused of violating these laws were often tried without a lawyer, fined, and sentenced to jail or public lashings— women journalists, women dissidents, and any woman who dared to criticize the regime were especially targeted.[49]

The very act of protesting required fierce courage on the part of women and girls not only because it put them at risk of retaliation by regime forces but also because many suffered severe consequences when they returned home. Most Sudanese actively avoided attracting al-Bashir's wrath. Often, protesters were beaten by family members, forced into home confinement, or, worse, shunned and exiled for participating in the revolution. This avoidance and punitive attitude toward the protesters is another demonstration of how misogyny serves to enforce patriarchy's institutional power by violently policing rigid gender norms that suppress women's power. Many girls and women, however, felt they had nothing left to lose. Some said they would rather die in the streets than return home and continue under intolerable conditions. Throughout the revolution, UAF-Africa supported Sudanese women's human rights defenders and groups ranging from evacuation and relocation support, psychosocial support, and medical support.[50]

Despite the grim circumstances and the menacing military presence the protests provoked, joy was contagious in the crowds of women protesters in Khartoum. Hope for an end of the brutal dictatorship grew with the numbers of women uniting against it. In the dusk of April 8, 2019, 22-year-old activist Alaa Salah climbed up onto the hood of a car before the mass of protesters. "Women have a voice! It is our revolution!" she called out. "Revolution!" the hundreds thundered back. "They jailed … burnt us in the name of religion," she proclaimed. "Revolution!" the crowd roared as one.

There's a powerful alchemy present in movements. It was that unique mixture of hope, power, political intent, camaraderie, rebellion, and gratitude that moved Alaa to rise up to sing to the women and girls leading the revolution against al-Bashir. "I was in the Revolution area and found a group of girls behind the car. I asked the girls whether I could cheer them," explained Alaa, "I climbed on the car and chanted and cheered with them."[51] It's a long-practiced tradition in Sudan for women to sing to soldiers to defy ruthless leaders and to boost their morale. Alaa sang to the women and girls from the car hood, "The bullet doesn't kill. What kills is the silence of the people," which is a well-known protest chant during the 2018–2019 Sudanese protests and the earlier 2011–2013 Sudanese protests.[52] In that instant, a local photographer snapped a photo of Alaa, and it went viral on social media.

The image of Alaa, in a plain white traditional headscarf and dress, confidently pointing her finger up to the sky, evoked for many Sudanese memories of their mothers and grandmothers who had marched the streets demonstrating against previous military dictatorships in the 1960s, 1970s, and 1980s. She was dubbed "Lady Liberty" on social media and, within hours, news outlets throughout the world began reporting on the story behind the contagious image of the heroic and peaceful revolution being led by women.

Suddenly, Alaa became the international symbol of confidence in the face of powerful and horrifying male forces. She personified the modern-day revolution: women-led, peaceful, political, full of hope, and resolute. As her image gained media traction and spread throughout the internet, the throngs of women protesters in Khartoum grew. "Break the girls, because if you break the girls, you break the men" was the message from al-Bashir's government issued to its military officers in response to the women's protests against his regime.[53] The same day Alaa captured the world's attention, the military turned on the brutal dictator, defying his orders.[54]

Al-Bashir was soon after taken into custody to await extradition to face the consequences of his horrific crimes. Six months later, Alaa stood before the UN Security Council giving a speech to world leaders on why women must be equally represented in the now-forming civilian Sudanese government.[55]

By funding the frontlines, as with the Sudanese women's movement, women's funds are adept at detecting the morphing threats, such as continued violence against women human rights defenders, and at identifying emerging opportunities for women's leadership. Urgent Action Fund-Africa quickly deployed financial and capacity-building resources to ensure the women's movement leaders had continued meaningful involvement in the formation of the democracy, something the Sudanese women's movement made possible, including helping shape the laws and draft the new constitution. UAF-Africa advocated for women human rights defenders to be represented in the leading councils of the Forces of Freedom and Change, a wide political coalition of civilian and rebel groups that came together to lead a transition to the return to democracy.[56] UAF-Africa documented the continued military resistance to women's leadership in the transition.[57] Ndana Bofu-Tawamba, Executive Director of UAF-Africa, says:

> The mere fact that most people who work in women's funds and who are driving work within women's funds are not technocrats but activists themselves, I think that is at the core of what makes the work that we do different from mainstream philanthropy and other types of philanthropy.[58]

Huda Shafig of the Women of Sudanese Civic and Political Groups (MANSAM) coalition says:

> I understand change doesn't happen overnight, and we face resistance. But gender justice cannot be ignored and should be at the top of the government's agenda ... The same laws that were there under Bashir are still there now. Women continue to face discrimination and harassment even after the protests. So, for us, the revolution isn't over, but continues every day.[59]

Today, the country is again in the midst of a civil war triggered by conflict between the Sudan Armed Forces (SAF) and the paramilitary Rapid Support Forces (RSF). Civilians are caught in the crossfire, and women are especially impacted in this growing humanitarian crisis, so the work of women's movements remains critical, including in mobilizing for food and water security to address basic needs.

"Sometimes the work is just to hold the line, right?", says Melinda Wells, Vice-President Strategic Partnerships, Equality Fund:

> This notion of what you've achieved, sometimes it's just fighting back against the backlash, which is what we've seen. Certainly, we're not living in an unusual moment. There's been backlash throughout history facing women's movements, but sometimes just holding the line is the work, right?[60]

## Investing in Women's Leadership to Build the Movement

Women's funds cultivate women's movements by investing in the women leaders, like the Kandakas, who emerge to build the movements. Women's funds invest money in these diverse, intersectional, and intergenerational leaders. They also provide a wealth of connections and capacity-building know-how. Sometimes, it's precisely these non-financial investments that help turbocharge social justice efforts—building leaders' visibility and capacity through women's funds' deep and influential networks, which have been expanding for decades. Women's movement leaders typically emerge from the frontlines to sound the alarm over an issue affecting many. They come equipped with many skills, strategies, and solutions that are based on their unique first-hand experiences.

This kind of acutely lived experience is extremely valuable; however, to be effective, women's movements need connections to spheres of influence and access to philanthropists who can fund their critical efforts. Women's funds have long-standing reputations for championing bold and effective leadership within their communities and for innovating cutting-edge social justice strategies within philanthropy. In addition to providing grants, they can share a long list of deep connections to support activist leaders, connecting them to networks, resources, donors, and influential forums to lead transformational change.

According to the Women's Funding Network's 2022 Landscape Study:

> Each Women's Funding Network member is a critical enabler of local progress. Their cross-sector relationships and spheres of influence

include government, corporate, non-profit, entrepreneurs and venture capital partners, and civic engagement organizations. While not the biggest player at any of these tables—their trust-based social capital propels their success. Sitting at the intersection of philanthropy and advocacy means women's funds are both using data-driven insights to educate policymakers about expanding public goods while they are also funding the incubation of grassroots-led strategies that lead to building their community's power of economic self-determination and dignity.[61]

As Stephanie Clohesy, founding member of the Iowa Women's Foundation, has said, women's funds are not the gatekeepers of wealth, but the gate openers.

Françoise Moudouthe, CEO of the African Women's Development Fund, reflects:

> I think women's funds and feminist funds can really be opener of doors in terms of, for us in African communities and movements, amplifying their own narratives, lifting those voices that are too often ignored. We have a very big and global stage that we can speak on.[62]

In 2006, the New York Women's Foundation was funding the group, CAAAV: Organizing Asian Communities. Their mission is "to build grassroots community power across diverse poor and working-class Asian immigrant and refugee communities in New York City." Founded in 1986 by Asian working-class women alarmed by the spike of hate violence in Asian communities, CAAAV set out to stop the abuses at their source by organizing Asian communities to specifically address institutional racism and fight for institutional change.[63]

Ai-jen Poo, was an organizer on the staff of CAAAV at the time, who had an idea of addressing institutional change from a different angle. Ai-jen wanted to build a movement of domestic workers—a challenging task since domestic workers typically have no common workplace to gather. Domestic workers, which include nannies, home care workers, and house cleaners in private homes, all provide care and cleaning services. They typically work alone, in isolation, in their bosses' homes, with no labor protections while receiving a below-minimum wage. These work conditions create tremendous risk for abuse. In the U.S., most (91.5%) domestic workers are women, and just over half (52.4%) are Black, Hispanic, or Asian American/Pacific Islander women. The entire global economic system relies on this unacknowledged and undervalued workforce that ensures offices are cleaned, children, people with disabilities, and the sick elderly are taken care of, and food is prepared for families and workers.

In 2006, Ai-jen had ideas on how to organize domestic workers to fight for minimum wage and worker protections:

> One of the first things I did when I started in this line of work was try to invite these women to come together collectively. It's not like there's a water cooler or co-workers around for a lot of these jobs.[64]

According to Ana Oliveira, CEO of the New York Women's Foundation (NYWF):

> Ai-jen approached the Foundation and said, "I am working with domestic workers. I'm looking to organize them. I already run a group or two. For me to dedicate more time, I need more investments. Would you support that? I haven't been able to get others to see that I can organize them because, typically, people look at organizing people that are physically in one location and domestic workers are not. But that is not the case. I'm organizing them regardless of their physical location." We considered that, and we began to fund her.[65]

Having secured $30,000 from her first funder, NYWF, Ai-jen got busy organizing, protecting, and empowering this scattered workforce. She explains:

> We held health fairs so people, specifically undocumented workers, had access to health care and preventative care. We had "Do you know your rights?" clinics for people who had legal questions. We would have meetings where people would come together, have food, and share their stories. We had open mics where people would talk about their weeks, which was really powerful. There is a confidence that comes through working collectively.[66]

Bringing domestic workers together in a movement was key, Ai-jen explains:

> This helped them break out of that isolation and realize that there's so many others who experience the same vulnerability, the same types of struggles and challenges they're facing. It gave them a chance to not only support each other in the short term but to work together to change the root issues.

The seed funding from New York Women's Foundation was the jet fuel Ai-jen needed to propel her efforts. She was able to quickly unify domestic workers in massive numbers behind a common agenda, which convinced other funders to invest in the domestic workers movement too. Ai-jen helped to organize the first national meeting of domestic worker organizations in 2007, which resulted in the formation of the National Domestic Workers Alliance that year. She has been NDWA's director since April 2010. Ana explains:

> We funded her, and she rapidly grew Domestic Workers United. After we funded her work, it was much easier for her to get other people to fund, which is exactly the goal that we have. We have a goal of stepping in and seeing people and seeing the value of them and their work before others do. That is a very important role that we perform. She passed the Domestic Workers Bill of Rights in New York State and then went to California and then the rest is history.[67]

Under Ai-jen's leadership, the National Domestic Workers Alliance has become an advocacy powerhouse for the 2.5 million domestic workers who work as nannies, home care workers, and house cleaners in private homes, providing care and cleaning services. NDWA operates as a movement that's powered by over 250,000 domestic workers who are its active members, representing all 50 states, and more than 70 local affiliate organizations.[68] NDWA has achieved tremendous victories in a very short span of time, starting with the passage of the Domestic Worker Bills of Rights, first in New York State, and then in ten more states, as well as in the cities of Seattle and Philadelphia.[69] NDWA has established minimum wage protections for close to 2 million home care workers – a policy that is linked to dramatic declines in poverty rates.[70]

The partnership between the NYWF and Ai-jen is a powerful example of how women's funds invest in women leaders to build movements that address the root causes of oppression and replace them with systems that deliver economic, racial, and gender justice.

In 2011, Ai-jen founded Caring Across Generations to unite family caregivers, care workers, people with disabilities, and older Americans with a mission to build a strong care infrastructure so that we can all live, work, care, and age with dignity. As Ai-jen has built the domestic workers movement and has led a cultural shift around how we value care, she too has grown in influence. Her reputation as a champion of domestic workers enables her to move at greater speeds in spheres of power, and her voice is more prominent in the national discourse on many critical social issues. "She even went to the 2018 Golden Globes with Meryl Streep because of her crucial involvement in the MeToo movement."[71]

After the 2016 U.S. Presidential Election, Ai-jen and other leading activists were regularly stopped on the streets by women asking what they could do next. Knowing the Trump administration's harmful policies would require women across the country and across demographics to unite, organize, and vote, in 2017, Ai-jen teamed up with Aliza Garza, a co-founder of the Black Lives Matter movement, and Cecile Richards, former president of Planned Parenthood Federation of America, and they launched Supermajority to "create a voting advocacy hub focused not only on protecting women's rights, but on bringing women together as a political force that transcended age, race, and background."[72]

Movements are born when many leaders unite behind a common effort. Ai-jen and Aliza are united on numerous social justice movement frontlines. Aliza is also now the Special Projects Director for the National Domestic Workers Alliance. [73]

## Funding Systemic Change That Includes Reproductive Justice

Just as Ai-jen and Aliza unite and collaborate on synergistic social justice efforts, the Global Women's Funding Movement works as a highly collaborative movement too. Women's funds often unite to address the biggest threats against women, girls, and gender-expansive people, share strategies, recruit other philanthropic leaders, and unite with other movements to be more impactful.

No matter how safe we consider ourselves, protecting women's rights requires constant vigilance and new approaches wherever women, girls, and gender-expansive people are. The Global Women's Funding Movement has long been at the forefront as funders in defending reproductive freedom and sexual freedom and in pursuing reproductive justice, and this commitment has also contributed to building a diverse and inclusive movement. Many of the innovations that grew out of grants received from the women's funds have resulted in systemic reproductive rights victories in the most hostile climates. These include countries in the Global South, like Colombia, Mexico, and Argentina, who struggle under the powerful grip of patriarchal, religious, and cultural forces. But with the aid of the persistent and well-resourced women's movements, these countries recently ushered in a victory for universal abortion rights.

Amelia Wu, a former senior director at the Global Fund for Women, reflects:

> Beginning in the early 1990s, there was a consortium of US funders that pooled resources to advance abortion rights in Mexico over a period of 5–10 years. The long-term funding contributed to the strengthening of a movement that has led to the legalization of abortion in Mexico.[74]

The patriarchy moves swiftly and often stealthy with their assaults—this truth is best exemplified by the 2022 stealth strategy reversal of the *Roe v. Wade* decision in the U.S. This half-century-old Supreme Court ruling established a federal legal framework for abortion rights. *Roe*'s reversal triggered the end of federal abortion rights in the United States. Since then, a total of 21 states have moved to ban or restrict abortion.[75] In many states, exceptions do not exist for abortion in cases of rape or incest, which violates international law. Black and brown people and individuals below the poverty line—the people who already face limited access to sexual and reproductive health services such as contraception and who also experience inequities across broader social and economic dimensions—are the ones the bans will impact most severely as they make up the majority of those who obtain abortions in the United States.[76]

Women's funds used their own stealth strategies to try to get ahead of the curve, and with some success. Lauren Y. Casteel, President and CEO, Women's Foundation of Colorado, says:

> We were very active in the passing of the Reproductive Health Equity Act, and that was before the *Dobbs* case and *Roe v. Wade* went down because we saw the writing on the wall. The legislation passed, and there will be a movement to get it into the constitution in 2024.[77]

According to the Center for Reproductive Rights, 41 percent of women worldwide live in countries with restrictive abortion laws. These restrictions have a significant impact on women's lives: each year, the World Health Organization estimates that 39,000 women and girls die from the consequences of unsafe abortions. However, even in countries where abortion is legal, barriers may still exist, such as high costs, waiting times, parental or marital consent requirements, and social stigma.[78]

In truth, *Roe* had long failed many pregnant people seeking abortion. *Roe* was never going to deliver reproductive justice—best proven by the fact that, for the half-century in which it was the law, it never did.

Monica Simpson, Executive Director of SisterSong, an Astraea Lesbian Foundation for Justice (and Ford Foundation) grantee and the largest national multi-ethnic reproductive justice collective in the U.S, explains:

> [I]t's important to keep in mind that Roe never fully protected Black women—or poor women or so many others in this country. That's because Roe ensured the right to abortion without ensuring that people could actually *get* an abortion. People seeking abortions in America must consider: Do I have the money? How far is the nearest

clinic, and can I get there? Can I take off work? Will I be safe walking into the clinic? For more privileged people, these questions are rarely a deterrent. But for many women of color and poor people, they are major obstacles. That's how white supremacy works."[79]

## Sustaining Funding for Rights and Movements Under Attack

For many in the Global Women's Funding Movement, the reversal of the *Roe v Wade* decision is a crisis that also presents an immense opportunity, and a mandate, to replace *Roe* with true, systemic reproductive justice. The loss in the United States contrasts starkly with Latin America and Africa which have experienced tremendous progress in sexual and reproductive justice. The Marea Verde or "Green Wave" movement for abortion rights began in Argentina and continues to sweep across Latin America, creating seismic culture shifts that are leading to long-fought reproductive rights victories that are making their way to U.S. shores now, too. The Green Wave and legalization of abortion throughout Latin America were the result of decades of movement building for abortion rights in Argentina. Vital here has been constant vigilance to sustain momentum. Its unifying force has been the Campaña Nacional por el Derecho al Aborto (National Campaign for the Right to Legal, Safe, and Free Abortion), which was created in 2005 and, itself, was built on almost two decades of activism.[80] Argentina is a Catholic-majority country, with 92 percent identifying as Catholic.[81] This is why Catholics for the Right to Decide-Argentina (CDD-Argentina), a longtime grantee partner of the then International Women's Health Coalition (IWHC), was one of the leaders of the national coalition.[82]

In 2021, the same year as the Green Wave victory in Argentina, the International Women's Health Coalition (IWHC), the International Planned Parenthood Federation Western Hemisphere Region (IPPFWHR), and the Center for Health and Gender Equity (CHANGE) merged together into a feminist alliance to "aspire to co-create a feminist future where all women, girls, and gender-diverse people have the support, information, and services they need to make their own choices about their bodies, their sexuality, and their lives." They named the alliance "Fòs Feminista," with "Fòs" signifying strength in Haitian Creole and "Feminista" meaning feminist in many languages.[83] Today, the Fòs Feminista alliance includes more than 170 organizations worldwide,[84] focused on sexual and reproductive health care and activism. Fòs Feminista is on a mission to spread the power of the Green Wave that began in Argentina to expand abortion rights in other parts of the world. In 2021, Mexico's Supreme Court also ruled that criminalizing abortion is unconstitutional, paving the way for Mexico to become the most populous Latin American country to legalize abortion.

To fortify the victory in Mexico, Fòs Feminista now supports more than a dozen local organizations to ensure the ruling results in increased access to safe abortion for pregnant people. The Green Wave continues to have success with Uruguay, Cuba, and Guyana each having enacted laws to increase access to abortion care.[85] The Green Wave provides inspiration for other feminist movements and is also providing its expertise and modern-day knowledge on how to push back against abortion bans and protect those seeking safe abortion care in illegal conditions.

Indeed, the loss of the *Roe* decision in the U.S. has triggered a powerful demonstration of how the Global Women's Funding Movement works as a movement, uniting across borders to quickly strategize on ways to furnish those seeking abortion in the U.S. with safe options. The reproductive rights victories in the Global South immediately became a source of options—and strategic perspective—for those fighting for the right to abortion care in the U.S. Countries that had struggled for decades under illegal abortion conditions have now, with newly won abortion rights, stepped up to help those seeking abortion care from the U.S. The frontline activists who have been addressing the denial of access for specific groups of people, both in the US and throughout the world, have unique solutions and expertise on how to provide safe abortion care in the context of its inaccessibility and criminality.

Following the Supreme Court ruling around abortion in the U.S., it became instantly dangerous for many abortion providers in the country to continue offering services. Consequently, collectives that had formed an abortion accompanying network in Mexico, such as one of Fondo Semillas' grantee partners Necesito Abortar, began to receive an increasing number of requests for help from women and girls in the U.S.[86] They call the service they provide the "acompañimiento," or accompaniment model. Health workers, often linked up through reproductive rights groups, guide patients, either virtually or in person, through the medication abortion treatment, providing information and, in some cases, the abortifacient.[87]

Giselle Carino, an Argentinian political scientist who took part in the campaign for legal abortion in her country, now serves as CEO of Fòs Feminista. "I look at Argentina with a lot of pride, of course, because that was a truly democratic effort," Carino explains, "It took decades for us, and we had many defeats. When we succeeded, it was because mobilization was huge: People would talk about abortion at the dinner tables, in bars, and cafes—and at the same time, we managed to put women in positions of power. We elected feminist representatives who would try to expand our struggle," she said. "Those were the two lessons: To make abortion a mainstream topic and to advance through political victories, bit by bit."[88]

Carino does not consider the striking down of *Roe v. Wade* to be a defeat. Instead, she sees it as an opportunity to advance feminism and to realize full reproductive justice. "Now it's the time to elect feminist leaders,"[89] she explains.

> A stronger feminist voice is needed now more than ever. The growth of right-wing authoritarianism and anti-gender movements, the climate change crisis, and the ongoing pandemic all disproportionately affect women and girls, with negative consequences for their sexual and reproductive health and rights. By acting in solidarity, we can meet these challenges with creativity and resilience.[90]
>
> Before this moment, the world was divided between the Global South and the U.S. Only now, after this moment, we receive a lot of requests from organizations in the U.S. to connect with folks in the Global South, to share strategy, to have dialogue, to share intelligence, to get together. But that's a new thing. It's not something that happened before.[91]

Given this, it makes sense that the leadership that helped create Fòs Feminista would be the ones now helping those in the U.S. states where abortion is now outlawed. Serra Sippel is interim executive director of the Brigid Alliance, an organization that was established to offer all-inclusive support to people in the U.S. traveling to reach an abortion provider. They book and pay for travel expenses, including childcare.[92] In the first nine months after *Dobbs*, the Brigid Alliance helped 30 percent more clients compared to the same period before the decision.[93] The average cost is $1,400 which does not include the cost of the procedure.[94] "Our clients are traveling farther. They travel an average of 1,300 miles round trip to get their abortion care," Sippel explains, "Research and experience also show that forcing people to travel long distances to receive abortion care frequently causes them to undergo a range of negative emotions, including distress, stress, anxiety and shame."[95] As the Brigid Alliance website explains, "Wherever someone needs to get to abortion care in the U.S., we find a way to get them there—through direct support and in collaboration with our network of partners."[96] Serra has two questions at the forefront of her mind, "How do we ensure safe abortion access when it's illegal? And what can we learn from the pro-abortion Green Wave in Latin America on social mobilisation?"[97]

Carino of Fòs Feminista brings an air of victory to all the organization's efforts:

> As an Argentinian woman, I'll never forget what it was like to march through the streets of Buenos Aires with thousands of women and girls in pañuelos verdes (green handkerchiefs), fighting for our human right to safe and legal abortion. I didn't yet know that these demonstrations would inspire an international movement that continues to grow in size and strength to this day. In just the last three years, we have won the right to abortion for millions of women—including in Argentina. Now, as abortion rights are under renewed attack in the United States, the Green Wave is a reminder of what we can achieve when we stand together.[98]

It's also a reminder of the crucial importance of providing flexible funding to women's and feminist movements and amplifying diverse voices for justice within these movements. This is the strength of women's funds. In building the Global Women's Funding Movement, these funds demonstrated the importance of reimagining philanthropy and shifting power to activist leaders and movements to redefine the issues and build momentum for a just, equitable, and transformed world. This includes supporting women's movements to hold ground as well as gain ground. These feminist philanthropic visionaries had shown how to build a diverse and inclusive global women's funding movement. The challenge now was how to sustain it.

## Notes

1  Jessica Horn, personal voice note via WhatsApp exchange with Laura Risimini, September 21, 2022.
2  Leymah Gbowee, "Liberian Nobel Peace Prize Laureate Leymah Gbowee: How a Sex Strike Propelled Men to Refuse War," Interview by Amy Goodman, *Truthout*, April 28, 2015, accessed on November 25, 2023, https://truthout.org/video/liberian-nobel-peace-prize-laureate-leymah-gbowee-how-a-sex-strike-propelled-men-to-refuse-war.
3  Dominique Bouchard on behalf of Abigail Disney, personal email communication with Jane Sloane, October 30, 2022.
4  Leymah Gbowee, *Mighty Be Our Powers: How Sisterhood, Prayer, and Sex Changed a Nation at War* (New York: Beast Books, 2011), Prologue.
5  Muriel Rukeyser, "Käthe Kollwitz," *The Collected Poems of Muriel Rukeyser* (University of Pittsburgh Press, 2006).

6  Charlotte Alter, Suyin Haynes, and Justin Worland, "Greta Thunberg: TIME's 2019 Person of the Year," *TIME Magazine*, 2019, accessed on November 25, 2023, https://time.com/person-of-the-year-2019-greta-thunberg.

7  Charlotte Alter, Suyin Haynes, and Justin Worland, "Greta Thunberg: TIME's 2019 Person of the Year," *TIME Magazine*, 2019, accessed on November 25, 2023, https://time.com/person-of-the-year-2019-greta-thunberg.

8  Hinde Pomeraniec, "How Argentina rose up against the murder of women," *The Guardian*, June 8, 2015, accessed on November 25, 2023, www.theguardian.com/lifeandstyle/2015/jun/08/argentina-murder-women-gender-violence-protest.

9  Hinde Pomeraniec, "How Argentina rose up against the murder of women," *The Guardian*, June 8, 2015, accessed on November 25, 2023, www.theguardian.com/lifeandstyle/2015/jun/08/argentina-murder-women-gender-violence-protest.

10  Uki Goñi, "Argentine Women Call Out Machismo," Opinion, *The New York Times*, June 15, 2015, accessed on November 25, 2023, www.nytimes.com/2015/06/16/opinion/argentine-women-call-out-machismo.html.

11  Alba Ruibal, "Case Study: Abortion in Argentina Movement Expansion, the Green Wave and Legalization," Fós Feminista, September 2022, accessed on November 25, 2023, https://fosfeminista.org/wp-content/uploads/2023/05/Fos-Feminista-Policy-Brief-Argentina-ENG-v4.pdf.

12  Lucía Leszinsky, "#NiUnaMenos six years on: triumphs and new demands of Argentina's feminist movement," Global Voices, June 22, 2021, accessed on November 25, 2023, https://globalvoices.org/2021/06/22/niunamenos-six-years-on-triumphs-and-new-demands-of-argentinas-feminist-movement.

13  Olivia B. Waxman, "The Inside Story of Why Take Your Daughter to Work Day Exists," *TIME Magazine*, April 26, 2007, accessed on November 25, 2023, https://time.com/4753128/take-your-our-daughters-to-work-day-history.

14  Sara Gould, interview by Laura Risimini, October 11, 2022.

15  Patti Chang, interview by Christine Grumm, September 27, 2022.

16  Dawn Oliver Wiand, interview by Stephanie Clohesy, July 11, 2022.

17  "Iowa Women's Foundation launches child care assistance initiative," *Business Record*, November 30, 2017, accessed on May 24, 2024, www.businessrecord.com/iowa-womens-foundation-launches-child-care-assistance-initiative.

18  Lauren Y. Casteel, interview by Laura Risimini, September 29, 2022.

19  Women's Funding Network, "Women's Fund Funds Video Project 12 9 88," December 9, 1988, 23:17, www.youtube.com/watch?v=DkuhHxrTTOM.

20  Women's Funding Network, "Women's Fund Funds Video Project 12 9 88," December 9, 1988, 23:17, www.youtube.com/watch?v=DkuhHxrTTOM.

21  Tracy Gary, personal email correspondence with Helen LaKelly Hunt, January 24, 2023.

22  Anne Delaney and Michelle Coffey, interview by Christine Grumm and Laura Risimini, September 5, 2023.

23 Anne Delaney and Michelle Coffey, interview by Christine Grumm and Laura Risimini, September 5, 2023.

24 Anne Delaney and Michelle Coffey, interview by Christine Grumm and Laura Risimini, September 5, 2023.

25 Anne Delaney and Michelle Coffey, interview by Christine Grumm and Laura Risimini, September 5, 2023.

26 Anne Delaney and Michelle Coffey, interview by Christine Grumm and Laura Risimini, September 5, 2023.

27 Anne Delaney and Michelle Coffey, interview by Christine Grumm and Laura Risimini, September 5, 2023.

28 Anne Delaney and Michelle Coffey, interview by Christine Grumm and Laura Risimini, September 5, 2023.

29 Matt Broomfield, "Women's March against Donald Trump is the largest day of protests in US history, say political scientists," *The Independent*, January 23, 2017, accessed on November 24, 2023, www.independent.co.uk/news/world/americas/womens-march-anti-donald-trump-womens-rights-largest-protest-demonstration-us-history-political-scientists-a7541081.html.

30 Maya Salam, "A Record 117 Women Won Office, Reshaping America's Leadership," *The New York Times*, November 7, 2018, accessed on November 24, 2023, www.nytimes.com/2018/11/07/us/elections/women-elected-midterm-elections.html.

31 Strength in Numbers Consulting Group for the New York Women's Foundation, *The Fund for the #MeToo Movement & Allies Year Two Evaluation.* November 2021.

32 Strength in Numbers Consulting Group for the New York Women's Foundation, *The Fund for the #MeToo Movement & Allies Year Two Evaluation.* November 2021.

33 "Beyond #MeToo: Movements in Asia," Asian Pacific Institute on Gender-Based Violence, accessed on November 24, 2023, www.api-gbv.org/resources/beyond-metoo-movements-in-asia.

34 Georgetown Institute for Women, Peace and Security, "The Ms. Q&A: Black Lives Matter Co-Founder Opal Tometi on the Fight for Racial Justice," *Ms. Magazine*, February 1, 2021, accessed on November 24, 2023, https://msmagazine.com/2021/02/01/black-history-monthblack-lives-matter-opal-tometi-racial-justice.

35 Rashawn Ray, "Black Lives Matter at 10 years: 8 ways the movement has been highly effective," The Brookings Institution, October 12, 2022, accessed on November 24, 2023, www.brookings.edu/articles/black-lives-matter-at-10-years-what-impact-has-it-had-on-policing.

36 "Black Lives Matter: Lessons from a Global Movement," American Studies Association, accessed on November 24, 2023, www.theasa.net/black-lives-matter-lessons-global-movement.

37  Srilatha Batliwala, quoted in Global Fund for Women, *Movement Capacity Assessment Tool* (San Francisco: Global Fund for Women, April 2018), accessed November 25, 2023, www.globalfundforwomen.org/wp-content/uploads/2018/06/MCAT-Public-Version-English.pdf.

38  Cass R. Sunstein, *How Change Happens* (The MIT Press, 2018), 34.

39  Jessica Houssian, interview by Christine Grumm and Laura Risimini, November 14, 2022.

40  Paige Andrew, interview by Christine Grumm and Laura Risimini, December 5, 2022.

41  "About Us," The New York Women's Foundation, accessed on November 24, 2023, https://nywf.org/about.

42  Christine Grumm, personal email communication with Jane Sloane, September 8, 2023.

43  Claudia Samcam, interview by Christine Grumm and Laura Risimini, November 23, 2022.

44  Emilienne de León, personal email communication with Christine Grumm, October 31, 2023.

45  Ndana Bofu-Tawamba. "How to Create Gender Justice in Africa," *Alliance Magazine*, September 3, 2019, accessed on November 24, 2023, www.alliancemagazine.org/feature/how-to-create-gender-justice-in-africa.

46  "Omar al-Bashir: Sudan agrees ex-president must face ICC", BBC News, February 11, 2020, accessed on November 24, 2023, www.bbc.com/news/world-africa-51462613.

47  Yassir Abdulla and Raja Razek, "Ousted Sudan President Omar al-Bashir sentenced to 2 years in correctional facility," CNN, December 14, 2019, accessed on November 24, 2023, www.cnn.com/2019/12/14/africa/sudan-omar-al-bashir-prison-sentence-intl.

48  Vanessa Friedman, "'It's Going to Be the Image of the Revolution,'" *The New York Times*, April 10, 2019, accessed on November 24, 2023, www.nytimes.com/2019/04/10/fashion/demonstration-clothing-women-sudan.html.

49  Nita Bhalla, "'The revolution isn't over' say Sudan's frontline female protesters," Reuters, September 19, 2019, accessed on November 24, 2023, www.reuters.com/article/us-sudan-women-rights/the-revolution-isnt-over-say-sudans-frontline-female%20protesters-idUSKBN1W4369.

50  Masa Amir, personal email communication with Laura Risimini, October 10, 2022.

51  Ruud Elmendorp, "Sudan's Protest Icon Alaa Salah 'Just One of the Million,'" Voice of America, April 30, 2019, accessed on November 24, 2023, www.youtube.com/watch?v=erT2ftJmq0g.

52  "Kandake of the Sudanese Revolution," Wikipedia, last modified on November 23 2023, accessed November 25, 2023, https://en.wikipedia.org/wiki/Kandake_of_the_Sudanese_Revolution.

53   Mia Archambault, "A Women's Revolution in Sudan," *The McGill International Review*, April 19, 2022, accessed November 25, 2023, www.mironline. ca/a-womens-revolution-in-sudan.

54   "Kandake of the Sudanese Revolution," Wikipedia, last modified on November 23 2023, accessed November 25, 2023, https://en.wikipedia.org/wiki/ Kandake_of_the_Sudanese_Revolution.

55   "Kandake of the Sudanese Revolution," Wikipedia, last modified on November 23 2023, accessed November 25, 2023, https://en.wikipedia.org/wiki/ Kandake_of_the_Sudanese_Revolution.

56   "Forces of Freedom and Change," Wikipedia, last modified on November 25 2023, accessed November 25, 2023, https://en.wikipedia.org/wiki/ Forces_of_Freedom_and_Change#cite_note-Vox_TMC_FFC_deal-2.

57   Masa Amir, personal email communication with Laura Risimini, October 10, 2022.

58   Ndana Bofu-Tawamba, interview by Laura Risimini, August 31, 2023.

59   Nita Bhalla, "'The revolution isn't over' say Sudan's frontline female protesters," Reuters, September 19, 2019, accessed on November 24, 2023, www.reuters.com/article/us-sudan-women-rights/the-revolution-isnt-over-say-sudans-frontline-female%20protesters-idUSKBN1W4369.

60   Melinda Wells, interview by Laura Risimini, May 10, 2023.

61   *Landscape Study of Women's Funds and Foundations, Part I* (San Francisco: Women's Funding Network, October 2022), accessed November 25, 2023, www. womensfundingnetwork.org/wp-content/uploads/2022/10/LandscapeReport-Part-1_2022.pdf.

62   Francoise Moudouthe, interview by Christine Grumm, November 9, 2022.

63   "History of CAAAV," CAAAV, accessed November 25, 2023, https://caaav. org/about-us/history-of-caaav.

64   Mia Mercado, "How Labor Activist Ai-jen Poo Gets It Done," *The Cut*, April 4, 2022, accessed November 25, 2023, www.thecut.com/2022/04/how-ai-jen-poo-gets-it-done.html.

65   Ana Oliveira, interview by Laura Risimini, October 28, 2022.

66   Mia Mercado, "How Labor Activist Ai-jen Poo Gets It Done," *The Cut*, April 4, 2022, accessed November 25, 2023, www.thecut.com/2022/04/how-ai-jen-poo-gets-it-done.html.

67   Ana Oliveira, interview by Laura Risimini, October 28, 2022.

68   Rebecca Sun, "ICM Partners Signs Labor Activist Ai-jen Poo (Exclusive)," *The Hollywood Reporter*, June 14, 2022, accessed November 25, 2023, www.hollywoodreporter. com/business/business-news/ai-jen-poo-icm-agency-1235165277.

69   "Aijen Poo," Spokespersons, National Domestic Workers Alliance, accessed November 25, 2023, www.domesticworkers.org/press/spokespersons/ai-jen-poo.

70   Joseph Parilla and Sifan Liu, "A $15 minimum wage would help millions of struggling households in small and mid-sized cities achieve self-sufficiency,"

The Brookings Institution, March 17, 2021, accessed November 25, 2023, www.brookings.edu/blog/the-avenue/2021/03/17/higher-regional-minimum-wages-can-lift-half-of-struggling-households-into-economic-self-sufficiency.

71  Mia Mercado, "How Labor Activist Ai-jen Poo Gets It Done," *The Cut*, April 4, 2022, accessed November 25, 2023, www.thecut.com/2022/04/how-ai-jen-poo-gets-it-done.html.

72  "Our Story," Supermajority, accessed November 25, 2023, https://super-majority.com/our-story.

73  "Avengers of the Week: Black Lives Matter Founders Patrisse Khan-Cullors, Alicia Garza, and Opal Tometi," Action Alert, Gender Avenger, July 10, 2020, accessed November 25, 2023, www.genderavenger.com/blog/avengers-of-the-week-patrisse-khan-cullors-alicia-garza-opal-tometi.

74  Amelia Wu, personal email communication with Musimbi Kanyoro, October 21, 2022.

75  Oriana González, "Where abortion has been banned now that Roe v. Wade is overturned," *Axios*, July 17, 2023, accessed November 25, 2023, www.axios.com/2022/06/25/abortion-illegal-7-states-more-bans-coming.

76  Professor Terry McGovern, J.D., *Sexual and Reproductive Justice as the Vehicle to Deliver the Nairobi Summit Commitments*, 2022 Report of the High-Level Commission on the Nairobi Summit on ICPD25, November 10, 2022, accessed November 25, 2023, www.nairobisummiticpd.org/sites/default/files/HLC%20Report_11-01.pdf.

77  Lauren Y. Casteel, interview by Laura Risimini, September 29, 2022.

78  "Where Do Abortion Rights Stand In The World In 2023?" Focus 2030, accessed November 25, 2023, https://focus2030.org/Where-do-abortion-rights-stand-in-the-world-in-2023.

79  Monica Simpson, "To Be Pro-Choice, You Must Have the Privilege of Having Choices," *The New York Times*, April 11, 2022, accessed November 25, 2023, www.nytimes.com/2022/04/11/opinion/abortion-black-brown-women.html.

80  Alba Ruibal, "Case Study: Abortion in Argentina Movement Expansion, the Green Wave and Legalization," Fós Feminista, September 2022, accessed on November 25, 2023, https://fosfeminista.org/wp-content/uploads/2023/05/Fos-Feminista-Policy-Brief-Argentina-ENG-v4.pdf.

81  Uki Goñi, "Argentinians formally leave Catholic church over stance on abortion," *The Guardian*, September 9, 2018, accessed on November 25, 2023, www.theguardian.com/world/2018/sep/09/argentina-catholic-church-legalize-abortion-apostacy.

82  Shena Cavallo, "Argentina gets closer to expanded abortion rights," openDemocracy, April 3, 2018, accessed on November 25, 2023, www.opendemocracy.net/en/democraciaabierta/argentina-gets-closer-to-expanded-abortion-rights.

83  "About Us," Fós Feminista, accessed on November 25, 2023, https://fosfeminista.org/about-us-2.

84 "Fòs Feminista Board Member Search," Fós Feminista, accessed on November 25, 2023, https://fosfeminista.org/wp-content/uploads/2022/08/Fo%CC%80s-Feminista-Board-Elections-ENG.pdf.

85 "Latin America's Marea Verde movement secures new victory in Colombia," The Sigrid Rausing Trust, February 25, 2022, accessed on November 25, 2023, www.sigrid-rausing-trust.org/story/latin-americas-marea-verde-movement-secures-new-victory-in-colombia.

86 Tania Turner, personal email communication with Laura Risimini, November 21, 2022.

87 David Shortell, "A Mexican network is sending abortion drugs to American women," CNN, July 14, 2022, accessed on November 25, 2023, www.cnn.com/2022/07/13/americas/mexican-network-abortion-drugs-usa-intl.

88 Stefano Pozzebon, "Abortion rights activists in the US can learn from recent progress on abortion access in Latin America," CNN, May 12, 2022, accessed on November 25, 2023, www.cnn.com/2022/05/07/americas/abortion-analysis-latin-america-activists-intl-latam/index.html.

89 Stefano Pozzebon, "Abortion rights activists in the US can learn from recent progress on abortion access in Latin America," CNN, May 12, 2022, accessed on November 25, 2023, www.cnn.com/2022/05/07/americas/abortion-analysis-latin-america-activists-intl-latam/index.html.

90 "Fòs Feminista to Advance Sexual and Reproductive Health, Rights, and Justice Across the Global South," Fós Feminista, October 29, 2021, accessed on November 25, 2023, https://fosfeminista.org/media/fos-feminista-launch.

91 Giselle Carino, interview by Christine Grumm, October 18, 2022.

92 Serra Sippel, "Abortion restrictions cause mental health strains, too," The Washington Post, May 21, 2023, accessed on November 25, 2023, www.washingtonpost.com/opinions/2023/05/21/abortion-restrictions-mental-health-strains.

93 Serra Sippel, "Abortion restrictions cause mental health strains, too," The Washington Post, May 21, 2023, accessed on November 25, 2023, www.washingtonpost.com/opinions/2023/05/21/abortion-restrictions-mental-health-strains.

94 Rebekah Sager, "These abortion funds and practical support groups are bridging the gap for patients," American Journal News, June 15, 2023, accessed on May 15, 2024, https://americanindependent.com/abortion-funds-texas-practical-support-groups.

95 Serra Sippel, "Abortion restrictions cause mental health strains, too," The Washington Post, May 21, 2023, accessed on November 25, 2023, www.washingtonpost.com/opinions/2023/05/21/abortion-restrictions-mental-health-strains.

96 "We get people to abortion care, whatever it takes," The Brigid Alliance, accessed on November 25, 2023, https://brigidalliance.org.

97  Husna Jalal and Nadia van der Linde, "Backlash And Progress: Reflections About Recent SRHR Developments at the UN and in the USA," WO=MEN, Dutch Gender Platform, By, July 13, 2022, accessed on November 25, 2023, www.wo-men.nl/en/blog-post/backlash-and-progress-reflections-about-recent-srhr-developments-at-the-un-and-in-the-usa.

98  "A Brief History of the Green Wave," Fós Feminista, October 15, 2021, accessed on November 25, 2023, https://fosfeminista.org/media/a-brief-history-of-the-green-wave/#:~:text=In%20just%20the%20last%20three,achieve%20when%20we%20stand%20together.

# Nothing About Us Without Us

# 3

## Trust-Based Philanthropy

### Keeping It Real

Intersectionality is at the core of every great social justice advancement in history because the most powerful movements are led by those most affected by the injustice at hand. These movements are the ones who are the most aware of the intersecting problems, best poised to identify the solutions needed, and most motivated to find them.

Civil rights attorney, feminist legal scholar, and women's fund grantee, Kimberlé Crenshaw, coined the term "intersectionality" in 1989 to represent the theory that women's lives are influenced by many overlapping systems, or "intersections," of discrimination or disadvantage. Crenshaw explains in her seminal work, *Demarginalizing the Intersection of Race and Sex*, "Because the intersectional experience is greater than the sum of racism and sexism, any analysis that does not take intersectionality into account cannot sufficiently address the particular manner in which Black women are subordinated."[1]

The concept of intersectionality describes the ways in which systems of inequality based on gender, race, ethnicity, sexual orientation, disability, class, casteism, and other forms of discrimination "intersect" to create unique dynamics and effects. For instance, the burden of unpaid care carried by girls and women is further magnified when we also apply a racial lens to understand the even higher impact of unpaid care on girls and women of color. Its why women's movements are saying that climate justice isn't possible without care justice and why the global women's movement is funding such work.

DOI: 10.4324/9781003330455-3

It was feminist writer and activist bell hooks who said, "Intersectionality allow us to focus on what is most important at a given point in time."[2] The feminist theorist Judith Butler elaborated on this by saying:

> Intersectionality has made an important contribution to social and political analysis, asking all of us to think about what assumptions of race and class we make when we speak about "women" or what assumptions of gender and race we make when we speak about "class." It allows us to unpack those categories and see the various kinds of social formations and power relations that constitute those categories.[3]

Intersectionality is considered one of the most important contributions of feminist scholarship in the realm of human inquiry.[4] It provides a more revealing, stronger lens with a more precise focus to examine and respond to social inequity and humanity's most pressing issues. Intersectionality increasingly informs policy planning and implementation in fields as varied as health care, criminal justice, economic policy, and climate change solutions. This is the reason why intersectionality is under sustained attack by right-wing forces because it is a powerful and proven tool in strengthening democracy and delivering social justice victories.

Ise Bosch, co-founder of the Pecunia Network of Women with Inherited Wealth, and the German women's fund, filia, and a founder donor of Astraea, says, "As they like to say in the US, if it ain't horizontal, it ain't feminist. Right? Horizontal means intersectional. You think inclusively, and you think bottom up. And you include. You network. You network with that kind of 'bottom up' view. I think understanding feminism and understanding intersectionality almost equals out. If you're feminist, you take intersectionality really seriously."[5]

The Global Women's Funding Movement invests in intersectional leadership and innovates intersectional philanthropic practices that are guided by the expertise of those with lived experiences of intersecting injustices. With intersectional philanthropic practices, such as trust-based philanthropy, the most affected shape the vision, lead the movements, and direct the philanthropic dollars to where they determine they are needed most.

Committing to diverse staff, board, donors, and grantees of women's funds and inclusive work and funding practices, coupled with an active commitment to intersectionality, provides the vision and foundation for everything women's funds do. This has been true since the Global Women's Funding Movement's earliest origins. Intersectionality is a feminist funding principle because it connects the intersections of injustice to reveal a more complete and precise roadmap to social justice solutions.

As Latanya Mapp Frett, the former CEO of the Global Fund for Women, says:

> [G]rassroots movements, in my opinion … really get to the corner-stone of intersectionality … You can't say, Oh, here's some resources for HIV/AIDS, but don't do women's health, don't do infant health, just do HIV/AIDS in your organization and in your community. And there's just the pushback that comes is because women know that we don't live sectional lives, right? We do all of it. We all have to do all of it. So, we have to get the kids to the doctors. We have to get the kids to the school. We have to educate ourselves. We have to take care of the house. We got to get to the job. So all of those things are relevant. We can't just say we're going to do one thing.
>
> I think the value of having grassroots led movements is because they understand very well this intersectionality and can do programs on food security the same time they're doing programs on women's health, and at the same time that they're down at down at the PTA at their schools trying to fix what's happening at the schools. So, for me, this privilege that comes with being very sectional doesn't exist very much at the community level.[6]

Esther Mwaura Muiru, Founder and Coordinator, GROOTS Kenya (Grassroots Organizations Operating Together in Sisterhood), speaks of the critical importance in investing in the collective organizing of women, saying:

> Women don't have that privilege [of organizing on one issue at a time], those who are living in poverty. They cannot decide, today, I will deal with the health of my children and my community, and tomorrow I will deal with food security. They deal with all those issues every day at every given hour. We are one of the organizations that had to really focus the donors to see the connectivity of those issues and to stop fragmenting the work.[7]

Language also matters when it comes to an intersectional lens. Tania Turner, former Executive Director of Fondo Semillas says:

> We labeled our programs as broad as we could imagine (Body, Land, Work, Identities) so everything can fit in them. We want to respond to the needs of the activists in the field and the issues that movements identify as priorities, instead of predefining an

agenda with a narrow perspective about what to support. All these programs are related and intertwined. Activists can request funding for any topic they are working on, and we know they work on many topics in an intersectional way. This strategy provides us with a good mapping tool to respond to movements that is useful to make decisions, but also to advocate with other donors so we all can respond to the movements and not the other way around. This is fundamental for shifting power.[8]

Intersectionality factors the political, social, and historical contexts in which oppression and injustice happens, whether based on race, gender, class, caste, sexuality, religion, or disability, and identifies how the intersecting oppressions create unique and compounding inequalities in women's and other marginalized people's lives. High rates of asthma in children in the poorest parts of the inner city can be better addressed when factoring that racism designed the layout of residential areas. Indigenous people, people of color, and those who are poor are often "redlined" into environmentally toxic regions with high levels of contaminated air and lack of trees and into "food deserts" where affordable healthy options are unavailable—all contributing to high rates of asthma.[9,10] Without applying the lens of intersectionality to data sets, these compounding injustices—and the paths to solutions—are frequently unseen. As a result, the actual cause of the toxic problem goes unaddressed, worsens, and becomes endemic. Today, intersectionality is used as an analytical framework to discuss the most critical issues of our time in nearly every facet of society including in philanthropy, academia, health care[11], law,[12] and career development.[13] And yet gender is often missing when it comes to philanthropic organizations applying an intersectional lens to issues and opportunities.

In an article written by Surina Khan, former CEO of the California Women's Foundation, and Lucia Corral Peña, Senior Program Officer with Blue Shield of California Foundation, they said:

> The philanthropic community has made great strides to include a race and class analysis in our research and grantmaking, and the time has come to elevate gender into our analyses. To move beyond what is, to what can be. If we are to truly achieve transformative systems change, using an intersectional approach that includes gender along with race and class in all aspects of our work will be key to transforming culture towards justice, liberation, and our nation's fundamental value that all people are created equal.[14]

## Applying a Gender and Racial Equity Lens for Giving

Women and girls of color are pivotal frontline leaders and organizers in the powerful social change movements that pave the way for a more equitable and just democracy. As part of its commitment to applying a gender and racial equity lens to its philanthropy, the Ms. Foundation commissioned a report, *Pocket Change: How Women and Girls of Color Do More with Less*,[15] to better understand how they do this work and to ask critical questions of philanthropy and donors: How is philanthropy supporting or not supporting women and girls of color? Are philanthropic practices in alignment with the breadth of advocacy and services that women of color-led organizations provide? How can we change our practices to center women and girls of color in our giving and hold ourselves accountable?

The report included this analysis:

> As a group, women and girls of color live at the intersection of multiple systems of oppression, and we already know that the Covid-19 pandemic is having a disproportionate impact on them. Our research reveals that, although philanthropy's response to the pandemic has been extraordinary, most of the funding flowing in this moment will not reach women and girls of color. In fact, shifting philanthropic priorities already suggest that funding to this group may substantially diminish in the aftermath of the public health and related economic crises.[16]

Moreover, the report found that:

> [O]f the seventeen foundations reporting that they "very much" prioritize giving to particular populations in their work, only seven (41.2%) track their giving to women and girls of color in a database. This absence of formal tracking contrasts with the report by ninety percent of foundations that women and girls of color are a priority in their internal strategy documents.[17]

The report is a call to action to step up and fund initiatives and organizations led by women and girls of color and to track this commitment.

## Moving at the Speed of Trust

Since the Global Women's Funding Movement has always been guided by intersectionality, it has been able to innovate practices, that are more effective approaches to philanthropy. Trust-based philanthropy is a philanthropic innovation developed by women's funds. It is the practice of giving philanthropic power to those with the vision and solutions and who are closest to the issues. The goal of trust-based philanthropy is to change funders' core organizational culture and enable them to better express their values through their work.

Trust-based philanthropy is practiced in many ways. It may include unrestricted funding, meaning that money is provided to grant partners who decide how to spend it. Funders may also modify reporting requirements or change the process to be more like a two-way conversation between the funder and the grant partner than a report. This may include reporting using video or a verbal report or storytelling rather than written reporting. Another approach, called participatory grantmaking, involves the grant partners and communities that are intended to benefit from funding in the decision-making processes around the grant making. These are revolutionary departures from traditional philanthropic practices.

The adoption of trust-based philanthropy proliferated throughout the philanthropic sector during the Covid-19 pandemic starting in early 2020. Foundations of every type and mission rushed to meet the fast-changing needs of the grant partners that they already supported, as well as new ones. Funders had to immediately reinvent their funding requirements, incorporating many of the trust-based practices women's funds had innovated, to meet the new challenges facing their grant partner networks.[18] As the pioneers of trust-based philanthropic practices, women's funds have been agile funders during the toughest times, including through the pandemic. This has meant they've been better able to respond to the emergency needs of women's networks and movements while also supporting these movements to hold ground on important gains made through long-term flexible funding.

Françoise Moudouthe, CEO, African Women's Development Fund (AWDF), says:

> [In] the evolution of AWDF, there's been this realization that the grant alone is not enough. First, there was a layer added of capacity building, and then there was a layer added that you need to lift the voices, the knowledge. There's another layer of solidarity, which we've been calling movement building, and we've learned a lot about the fact that we can't say that movements only need to be resourced by financial resources. We need competencies, agency resilience, solidarity, and care.[19]

Women's funds have gone on their own journeys to appreciate the game-changing work of women's movements and how they can best support this work. In 2011, the Women's Funding Network presented feminist funder

Anne Delaney, founder of the Starry Night Fund and Lambent Foundation, with its LEAD Award. In presenting the award, Abby Disney said:

> Anne Delaney has built our [global women's funding] movement here and around the world and she has worked so hard to make sure in this country we don't forget what democracy means. She makes it possible to imagine what living a real feminist life is all about.[20]

In accepting the award and speaking about the Global Women's Funding Movement, Anne Delaney said:

> [In our funding] we wanted a women's part of our docket, which became known as the women's pool. We kept adding groups into it because there was such incredible bold, strategic thinking going on in the women's movement. ... It was this groundswell and we realized that our women's [funding] pool was really the avant-garde of the social change movement.[21]

What has also been a hallmark of women's funds has been representation on their boards and staff by women from the communities where they fund, whether they are U.S. or global funds. Speaking about her experience as a board member of the Global Fund for Women, Jacqueline Pitanguy said:

> From the day I joined the board, the Global Fund for Women became an important part of my international work for women's rights. I have learned, shared, and influenced the Global Fund for Women by bringing a perspective of a woman from the South who believed there should not be a hierarchy of relationship between North and South, or between donors and grantees, since a more accurate perspective of challenges and opportunities should combine all of them. I also understood the huge potential of the Global Fund for Women and of the necessity to find the intersections between local and global needs from the agendas of our partners and grantees. In this way, we could build a road map on how to be more effective in local, regional, national, and international advocacy. More and more, the Global Fund for Women became a key political actor in the sense that being a donor is not a neutral position; a donor is also a protagonist and thus needs to understand the critical role of grant making in shaping gender equality in national and international arenas.[22]

These values of trust, intersectionality, and inclusion have been essential to the success of the Global Women's Funding Movement. Jessica Houssian, former co-CEO (with Jessica Tomlin) of the Equality Fund, says:

> I think one of the things, less lately, but one of the things that doesn't work is when we are moving faster than our relationships and then the trust of our relationships can handle. The founders of Black Lives Matter coined this term that Gloria Steinem has borrowed, which is "moving at the speed of trust." We fall down when we are moving at a speed that doesn't align with ourselves as an organization internally or with any number of our partners who are at the core of everything we're building.[23]

When being honored with a 2019 Mary Lee Dayton Catalyst for Change Award, the phenomenal women's fund leader, Lee Roper-Batker, speaking about her 19 years of tenure and impact as President of the Women's Foundation of Minnesota and what she learned, said:

> I learned that systems don't exist outside of us—that *we* are the systems—our collective behaviors either reinforce systems of inequity or create new, fair systems. I learned that overweighting evidence-based outcomes in systems change work can perpetuate the status quo, or—let's name it—white supremacy—and squelch community innovation. I learned about the power of cross-sector collaborations to solve complex problems. And I learned that equity is a long game, and our rewards are the wins along the path.[24]

## Pioneering Intersectionality and Trust-based Philanthropy in a Time of Pandemic

A good illustration of how and why women's funds pioneer intersectionality in philanthropy and practice trust-based philanthropy is the story of ELAS+, a Brazilian women's fund. ELAS+ was one of the first social justice funds created in Brazil in the twenty-first century and is the first fund led by women to mobilize resources to promote and support the empowerment of women and LGBTQIA+ organizations in Brazil.

Its primary mission was to support social movements, such as gender equity and women's rights, not otherwise supported by mainstream philanthropy and the larger social investment ecosystem. National foundations and corporations in Brazil mostly focused on "charitable work," with immediate impact such as raising funds for education, children, and churches, and addressing urgent issues in times of catastrophe such as floods, a long-standing problem in Brazil. For example, in the first year of the Covid pandemic in Brazil, 10.3 billion reais were donated, which is 0.14 percent of Brazil's GDP for that year.[25] ELAS+ has worked diligently to create a feminist-centered philanthropy that is at once strategic, pioneering, resilient, and innovative.

ELAS + was one of the first women's funds in Latin America to successfully collaborate with private sector institutions, Chevron and Avon, resulting in ELAS+ being seen as an effective model to reference in grantmaking on gender equity and women's rights. ELAS+ obtained its first million reais by consulting for Chevron on their Program of Gender Equity and its first million dollars from its the partnership with the Avon Institute.

In March 2020, Covid was officially declared a pandemic in Rio de Janeiro, and everything shut down. At the same time, threats from the federal government escalated. As a feminist fund, ELAS+ was used to these kinds of threats coming from a right-wing regime that had a policy of persecuting progressive activists. Anyone perceived to be involved in a social movement such as feminists, indigenous, Black, LGBTQIA+, and young people were seen as a threat.

In the early days of the pandemic, ELAS+ was not yet fully online, meaning grant proposals were still being received through the regular postal system. At the same time, most of their resources were designated for specific issues and there was no flexibility in how to distribute funding. This hampered efforts to reach those who needed immediate aid, so ELAS+ began discussions with their funders to reallocate grants toward general support to work around these limitations.

The pandemic was taking a toll and the fund had to quickly adjust. Within six months, the fund fully transitioned to a virtual organization and created a website where proposals could be accepted. Next, ELAS + looked inward and took a hard look at their staff who were by now emotionally drained. It was decided that everyone needed a 15-day break to spend with family in a safe place and come back to work less stressed.

During this break, the former Executive Director, K.K. Verdade, and Amalia E. Fischer, co-founder of ELAS+, put their creativity to work. Amalia remembers:

> One day when K.K called me, distressed, asking me how we could cope with these moments, because she hadn't ever experienced a situation with so much urgency. For my part, I had already experienced three earthquakes and the consequences of war. Even so, I replied that

I had never experienced a pandemic, but from my other experiences I could envision two main approaches: 1) we had to differentiate between urgency and emergency, as we needed to think about here and now, 2) we also needed to plan for additional future emergencies. We discussed that we needed to focus on the here and now, but also needed to mobilize and bring more resources to feminist philanthropy—the consequences of the pandemic would affect the economy, health, and all support and social assistance services. Emergencies would evolve over months and could last for years. We thought it was essential for ELAS+ to ensure that women's organizations would remain active and, as always, at the forefront of the solutions. ELAS+ would need to support the building of new futures.[26]

From these reflections, an idea emerged to make a video that would act as a call for new proposals but with a new approach. Amalia recalls:

We talked also about generosity, empathy, solidarity, courage, emergency, urgent and emergency situations, and we posted the video on our website.[27] We anticipated that the pandemic emergency would last for many years, but we were careful not to allow that to impede our vision of a future, which for us meant investing in a good and fair life for all people and living beings.

We knew that women would have to be at the center of rebuilding and transformation because they are always at the forefront of social protection, in all spaces and historical moments. We always had radical trust in women's organizations because they embrace and promote qualities such as altruism, empathy, generosity, and solidarity. Through this video, we launched the call for proposals in 2020 with the modality of flexible support for the institutional strengthening of groups, and direct philanthropic support to community.

Shortly after, an offer came from the Global Fund for Women. The situation in Brazil was difficult because the federal government refused to promote vaccines. The governor of São Paulo took the bold step of promoting the purchase and production of vaccines. We had requested funding from the Global Fund for Women to be used as a resource for the team's resilience and resistance during the pandemic. A significant portion of the Global Fund's resources was used for cleaning ELAS+ headquarters and for creating a safe environment for the team to return to work after their much-needed break. There was also a budget allocation for the team and board member to purchase vaccines in case vaccines were only available in São Paulo.

In the three years of the pandemic, the number of proposals grew and so did ELAS+'s grantmaking. In 2020, ELAS+ received 1,575 proposals, in 2021, 1,434 proposals, and in 2022, 1,523. In 2019, they were already funding 91 groups, totaling $762,000. In 2020, it rose to $841,000, and in 2021, it reached $1,400,000 to 133 groups. In 2022, ELAS+ donated $3,555,000 to 259 groups.

In November 2021, the fund conducted research on how women's organizations responded to their communities during the worst moments of the pandemic. The name of the research is "Activism and Pandemic in Brazil."[28] Besides the health problems during the pandemic, other social challenges increased, such as violence against women and girls. According to data from the Brazilian Public Security Forum, femicides increased by 22.2% in 2021, compared to the same period in 2019.[29] During the pandemic, four women were killed every 24 hours.

In general terms, all research states that women have been at the forefront of problem solving during the pandemic.

## Funding Movements Responding to Intersectional Crises

Women's funds have also responded to intersectional crises that compound the erosion of women's human rights and gender justice – in this case, the intersecting impacts of Covid, climate change, and conflict. Getting funds to women-led organizations in such circumstances has been crucial, such as to Dr. Sakena Yacoobi, founder and Executive Director of the Afghan Institute of Learning. The August 2021 Taliban takeover of Afghanistan has devastated all Afghan people. It resulted in many men being killed and tortured, and human rights violations against women and girls have been mounting steadily. Despite initial promises that women would be allowed to exercise their rights within Sharia law—including the right to work and to study—the Taliban systematically excluded women and girls from public life. Women hold no cabinet positions in the de facto administration, which abolished its Ministry for Women's Affairs, effectively eliminating women's right to political participation. The Taliban also banned girls from attending school past the sixth grade and barred women from working most jobs outside the home. Women were banned from traveling long distances without a male chaperone, and unchaperoned women were denied access to essential services.

With Covid-19, the Taliban were confronted with a crisis of how to provide vaccinations to the population. They called on community leaders such as Dr. Yacoobi who could tap a network of health workers to implement a vaccination rollout and accompanying health services. Sakena insisted on female health workers representing at least half the health workers, and the Taliban agreed. However, there still weren't enough female health workers to deal with the intersecting crises of Covid and a climate emergency to provide support to women affected by the devastating earthquake there in June 2022 since women could only see female health workers.[30]

As a trusted community leader, Sakena did what some felt was impossible. With support from women's funds and other donors, Sakena and her team created a TV channel to reach Afghan people and provide education to girls on this channel so they could access this learning from their homes. This was a pivot for an organization that previously ran schools for girls across the country, and while not ideal, it does at least give girls access to basic education support. This story reinforces the importance of sustaining core funding for grassroots women's organizations and networks so that they can mobilize, assess, and pivot accordingly during a crisis and during intersectional crises such as Covid, climate change, and conflict.

As Sakena Yacoobi underscores, "If we are to overcome terrorism and violence, we need education. That is the only way we can win."[31] And "when women rise, the nation rises."[32]

## Mobilizing Resources for the Black Feminist Movement

Intersectional leadership is a pattern that can be traced through the most seismic social justice movements in history. The Black feminist movement in the U.S. is where the phenomenon of intersectionality was first identified and where it is voiced most clearly, consistently, and over centuries. Indeed, the powerful intersectional vision and leadership of Black women can be traced to the origins of many of the most massively transformative social justice movements in history including the anti-rape movement,[33] the civil rights movement, the movement to defend voting rights, the LGBTQI+ movement, the women's funding movement, the #MeToo movement, the Black Lives Matter movement, the reproductive justice movement, and beyond.

Grounded in Black feminist history and activism, the concept of intersectionality has been voiced throughout time by Black feminist leaders of many of the most transformative social justice movements in history, including the Global Women's Funding Movement. Kimberlé Crenshaw explains:

> So many of the antecedents to it are as old as Anna Julia Cooper, and Maria Stewart in the 19th century in the US, all the way through Angela Davis and Deborah King, In every generation and in every

intellectual sphere and in every political moment, there have been African American women who have articulated the need to think and talk about race through a lens that looks at gender, or think and talk about feminism through a lens that looks at race. So, this is in continuity with that.[34]

When U.S. Black abolitionist and suffragist Sojourner Truth rose in 1851 to rhetorically ask "Ain't I a woman?"[35] to her white female and Black male suffragist counterparts, she voiced an intersectional vantagepoint that no one else present did or could. Truth offered, especially clear in hindsight, a more immediate and complete strategic path to voting rights, democracy, and justice. "If black women were free, it would mean that everyone else would have to be free since our freedom would necessitate the destruction of all the systems of oppression," reads the Combahee River Collective Statement, written a little more than a century later, in 1977, by the Combahee River Collective (CRC), a Boston-based Black feminist lesbian socialist organization that was active from 1974 to 1980. Now considered a seminal document of Black feminism, in it the Collective argued that neither the feminist movement nor the civil rights movement represented their issues and needs as Black women and as Black lesbians. Racism plagued the mainstream feminist movement while much of the civil rights movement was mired in sexism and homophobia.[36] The members of the Collective were all living at the intersection of at least three deeply oppressed groups.

The Combahee River Collective Statement asserts that the oppression that Black women endure is rooted in interlocking oppressions based on race, gender, class, and, because many of the women who comprised the Collective were lesbians, sexuality too. In the statement, the Collective "committed to struggling against racial, sexual, heterosexual and class oppression" through the "development of integrated analysis and practice based upon the fact that the major systems of oppression are interlocking. The synthesis of these oppressions creates the conditions of our lives."[37] The CRC statement is considered a perfect example, among many examples throughout history, of intersectionality voiced like a mantra by Black feminists before it had a name.

Sojourner Truth also said:

If the first woman God ever made was strong enough to turn the world upside down all alone, these women together ought to be able to turn it back and get it right side up again! And now they is asking to do it, the men better let them.[38]

Truth was also conscious of intersectionality in her oration and advocacy:

> There is a great stir about colored men getting their rights, but not a word about the colored women; and if colored men get their rights, and not colored women theirs, you see the colored men will be masters over the women, and it will be just as bad as it was before.[39]

Women's rights and feminist leaders and movements stand on the shoulders of powerful Black activists such as Sojourner Truth.

Being guided by intersectional leadership has been possible because the Global Women's Funding Movement was founded by diverse groups of women across the world and invested in its diversity as a core strength from the start. Also:

> [A]s social justice institutions predominantly founded by women of color in the early 1980s, many women's funds connected to the Women's Funding Network (WFN) have been practicing philanthropy through an intersectional lens since before Kimberlé Crenshaw articulated the theory in 1989. Additionally, members of WFN have pioneered participatory grantmaking and other trust-based philanthropic practices. In the past 40 years, WFN has documented and amplified the work of these funds in the broader philanthropic sector.[40]

## Funding the Most Marginalized to Lead Solutions

As a result of the skills those facing injustice have formed to confront and/or adapt to its eroding impact, people at these multiple intersections often have knowledge and insights from having endured harmful and traumatizing experiences that others do not. Women of color, trans and gender-expansive people, low-income people, girls and people with disabilities, people who are undocumented refugees, and those who have been or are currently incarcerated see through multiple lenses of marginalization. The multitude of injustices often compound into mounting problems and escalating predicaments in their lives. This means that those with intersectional experiences of injustice are the knowers of often never-before considered social justice solutions. Sometimes, their visions of justice are so crystalized and powerful that, when generously invested in, they can rapidly change whole societies and cultures and dramatically improve life on earth as we know it.

In 1867, in the immediate aftermath of the end of slavery, Black women in the U.S., including civil rights legend Ida B. Wells, established the first anti-rape movement, identifying organized sexual violence against Black women as part of the same system of violence, including lynchings, being committed by organized white supremacists to intimidate, terrorize and murder free Black people.[41] Iconic activist Rosa Parks began her activist career as a sexual assault investigator for the NAACP, 12 years before her fateful and historic bus ride.[42] Martha P. Johnson, a Black trans woman and sex worker, is identified as the instigator of the uprising that birthed the LGBTQI+ movement.[43] The power of intersectionality is why these leaders were the ones to first hear the call. They witnessed and experienced the critical issues and need and were able to devise the best strategies, lead the charge, and deliver the seismic social justice victories that still reverberate in society today. Intersectional leaders are the world's greatest social justice warriors and the makers of enduring social justice movements because their justice instincts are sharp, and their unique knowledge of oppression is deep. The Global Women's Funding Movement has seen it happen many times because it is often the first funder of intersectional movements.

It is natural that when an injustice is shared by many, they often unite to address it. Movements of people manifest to find solutions to their common affliction. Collectively, they summon the strength to overcome injustices that are often too large and systemic to tackle without a movement-sized response. Movements are built and led by the most affected, marginalized, and silenced who think and work politically as they mobilize and organize. For this reason, movements are naturally intersectional and solutions rich. Movements are the most effective vehicles for change because they are led by those most invested in, and knowledgeable about, the solutions to their own suffering. As Christian Giraldo, formerly of Third Wave Fund, explains:

> As of now, I think the biggest obstacle we're encountering is the mounting attacks on trans communities that we call our families and that are at the center of so many of our movements. Folks that are showing up hard in trans liberation and fighting for the rights of trans folks have also been showing up the entire time for sex worker liberation. For the trans community to be under attack almost inherently means that the sex worker community is right there being attacked with them.[44]

Those who don't suffer from a given injustice are rarely the ones to identify it, let alone sound the alarm about it, risk their lives, their safety, and security to change it, or inspire others to join. It's those whose lives are most impacted by a given injustice who are the people who act, especially people who are living under compounding, intersecting injustices. Those who can lead from an intersectional lens often bring a broader vision for more trans-formative and more broadly inclusive social change.

Intersectionality is only possible when diversity is coupled with the prac-tice of inclusivity. The Global Women's Funding Movement invested in its diversity and the practices of inclusivity from the start, recognizing these were the movement's core strengths. Over the last half-century, the active combination of diversity and inclusivity in the Global Women's Funding Movement has enabled the philanthropic practice of intersectionality to emerge through individual women's funds across the world and, from there, spread as best practices through all of philanthropy.

When the National Network of Women's Funds (NNWF), today the Women's Funding Network (WFN), was formed in 1985, the diversity among its members was prized as a core strength. To enshrine this commitment, the members, board, and staff created a "Statement of Values" which were reaffirmed and made actionable in 1990 through the organization's strategic plan entitled "Multiculturalism: Accomplishments and Plans."[45] The docu-ment says:

> Those who have experienced the greatest oppression in our society have been women, people of color, people with disabilities, lesbians and gays, and those in poverty. These groups have been disenfranchised in every segment of societal intercourse, including philanthropy. Consistent with its underlying values, the Network and its members are committed to giving voice and respect to those individuals most impacted by philanthropic decisions which affect their lives.

## Translating Commitments into Action

To achieve this vision, the Women's Funding Network invested in a range of deliberate approaches. The strategies were both broad-based and extremely specific, ranging from "Encouraging cooperation across race and ethnic origins, socio-economic and class lines" to "Explore different organizational models for decision-making, board and staff roles, responsi-bilities, and relationships." This meant supporting leadership by women of color, women isolated by geography, sexual orientation, disability, age, and class. This seminal document of the Women's Funding Network reveals its mission to forge a new model of philanthropy based on intersectional principles. It explains, "We seek to develop new, more inclusive models for philanthropy, recognizing that our decisions will be much wiser if they are based on many perspectives. We are proud to be creating a different model for philanthropy." WFN committed to at least 50 percent of board members being women of color, diverse in sexual orientation and class background, and to have participation from each geographic region, and different types of funds. WFN developed "how-to" tools with suggestions for concrete steps for diversification of board, staff, fundraising, grantmaking, etc. Through its newsletter and research clearinghouse, WFN collected and disseminated information on the experiences of women's funds in reaching their diversity goals, practical tools, and "think pieces" regarding diversity in their organizations.

WFN mapped out a plan to organize the southern region of the U.S. and incorporate new women's funds emerging. Additionally, WFN created diversity benchmarks and reviewed the network's progress in meeting them through annual surveys of member funds to report on their changing board and staff demographics. WFN established a database on each fund's specific challenges and organizational objectives around diversity and used the information to offer technical assistance to members with board recruitment and selection, hiring processes, and other steps toward achieving individual diversity plans.

The Women's Funding Network raised the budget needed to accomplish all of this and created and staffed a phone tree to contact members to assess their specific needs in achieving the network's common diversity goals. Travel subsidies for low-income women were included so they could attend WFN conferences. At these conferences, workshops addressed the need for, and power of, diversity, and ways to confront racism, homophobia, classism, and ableism through the work of women's funds. The WFN diversity plan was both granular in detail and expansive in scope. WFN detected and addressed issues confronted by individual funds in achieving diversity. WFN also focused on transforming the entire sector of philanthropy by fostering the leadership of diverse groups of women and creating philanthropic best practices using intersectionality. WFN worked with the Council on Foundations, National Network of Grantmakers, the Funding Exchange, Hispanics in Philanthropy, Asian Americans in Philanthropy, Native Americans in Philanthropy, Black United Funds, and others to strengthen diversity and women's leadership throughout the entire realm of philanthropy.[46]

At the time of the creation of their diversity plan, WFN and women's funds were newcomers in philanthropy and had fresh, new approaches never considered before. As one of the four founders of the Ms. Foundation for Women, Gloria Steinem, says, "For perhaps the first time in the history of the world, women were funding our own advancement."[47] The WFN's diversity document says:

Women's funds were created to expand the process of raising money and giving it away; to bring new voices into philanthropy; to provide a vehicle for women to join together in solving critical problems of women and girls ... We can create organizations in which there is congruence between our stated values and the strategies we employ, so that as we work to redistribute resources, we do not reinforce old models. This requires us to rigorously commit to testing our actions against our values and working to create structures in which each participant is welcomed and valued.[48]

Today, 33 years after this strategic plan was begun, the Global Women's Funding Movement has much to show for valuing, investing in, and nourishing the diversity within its networks. According to the 2022 WFN report, by 2020, over half of place-based women's funds in the U.S. were led by women of color, 73 percent of whom are Black women. The percentage of women of color leaders within the network is continuing to grow, increasing by 11 percent since 2020, and they are leading the largest funds. Women of color executive leaders are working with the largest operating and grantmaking budgets among place-based women's funds in the U.S. according to the Women's Funding Network. Women's funds are mindful to sustain and grow this leadership. According to the 2022 WFN report, "Whereas eight organizations have transitioned from a white executive leader to a woman of color executive leader in the past three years, no women's funds have transitioned from a woman of color executive leader to a white executive leader."[49]

## Transformational Grantmaking for Movement Transformation

The Global Women's Funding Movement has existed as an intersectional movement since its inception with a trust-based model as a counterpoint to traditional philanthropy. Beyond providing funding, the Global Women's Funding Movement actively works to elevate diverse women's views and voices in key forums and facilitating opportunities for women and feminist leaders to be at policy dialogues and decision-making tables. Many grantmakers who use strictly traditional approaches to their giving don't just hamstring activists and social justice movement makers from implementing their vision; their grants can completely prevent them from achieving it. The traditional philanthropic model dictates a work plan based on what change the grantmaker seeks, with strict parameters to meet, often not allowing for an approach that's led and designed by the grantee.

Traditional philanthropic funding is often confined to "project deliverables" that make it hard to sustain the infrastructure of staff and operations to ensure the continuity of organizing for justice. Instead, a stop-start project approach hampers the transformational impact possible when core funding is provided. In fact, the traditional grantmaking format has been traced as the cause for the demise of many social justice movements around the world. As Françoise Girard, who led the International Women's Health Coalition, an international women's fund that is now Fòs Feminista, says:

> Social change takes time. To be effective, activists must be nimble and able to respond strategically to changing conditions. As such, they require flexible, long-term funding that allows them to control the direction of their work. Numerous studies have shown that this pattern of funding cripples vibrant social movements. The weakening of women's organizations by donor funding has been documented in Brazil, Chile, Peru, Colombia, Ghana, Palestine, and Egypt from the late 1990s to the present.[50]

Instead, it's critical to invest in feminist networks and movements so that those most affected are leading the way to the solutions with sustained funding to achieve the level of change sought.

Surina Khan, former CEO of Women's Foundation California, says:

> The way with which we approach our grantmaking now is really through trust-based practices, which means that we really want movement leaders to be focusing on their movement work and less on the bureaucracies of applying for funding. Part of the reason that we can do that is we have very deep authentic relationships with our partners. Over time we have gotten to know them. They feel comfortable coming to us with their problems in addition to their successes. We feel confident that we can just do the most minimal, whether that's taking an application over the phone, they can send us a video, they can do an online traditional application if they wish, but we're very flexible in the way that we accept information and we try to do the bulk of the work in terms of writing up the grant proposal for them.[51]

Jessica Horn, former Director of Programmes, African Women's Development Fund, and now Regional Director, East Africa with the Ford Foundation, offers her own assessment:

> I think that women's funds are actually *of* the women's movement. All the women's funds were founded by people who were active in the

women's movement and particularly feminist organizing in different ways. For example, Mama Cash was founded by women who were part of the squatter movement in Amsterdam and anarchists with inherited wealth.[52]

This reality has helped forge trust-based practices based on the solidarity of those mobilizing the funds with those leading movements for justice.

Recognizing the different countries and contexts in which women's funds operate is crucial to understanding their development, political intent, and commitment to shifting power. Alexandra Garita, Executive Director, Prospera, explains:

> Philanthropic cultures in the Global South and East tend to be quite diverse and different to those developed in industrialized wealthy countries of the North. Women's funds in these regions have developed concepts of philanthropic sharing and giving that are deeply political in that they often come from struggles of independence, liberation, and decolonization. The staff of funds are deeply embedded in and come from feminist movements themselves, and they are able to engage communities of individual women and activists to engage not only in resourcing but in participating in larger social justice struggles within their countries and regions. Philanthropy in the South, therefore, requires collective community building, joint understandings of seats of struggles for sharing power, and in designing common strategies for resourcing activism.[53]

## Investing in the Long Game of Gender Justice for Women in Sport

Trust-based philanthropy was also at the heart of the Women's Sports Foundation and its approach to activist-engaged philanthropy and its support for a rising movement for justice by women in sport. Tuti Scott, Founder of Changemaker Strategies (formerly Imagine Philanthropy) and an iconic women's funds leader and coach, was former co-CEO of the Women's Sports Foundation founded by Billie Jean King. Tuti observed that:

> With a matriarchal approach the sports movement and sector would look different in leadership roles with more people of color and women's voices at the table. Athlete voices would be listened to and respected as activists and leaders of just communities and organizations.[54]

That's particularly relevant given that the fight by women's sports for pay equity and to address the systemic sexual harassment in sport has been a decades-long battle for justice, equality, and respect. The role that women's funds have played in resourcing this work and propelling change has been significant.

Tuti says:

> [A]ccess and funding in sports by gender and race has been an ongoing battle for justice at all levels of sport since inception. Over the decades, many athletes have used their social, moral, and physical courage to break barriers or advocate for justice (Jackie Robinson, Kathrine Switzer, Women's National Basketball Association) or have fought for pay equity (Venus Williams, Billie Jean King, and the original nine founders of the Women's Tennis Association, the United States Women's National Soccer Team). With the advent of social media, the misogyny and overt discrimination cannot be hidden with the willingness of people to reveal the disparities in how women are poorly resourced, and how women, and especially women of color, are hypersexualized and abused. Globally, women's funds continue to remind people of the abuses and inequities of women in the workplace and the sexual violence that is becoming more prevalent as women push back. Decades of awareness building, advocacy, grantmaking and taking actions to shift power has provided the setting for sports to be a rallying cry for ALL women fighting for fairness and safety. In 2023, the Women's World Cup had multiple countries (France, England, Haiti, Jamaica) coming to the pitch without adequate funding for preparation, time together as a team, equipment, coaching, and more. Others dealt with ongoing and blatant coaching harassment and poor working conditions (Spain). And yet, the crowds surpassed all records, the competition and level of play was superb, and the fever pitch drove the Australian government to make a bold $200 million commitment to women's football.[55]

According to research conducted by the Women's Funding Network in 2018, of women's funds studied, 74 percent involved community members in funding decisions including site visits and evaluating grants. Women's funds also lead listening tours to engage communities in the grantmaking process to inform the direction and advocacy of women's funds. A total of 88 percent of women's funds reported engaging in advocacy, with 75 percent engaging at the state level. Movement building through the creation of coalitions is another way women's funds advocate, with 96 percent stating they used coalition building to advocate for systemic change.[56]

## Learning from Women Who Are the Most Impacted by Injustice

When the Women's Fund of Greater Cincinnati Foundation was taking steps to address the "cliff effect," they asked Mary Moss to serve on their advisory board. Moss, a poor, Black, single mother was navigating around the treacherous cliff effect, the predicament in which parents who are struggling to support their families are trapped by policies in the U.S. that withdraw government support as soon as they begin to become self-sufficient. Mary and her daughter were on their own, and she relied on government-funded health care and vouchers to help pay for childcare while she worked for self-sufficiency. But getting a small raise meant she earned too much to qualify for the assistance, leaving her worse off financially than before the modest bump-up in pay.

The Women's Fund of the Greater Cincinnati Foundation learned of Mary's story and recruited her to their advisory board where her experiences informed solutions supported through their "Cliff Effect Grantmaking Program." Meghan Cummings of the Women's Fund for a Greater Cincinnati Foundation explains:

> We decided we wanted to create this Women's Fund Advisory Council, different than our board, but comprised of women, mostly women of color, who were working these lower wage jobs, who had childcare and transportation needs, who were facing the cliff effect. And they became a central, central part of our work … For a lot of these women, this is the first time they've ever been asked to be involved in something like this. They might have been asked for their opinion before, but as far as making decisions or giving them agency, it's probably not something that has happened for many of these women, which is so sad, because our community has missed out on just the most amazing insights and helpful insights. They are the people at the end of the day all of our work hopes to benefit. We brought them together to completely decide our grants every year. They absolutely read all the applications and make all the decisions about who will get funding.[57]

Knowledge sharing about feminist approaches is also a crucial part of the Global Women's Funding Movement. Caroline Sakina Brac De La Perrière, Executive Director, Mediterranean Women's Fund, introduced the idea of a Feminist School to fund grassroots feminist leaders in the Mediterranean to build self-esteem, self-awareness, connections, networks, knowledge, and collaboration in support of feminist movements for justice in different communities and countries.

The curative and constructive power of feminist and intersectional approaches and the seismic impact of movements in leveraging massive social justice victories is undeniable. Yet Black feminist movements constantly struggle for adequate funding, despite being traced to so many of our most transformative social justice victories throughout time and place. This motivated the Global Women's Funding Movement to take deliberate steps to reverse the disturbing pattern by fully centering Black women as women fund leaders, donors, board members, staff, and grant partners. One of WFN's earliest diversity documents envisioned, "We can create organizations which give attention to how we do our work, as well as what we do." This vision was again made real by the Global Women's Funding Movement with the 2021 founding of the Black Feminist Fund, "the first global institution of its kind, created to ambitiously fund the powerful, transformative, and intersectional work of black feminist movements."[58]

## Shifting Power and Resources to Black Feminist Activists and Movements

Before founding the Black Feminist Fund, its three co-founders, Amina Doherty, Hakima Abbas, and Tynesha McHarris, had spent a decade having discussions within Black feminist movements and in philanthropic arenas throughout the world about Black women's and gender-diverse people's social justice efforts going unrecognized, disempowered, under-resourced. In 2016, the Association for Women's Rights in Development (AWID) in Brazil held a 2,000-person Black Feminist Forum where Doherty presented the idea for the Black Feminist Fund which inspired "so much support, so much affirmation, real encouragement and agreement," Doherty says, "everyone saying that, absolutely, yes, there needs to be a fund like that."[59]

In 2021, the Global Fund for Women stepped forward to provide critical infrastructure support, becoming the fiscal sponsor to the Black Feminist Fund (BFF), establishing it as the first global women's fund singularly devoted to Black women and Black feminist agendas.[60] Now the fund is on a mission to raise $100 million for Black feminist movements worldwide over ten years, and to grant it all within the next ten years too. The founders anticipate that this can set in motion waves of funding to Black feminist movements at the levels that meet Black feminists' proven justice-delivering abilities.

Within two years of getting the fiscal sponsorship from the Global Fund for Women, the BFF had raised nearly $35 million of its goal of

$100 million.[61] The BFF supports work that benefits and engages Black women, girls, trans, intersex and gender non-conforming people.[62] "The amount of philanthropic resources that go to women's issues, period, is just embarrassing," said Latanya Mapp Frett, former CEO and president of the Global Fund for Women, and continued:

> But when you start breaking that number down to women of color, then Black women, the numbers get more and more dismal. The necessity of BFF is to ensure we don't go backwards, so we can work across the diaspora as Black feminist women, because we know that together we're stronger.[63]

Out of nearly $70 billion in foundation giving globally, less than half of 1 percent goes to Black feminist social movements.[64]

Black feminist activists are consistently the founders and leaders of social justice movements worldwide, but they receive a minuscule amount of global philanthropic dollars. The BFF is set on ending the funding gap with a trust-based approach to philanthropy that's Black women-led. It is a connection point for Black women donors and their allies to organizations rooted in Black feminist principles and centered on Black women and gender-expansive people, and their vision and solutions. BFF funding concentrates on Black feminists and gender-expansive people in Africa, North America, Latin America, the Caribbean, and Europe. Hakima Abbas, BFF co-founder, reflects on the momentum underway: "Black feminists are changing the world and we deserve resourcing that matches the boldness of our visions."[65]

McHarris explains:

> There's never been a fund singularly focused on the leadership of Black women, Black trans and Black nonbinary people around the world. Our grantees reflect that, our movement partners reflect that, our staff reflects that, and so do the folks who make up our advisory board—we're really reflecting the Black global community.[66]

McHarris continues, "We imagine a world where our movement leaders can focus on the work of world-building, rather than on reports and applications and trying to respond to funder requests," she said. BFF co-founder, Amina Doherty agrees:

> So many of our leaders have to worry about how they're going to resource their own staff and how they're going to fund the minimal things necessary in order to operate an organization. That reality is

sucking the energy from our movement. We know that the kinds of organizations that we intend to support are the ones leading social change and therefore should be trusted and should be resourced well with the core funding that pays staff, keeps the lights on, enables activists' wellbeing, and supports the work to get done. We want to provide core, long-term grants. For us, when we say long-term, we're not talking about one to three years. We're looking at five to eight years of funding, recognizing that it takes about 10 years for even the smallest change to really come forward. We certainly will prioritize trust-based giving. We absolutely want to have a participatory model to our grantmaking.[67]

Women's funds recognize who leads matters, and that is why participatory grantmaking has been an essential practice of women's funds. It shifts philanthropic power to the most affected communities. Surina Khan, former CEO of Women's Foundation California says:

If people who are closest to the problems are closest to the solutions, they shouldn't just be recommending grants, they should be in a decision-making role. It's not to say that this hasn't been true in the past, but now with great intention, we have activists, whether they're grant partners or policy institute alums on our board. They govern the foundation, they're my boss, and they are ultimately the decision makers about all our program strategy, including grantmaking."[68]

## Amplifying Voice and Shifting Power

Shifting power is about much more than just funding. It requires sustained dialogue and action on effectively resourcing movements and effective ways to disrupt the traditional, colonial, and patriarchal practices that persist throughout philanthropy. Mama Cash was the first women's fund established outside the U.S. Founded in the Netherlands in 1983, it began as a small-scale visionary initiative of five feminists around a kitchen table in Amsterdam and has since then grown into a leading international women's fund.[69] Mama Cash was one of the first women's funds to experiment with trust-based philanthropic practices. It's easy to be convinced that trusting those most affected to lead and design the solutions for their communities and movements is the most effective approach when one considers the work of Mama Cash grant partner, Svjetlana Timotic. Timotic co-founded Iz Kruga Vojvodina in Serbia in 2007 with the goal of supporting women with disabilities who face violence and abuse. The organization's name translates to "out of circle," as in out of the circle of violence.

In 2021, Mama Cash published a booklet entitled *If You Stay Quiet, You Stay Invisible: Feminist disability rights activists share their stories of working for justice*. One of the feminist disability rights activists featured was Svjetlana Timotic. Throughout her life, Timotic noticed the way language created false societal constructs that resulted in harmful boundaries for, and limitations on, her and other people with disabilities. She recalls:

> The hidden message behind the word 'invalid' was that I was not able to educate myself. I was not able to work. I was not able to do a lot of things that people without disabilities could do. I was not a complete person. What's important about the term 'person with disability' is that it gives you the right to think about yourself as a person—a person with a disability, and with a lot of other traits.

When Svjetlana Timotic became a college student in the early 2000s, she found a group of activists for disability rights on campus and quickly realized it was society that had been marginalizing people with disabilities by using this limiting language. The activist group that Timotic joined was advancing an entirely new framework, a "social model" of disability, in which the focus is on society's role to take people's needs into account. Joining with other activists with disability gave Timotic a new perspective, positioning her disability as an essential, and positive, part of her identity.

Since its founding in 2007, the Serbian organization Iz Kruga Vojvodina has campaigned for increased recognition of the problem of violence against women with disabilities. The organization has nine full-time staff members and engages as many as 100 women activists each year to carry out specific activities. Iz Kruga Vojvodina maintains a helpline that serves women with different types of disabilities, including those with a hearing disability. Iz Kruga Vojvodina also maintains a media outlet called "Disability Portal" that covers issues affecting women with disabilities. It is one of the only places where the perspectives of women with disabilities are voiced. Iz Kruga Vojvodina works to improve access to gynecological health care for women with disabilities by organizing gynecological check-ups in collaboration with health institutions.

One of Iz Kruga Vojvodina's first successes was getting Vojvodina's main medical center to purchase a hydraulic chair, thereby removing one of the major barriers for women with disabilities to accessing gynecological exams. Another mission of Iz Kruga Vojvodina's work is to impart activism skills to women with disabilities so they can advocate for their sexual and reproductive health and rights. Iz Kruga Vojvodina has expanded its activist work to 11 regions of Serbia and graduated 29 women as disability activists from their training program.

Timotic has experienced fundraising challenges when leading Iz Kruga Vojvodina's work, including funders who try to shape the group's agenda. She explains, "A lot of funding is for projects. Funders expect us to address other problems or change our course. It makes our work more difficult." Some donor reporting requirements were so burdensome, especially in comparison to the small amount of funding offered, that she no longer applies. Timotic prefers when donors ask good questions that give the organization the opportunity to reflect on their work and the future. She uses Mama Cash's structural assessment tool as a great example:

> It asks us questions about our mission, our structure, where we are and where we want to go. When we filled it out, it helped us see all the conferences we've participated in, all the services we've provided, all the actions we've done. It made us really proud. It also gave us insight into the strengths and weaknesses of our organization and prompted us to think about how to improve our governance and operations.[70]

In speaking about the type of funding works best, Timotic explains that it's funding that will sustain the organization: "We need support that enables continuity. We have issues we want to solve."[71]

Raising the money was only part of the equation for the Global Women's Funding Movement as it worked radically to share power, reconceptualize giving, amplify diverse women's views and voices, and fund feminist movements with a fierce commitment to a new world imagined and underway. As Ndana Bofu-Tawamba describes it, it's a story of "how women's funds, feminist funding agencies and activists, and philanthropic actors came together to build a bolder power and voice for the work that we do and for the causes that we are fighting for."

At the time, the founders of these women's funds could not know the challenges ahead and how much the courage, creativity, and commitment of the leaders of these movements for women's rights and gender justice would be tested. How women's funds have provided solidarity and rapid resourcing for these movements to respond to more frequent crises and emergencies is the story of the next chapter.

# Notes

1   Kimberle Crenshaw, "Demarginalizing the Intersection of Race and Sex: A Black Feminist Critique of Antidiscrimination Doctrine, Feminist Theory and Antiracist Politics," *University of Chicago Legal Forum*, Vol. 1989, No. 1, Article 8, accessed November 24, 2023, https://chicagounbound.uchicago.edu/cgi/viewcontent.cgi?article=1052&context=uclf.

2   bell hooks, "How Do You Practice Intersectionalism? An Interview with bell hooks," interview by Randy Lowens, Black Rose Anarchist Federation, February 14, 2018, accessed November 24, 2023, https://blackrosefed.org/intersectionalism-bell-hooks-interview.

3   Judith Butler, "Gender Performance: The TransAdvocate Interviews Judith Butler," interview by Cristan Williams, The TransAdvocate, accessed November 24, 2023, www.azquotes.com/quote/1556621?ref=intersectionality.

4   K. Davis, "Intersectionality as buzzword: A sociology of science perspective on what makes a feminist theory successful," *Feminist Theory*, Vol. 9, No. 1 (2008), 67–85, accessed November 24, 2023, https://doi.org/10.1177/1464700108086364.

5   Ise Bosch, interview with Christine Grumm and Laura Risimini, November 1, 2022.

6   Mapp Frett, Latanya, "Altering the Course of History for Women and Girls Around the World, with Latanya Mapp Frett, President and CEO of Global Fund for Women." Interview by Jennifer Simpson Carr, *On Record PR*, Season 2: Episode 59, accessed November 25, 2023, www.furiarubel.com/podcasts/altering-the-course-of-history-for-women-and-girls-around-the-world-with-latanya-mapp-frett-president-and-ceo-of-global-fund-for-women.

7   Esther Mwaura Muiru, interview with Laura Risimini, September 22, 2022.

8   Tania Turner, interview with Christine Grumm and Laura Risimini, November 18, 2022.

9   Natalie Kane Ph.D., "Revealing the racial and spatial disparity in pediatric asthma: A Kansas City case study," *Social Science & Medicine*, Vol. 292 (January 2022), accessed November 25, 2023, www.sciencedirect.com/science/article/abs/pii/S0277953621008753.

10  Myron Zitt, M.D., "Children living in urban 'food deserts' at higher risk for asthma," *Healio*, November 14, 2016. accessed November 25, 2023, www.healio.com/news/pediatrics/20161114/children-living-in-urban-food-deserts-at-higher-risk-for-asthma.

11  S. Vohra-Gupta, L. Petruzzi, C. Jones, and C. Cubbin, "An Intersectional Approach to Understanding Barriers to Healthcare for Women," *Journal of Community Health*, Vol. 48, No. 1 (February 2023): 89–98, accessed November 25, 2023, www.ncbi.nlm.nih.gov/pmc/articles/PMC9589537.

12 Grace Ajele and Jena McGill, "Intersectionality in Law and Legal Contexts," *Women's Legal Education and Action Fund (LEAF)*, 2020. Accessed November 25, 2023, www.leaf.ca/wp-content/uploads/2020/10/Full-Report-Intersectionality-in-Law-and-Legal-Contexts.pdf.

13 Anne-Mari Souto and Tiina Sotkasiira, "Towards intersectional and anti-racist career guidance," *British Journal of Guidance & Counselling*, Vol. 50, No. 4 (2022), 577–589, accessed November 25, 2023, www.tandfonline.com/doi/full/10.1080/03069885.2022.2073583#:~:text=For%20career%20guidance%2C%20adopting%20an,(2016).

14 Surina Khan and Lucia Corral Peña, "Announcing a New California Funder Collaborative to Advance Gender Justice," *Philanthropy CA*, January 15, 2019, accessed November 25, 2023, www.philanthropyca.org/news/announcing-new-california-funder-collaborative-advance-gender-justice.

15 Erin Howe and Somjen Frazer, *Pocket Change: How Women and Girls of Color Do More With Less* (New York: The Ms. Foundation for Women, June 2020), accessed November 25, 2023, https://forwomen.org/wp-content/uploads/2020/11/Pocket-Change-Report.pdf.

16 Erin Howe and Somjen Frazer, *Pocket Change: How Women and Girls of Color Do More With Less* (New York: The Ms. Foundation for Women, June 2020), accessed November 25, 2023, https://forwomen.org/wp-content/uploads/2020/11/Pocket-Change-Report.pdf.

17 Erin Howe and Somjen Frazer, *Pocket Change: How Women and Girls of Color Do More With Less* (New York: The Ms. Foundation for Women, June 2020), accessed November 25, 2023, https://forwomen.org/wp-content/uploads/2020/11/Pocket-Change-Report.pdf.

18 Emily Finchum-Mason, "Trust-based philanthropy is growing in popularity," *The Daily Record*, May 9, 2022, accessed November 25, 2023, https://thedailyrecord.com/2022/05/09/trust-based-philanthropy-is-growing-in-popularity.

19 Francoise Moudouthe, interview with Christine Grumm, November 9, 2022.

20 Women's Funding Network, "The LEAD Award—Presented by Women's Funding Network: Anne Delaney," YouTube, June 18, 2011, www.youtube.com/watch?v=6FA2YzrNuy4.

21 Women's Funding Network, "The LEAD Award—Presented by Women's Funding Network: Anne Delaney," YouTube, June 18, 2011, www.youtube.com/watch?v=6FA2YzrNuy4.

22 Jacqueline Pitanguy, personal email communication with Musimbi Kanyoro, September 4, 2023.

23 Jessica Houssian and Jessica Tomlin, interview with Christine Grumm and Laura Risimini, November 14, 2022.

24 "Lee Roper-Batker Honored with 2019 Mary Lee Dayton Catalyst for Change Award," Women's Foundation of Minnesota, accessed November 25, 2023,

www.wfmn.org/lee-roper-batker-honored-with-2019-mary-lee-dayton-catalyst-for-change-award.

25  "Confira os resultados da Pesquisa Doação Brasil 2020," IDIS, accessed May 15, 2024, www.idis.org.br/pesquisa-doacao-brasil-2020.

26  Amalia. E Fischer, personal email correspondence with Ana Oliveira, March 25, 2024.

27  "ELAS na Emergência do Futuro," YouTube, accessed May 16, 2024, www.youtube.com/watch?v=kHk_b07jgKI.

28  *Activism and Pandemic in Brazil* (Rio de Janeiro: ELAS +, 2021), 36, accessed November 25, 2023, https://fundosocialelas.org/ativismo-e-pandemia-no-brasil/uploads/activism-and-pandemic-in-brazil.pdf.

29  Amalia. E Fischer, personal email correspondence with Ana Oliveira, March 25, 2024.

30  Sakena Yacoobi, personal email correspondence with Jane Sloane, October 23, 2023.

31  Catalyst 2030, "20230503 Education as one of the top priorities for Afghanistan," YouTube, May 8, 2023, accessed May 16, 2024, www.youtube.com/watch?v=MfoAAYf-cxY.

32  Sakena Yacoobi in virtual private donor briefing, March 28, 2023.

33  Gillian Greensite, "History of the Rape Crisis Movement," *Valor US*, November 1, 2009, accessed November 25, 2023, www.valor.us/2009/11/01/history-of-the-rape-crisis-movement.

34  Bim Adewunmi, "Kimberlé Crenshaw on intersectionality: 'I wanted to come up with an everyday metaphor that anyone could use,'" *The New Statesman*, April 2, 2014, accessed November 25, 2023, www.newstatesman.com/politics/welfare/2014/04/kimberl-crenshaw-intersectionality-i-wanted-come-everyday-metaphor-anyone-could.

35  "Ain't I a Woman," Learning for Justice, accessed November 25, 2023, www.learningforjustice.org/classroom-resources/texts/aint-i-a-woman.

36  "Combahee River Collective," Wikipedia, last modified on November 6, 2023, accessed November 25, 2023, https://en.wikipedia.org/wiki/Combahee_River_Collective#:~:text=Combahee%20River%20Collective%20argues%20that,or%20interlocking%20system%20of%20oppressions.

37  "Combahee River Collective," Wikipedia, last modified on November 6, 2023, accessed November 25, 2023, https://en.wikipedia.org/wiki/Combahee_River_Collective#:~:text=Combahee%20River%20Collective%20argues%20that,or%20interlocking%20system%20of%20oppressions.

38  "Sojourner Truth," Sojourner Truth House, accessed November 25, 2023, https://sojournertruthhouse.org/sojourner-truth.

39  Truth, Sojourner, "Address to the First Annual Meeting of the American Equal Rights Association," New York City, May 9, 1867. Transcript of speech provided

by the Society for the Study of American Women Writers, accessed November 25, 2023, www.lehigh.edu/~dek7/SSAWW/writTruthAddress.htm.

40    *Landscape Study of Women's Funds and Foundations Part I* (San Francisco: Women's Funding Network, October 2022), accessed November 25, 2023, www.womensfundingnetwork.org/wp-content/uploads/2022/10/LandscapeReport-Part-1_2022.pdf.

41    Gillian Greensite, "History of the Rape Crisis Movement," *Valor US*, November 1, 2009, accessed November 25, 2023, www.valor.us/2009/11/01/history-of-the-rape-crisis-movement.

42    Ryan Mattimore, "Before the Bus, Rosa Parks Was a Sexual Assault Investigator," *HISTORY*, A&E Television Networks, last updated January 26, 2021, original published date December 8, 2017. Accessed November 25, 2023, www.history.com/news/before-the-bus-rosa-parks-was-a-sexual-assault-investigator.

43    "Life Story: Marsha P. Johnson (1945–1992) Transgender Activist," Women & the American Story, New York Historical Society Museum and Library. Accessed November 25, 2023, https://wams.nyhistory.org/growth-and-turmoil/growing-tensions/marsha-p-johnson/#resource.

44    Christian Giraldo, interview with Laura Risimini and Hadley Wilhoite, March 1, 2023.

45    *Report to Membership, April 1991* (Washington, DC: National Network of Women's Funds, April 1991).

46    *Report to Membership, April 1991* (Washington, DC: National Network of Women's Funds, April 1991).

47    Gloria Steinem, personal email communication with Helen LaKelly Hunt, December 6, 2022.

48    *Report to Membership, April 1991* (Washington, DC: National Network of Women's Funds, April 1991).

49    *Landscape Study of Women's Funds and Foundations Part I* (San Francisco: Women's Funding Network, October 2022), accessed November 25, 2023, www.womensfundingnetwork.org/wp-content/uploads/2022/10/LandscapeReport-Part-1_2022.pdf.

50    Françoise Girard, "Women's Movements Hold the Key to Gender Equality—So Why Aren't Donors Funding Them?" *Philanthropy News Digest*, July 18, 2019, accessed November 25, 2023, https://philanthropynewsdigest.org/features/commentary-and-opinion/women-s-movements-hold-the-key-to-gender-equality-so-why-aren-t-donors-funding-them.

51    Surina Khan, interview with Christine Grumm and Laura Risimini, October 25, 2022.

52    Jessica Horn, personal voice note via WhatsApp exchange with Laura Risimini, September 21, 2022.

53    Alexandra Garita, personal email correspondence with Laura Risimini, November 1, 2022.

54  Tuti Scott, personal email correspondence with Jane Sloane, September 9, 2023.

55  Tuti Scott, personal email correspondence with Jane Sloane, September 9, 2023.

56  Kiersten Marek, "Women's Funds Show Philanthropy the Way to Transparency, Diversity," *Philanthropy Women*, March 29, 2018, accessed November 25, 2023, https://philanthropywomen.org/womens-funds/womens-funds-show-philanthropy-way-transparency-diversity.

57  Alicia Miller and Meghan Cummings, interview with Laura Risimini, December 13, 2022.

58  Kylie Adair, "0.1 Percent Of The World's Philanthropic Money Goes To Black Feminist Activists - This Global Organization Is Working To Change That," *Future Of Good*, August 31, 2021, accessed November 25, 2023, https://Futureofgood.Co/Black-Feminist-Fun

59  Kylie Adair, "0.1 percent of the world's philanthropic money goes to Black Feminist activists—this global organization is working to change that," *Future of Good*, August 31, 2021, accessed November 25, 2023, https://futureofgood.co/black-feminist-fund.

60  Connie Matthiessen, "Funded to Win. These 11 Funders—and Counting—Are Stepping Up For Black Feminist Movements," *Inside Philanthropy*, January 30, 2023, accessed November 25, 2023, www.insidephilanthropy.com/home/2023/1/30/funded-to-win-these-11-funders-and-counting-are-stepping-up-for-black-feminist-movements.

61  Connie Matthiessen, "Funded to Win. These 11 Funders—and Counting—Are Stepping Up For Black Feminist Movements," *Inside Philanthropy*, January 30, 2023, accessed November 25, 2023, www.insidephilanthropy.com/home/2023/1/30/funded-to-win-these-11-funders-and-counting-are-stepping-up-for-black-feminist-movements.

62  Kylie Adair, "0.1 percent of the world's philanthropic money goes to Black Feminist activists—this global organization is working to change that," *Future of Good*, August 31, 2021, accessed November 25, 2023, https://futureofgood.co/black-feminist-fund.

63  "Meet the Black Feminist Fund founders out to transform philanthropy," Ford Foundation, September 15 2021, accessed November 25, 2023, www.fordfoundation.org/news-and-stories/stories/Meet-The-Black-Feminist-Fund-Founders-Out-To-Transform-Philanthropy

64  Connie Matthiessen, "Funded to Win. These 11 Funders—and Counting—Are Stepping Up For Black Feminist Movements," *Inside Philanthropy*, January 30, 2023, accessed November 25, 2023, www.insidephilanthropy.com/home/2023/1/30/funded-to-win-these-11-funders-and-counting-are-stepping-up-for-black-feminist-movements.

65  "Ford Foundation Supports Launch of First Global Fund Addressing Key Issues Facing Black Women," Ford Foundation, March 2021, accessed November 25, 2023, www.fordfoundation.org/news-and-stories/news-and-press/news/

ford-foundation-supports-launch-of-first-global-fund-addressing-key-issues-facing-black-women.

66  Connie Matthiessen, "Funded to Win. These 11 Funders—and Counting—Are Stepping Up For Black Feminist Movements," *Inside Philanthropy*, January 30, 2023, accessed November 25, 2023, www.insidephilanthropy.com/home/2023/1/30/funded-to-win-these-11-funders-and-counting-are-stepping-up-for-black-feminist-movements.

67  Kylie Adair, "0.1 percent of the world's philanthropic money goes to Black Feminist activists—this global organization is working to change that," *Future of Good*, August 31, 2021, accessed November 25, 2023, https://futureofgood.co/black-feminist-fund.

68  Surina Khan, interview with Christine Grumm and Laura Risimini, October 25, 2022.

69  "Our history," Mama Cash, accessed November 25, 2023, www.mamacash.org/en/our-history

70  *'If you stay quiet, you stay invisible': Feminist disability rights activists share their stories of working for justice* (Amsterdam: Mama Cash, 2021) accessed November 25, 2023, www.mamacash.org/wp-content/uploads/2022/02/if_you_stay_quiet_you_stay_invisible__mama_cash_disability_rights_report.pdf.

71  *'If you stay quiet, you stay invisible': Feminist disability rights activists share their stories of working for justice* (Amsterdam: Mama Cash, 2021) accessed November 25, 2023, www.mamacash.org/wp-content/uploads/2022/02/if_you_stay_quiet_you_stay_invisible__mama_cash_disability_rights_report.pdf.

# Women at the Frontlines of Crisis    **4**

## Funding and Supporting

### Investing in Women's Networks for Emergency Response

When Hurricane Katrina, a devastating Category 5 Atlantic hurricane, hit the U.S. Gulf Coast in 2005, it killed over 1,800 people and remains the costliest hurricane to date.[1] It unleashed a desperate flood of evacuees from New Orleans. Mostly women of color escaped the superstorm by setting a course north as far as they could reach. Some were desperately escaping the hurricane as well as other forms of violence exacerbated by the crisis. According to research conducted by the Institute for Women's Policy Research, a women's fund grant partner, in the immediate aftermath of Katrina and even a year later, women faced higher rates of domestic violence and sexual assault due in part to displacement and the difficulty lower-income women faced in finding a permanent home.[2]

The Center for Disaster Philanthropy reported:

> This vulnerability is also part of the intersectional nature of the gendered impact of disasters. For example, women and girls of color in the U.S. tend to have higher rates of poverty, greater challenges accessing health care, reduced access to education and employment opportunities and lower wages when they do find work. They often live in female-led households and are more likely to be tenants than homeowners. Before a disaster, women and girls usually have the primary responsibility for caring for a home and the people in it, including

DOI: 10.4324/9781003330455-4

children, older family members, and people with disabilities. Their caregiving responsibilities may prevent their ability to evacuate.[3]

When Katrina struck, Ruby Bright, the President and CEO of the Women's Foundation for a Greater Memphis (WFGM), saw the chaos unfolding. She knew that the city of Memphis would be strangled in red tape and would need the community's help to instill calm amid the tens of thousands of people who took refuge there. Having served in this position for nearly two decades, Ruby Bright was a recognized leader in Memphis and acutely aware of the needs of the most impoverished people in the U.S. South. Ruby's work in public–private partnership with the Memphis city government had already transformed the public housing system. The Women's Foundation for a Greater Memphis had an operating budget of less than $1 million, but Ruby and her team set about to raise $1.2 million to help the families through the term of the five-year rebuilding project and beyond.[4] They named this project Memphis HOPE and began innovating a "wraparound" social service approach to connect public housing residents with holistic services from one location. These wraparound services included transportation, access to medical care, jobs, retraining as required, and financial literacy.

Knowing the impact this work had in supporting Memphis's most vulnerable residents during their uprooting, the Mayor of Memphis Director of Housing was on the phone with Ruby within hours of Katrina making landfall, seeking her help in leading the Katrina response taskforce. The national network of women's funds, led by the Ms. Foundation for Women and the Women's Funding Network, was already gathering and directing the national outpouring of donations for the Katrina response to WFGM. Local leaders chose Ruby as one of the leading conveners for the emergency response.[5]

Walking alongside the long lines of people in Memphis waiting at the Red Cross pop-ups for immediate assistance, Ruby instantly recognized that those evacuating into Memphis were confronting the same issues as the women she had been working with in the local public housing community to address the needs of those dislocated in the city. Ruby knew the Memphis HOPE model would instill calm. As a movement of people with similar needs landed in Memphis due to Hurricane Katrina, Ruby quickly activated Memphis HOPE for those fleeing the disaster. The first thing evacuees needed was agency over their situation. Ruby helped to develop an intake form to be filled out by children and adults alike. It asked simple, obvious questions to gather information and quickly assess urgencies. What were their immediate needs? Housing? Food? Medication? Gas money to reach family members? Help to find a loved one? Deeply trusted by the Memphis community, Ruby could move fast and free of red tape. WFGM quickly directed the funding to where it was most needed, connecting evacuees with social service partners, and devising systems to harness the community's outpouring of help. They organized offers of temporary housing, established food banks where the evacuees were, and secured a wing of an unused area in one of the local hospitals to tend to the unique needs of those fleeing the hurricane. As a part of the City of Memphis's support to the City of New Orleans, Ruby was also tapped to help facilitate connections among community organizations. As soon as the crisis was contained, WFGM set about getting those needing to start a new life in Memphis integrated into the community with permanent housing, skills building, and job connections.[6]

## Bringing an Intersectional Lens to Emergency Response

The Ms. Foundation for Women and the Women's Funding Network also established the Katrina Women's Response Fund (KWRF) in response to the massive displacement caused by Hurricane Katrina. After the second funding cycle of KWRF, the Ms. Foundation for Women had awarded $811,000 to 35 grantees, mainly in Louisiana and Mississippi. With these funds, grant partners provided case management and direct relief in the form of clothing, food, furniture, transportation, and childcare to over 150,000 evacuees, as well as legal assistance, health and mental health services or counseling, housing assistance, job training, employment assistance, and youth services to thousands in the aftermath of the hurricane.

The KWRF grant partners brought an intersectional lens through which the public and policymakers could understand the role gender, race, and class played out in the ordeal. That same lens focused on the solutions for rebuilding that addressed systemic gender, racial, and economic injustice as the foundation of the problem.[7]

Helping a woman through a crisis in her life gives her the chance to stabilize her situation, which is a fundamental form of social justice. Many women's funds support women's emergency needs, such as funding domestic violence shelters, food banks, and access to medical support. Many provide this support episodically when an emergency severely impacts women, as with the "she-cession" during the Covid-19 pandemic or disasters like Hurricane Katrina.[8]

## Sustaining Important Gains During an Emergency

Several women's funds, like Urgent Action Fund, exist to provide women's and feminist groups with emergency funds wherever they are in the world, adapting to the ever-morphing nature of emergencies, whether a natural disaster, a complex humanitarian emergency, or a political crisis. Crucially, they support feminist groups and movements to sustain their organizing while also responding to the immediate crisis.

After the devastating earthquake in Nepal in 2015, TEWA, the Nepal women's fund, worked to get funds to local women's groups to reach the most marginalized and isolated while also committing funds to sustain the work of women leaders focused on ensuring that women's needs were represented and embodied in the new Constitution in Nepal. What's crucial at a time of emergency is supporting women's movements to hold ground on important gains made while also pivoting to address the impact of a humanitarian crisis or natural disaster.

Women's funds are well-suited for emergency response, moving with agility to get funding to the frontline leaders who know best how to deploy it. As Surina Khan, Former CEO of Women's Foundation California, says, "The basis of feminist philanthropy is that people closest to the problems in their communities are also closest to the solutions."[9]

## Funding the Solutions Proposed by Those Most Affected

A widely accepted belief within the Global Women's Funding Movement is that the solutions devised by those most affected by a problem are often very different and usually more effective than the solutions devised by those with little first-hand experience of a severe situation. Investing in women-led solutions, which women's funds do, in a society in which women's ideas, problems, and perspectives are often ignored, unleashes a rarely tapped female force with new perspectives, fresh ideas, and innovations. The Women's Fund of Hawaii demonstrated this by simply asking a woman who was unhoused what she needed to get off the streets. Her answer was "a bus pass." Without it, she missed her social service appointments, which were critical to getting housing. The Women's Fund of Hawaii was guided by her needs and perspective. They gave her the bus pass, which got her off the streets and helped her get into permanent housing, and, with it, they discovered a simple solution that lifted others out of the same predicament. Many women's funds are invested in letting the most affected, typically the most marginalized, lead the solution seeking, recognizing that their proximity to critical social challenges makes them best informed to solve them.

Due to its worldwide and local decentralized network structure, the Global Women's Funding Movement can act quickly and in highly focused ways to get funds to women's organizations and movements to realize justice gains including across borders.

The women's fund Fondo Semillas is a feminist fund in Mexico that believes in the transformative power of organized women, girls, trans, and intersex people. For 32 years, Semillas has been mobilizing resources and providing funds to organizations, networks, and collectives to advance girls, women, trans*, and intersex people's rights and strengthen social movements so that they can be sustainable, to disrupt power relations and recover historical memory.[10]

Dreamers Moms USA-Tijuana is a grant partner of Semillas and supports migrant women deported from the United States to Mexico who were separated from their families. Its mission consists of legally reuniting deported women with their families and intervening, so their children are not placed for adoption while deported. Dreamers Moms USA-Tijuana was founded and led by Yolanda Varona. In 2010, Varona was deported to Mexico, and she didn't even get to say goodbye to her children, who remained in the U.S. In a 2020 interview, Varona said:

> I was deported and separated suddenly from my kids. From that day to today, I fight every day to return to them and hug them. I fight for the rights of deported women, and I dream of the day I can return to hug my daughter. Now, today, I feel braver.[11]

In June of 2022, Varona was reunified with her family after more than a decade of watching her children grow up through a computer screen.[12] Varona requested parole under the Immigrant Military Members and Veterans Initiative (IMMVI) as a spouse of a former U.S. military member. Under the initiative, the U.S. considers parole requests case by case from certain noncitizen military service members and their qualifying family members, including those who seek entry to the U.S. With this, Varona and her children were united. While she was enduring this time and working for reunification with her children, Varona worked to help others in a similar situation, and this work had a huge impact. Varona's reunification with her children was covered by the *San Diego Union Tribune*, which commemorated the occasion, reporting:

> As an advocate for deportees and family reunifications, Yolanda Varona was able to witness some of the stories of deported veterans and mothers who after years of strife managed to return to the United States with their families. This Friday was her turn.[13]

Varona's daughter, Paulina Young, who was 31 when she was reunited with her mother, explained, "I was 19 when that happened [...] we're just getting to know each other again."[14]

"I think the willingness of donors to be political is critical," Jessica Houssian, Former Co-CEO of the Equality Fund says. She continues:

> There's your privilege at work again. Right? There's your privilege at work. If it was your child at the border in Texas, you would get political. That's also the power thing, and the privilege thing, and the lack of awareness thing. I do think that when donors can start seeing themselves as one piece of the puzzle rather than this binary, here are the haves, and here are the have-nots, and we're going to move money in this way, but actually, we're all moving together as an ecosystem.[15]

## Deploying Rapid Response Research

Addressing policy and legal change for justice also requires building the evidence base and conducting research to inform advocacy and action. Original research has been a critical foundation on which many Global Women's Funding Movement successes have been built. In 2021, the Women's Funding Network announced an exclusive research partnership with their grant partner, the Institute for Women's Policy Research (IWPR). This first-of-its-kind initiative, The Gender Point, provides on-demand data reports that equip women's funds and foundations with the research to leverage and enhance policy and funding priorities across the United States.[16]

Elizabeth Barajas-Román, President and CEO of the Women's Funding Network, explains the inspiration for the research partnership:

> The majority of our network said that, when they're doing their policy advocacy work, when they are making the case for certain support, funders would ask, "well, where's the data?" And they usually needed it quickly. We asked ourselves, "How can we provide that particular type of resource to our women's funds, and how can we afford it?" So, we proactively created the idea of Gender Point, a place for women's funds to request rapid research. For example, they could ask, "How many women in the state of New Hampshire access child subsidies?" They can request a rapid report, with a guaranteed turnaround of about 48 hours, and we turn it around to them in a formatted one pager that they can take to their funder, legislator, or whomever. These data sets will help build a long-term strategy for creating stronger systems and institutions that center the experiences and contributions of women in the workforce, society, and their families. This "rapid response" clearinghouse of gender equity research

in the 50 states enables WFN members to easily and quickly create a standard set of benchmarks that can be used by them and others, including policymakers and the media. Gender Point also makes the case for investments in women's funds, documenting how they move money faster than traditional philanthropic entities and are designed to produce a multiplier effect on investments [in] their communities.[17]

## Mobilizing Funds to Stabilize the Housing Emergency

Original research has also guided the work of the Texas Women's Foundation to address the unique housing issues low-income women confront in the U.S. As Dena L. Jackson, former Chief Strategy Officer of Texas Women's Foundation (TXWF), explains:

> 2014 was when the Texas Women's Foundation first published our Economic Issues for Women in Texas research report. It's always looked at four key pillars, childcare, health insurance or health care, education, and housing. Housing was just so important. We wanted to know, is it a gendered issue though? Is it a low-income issue? Is it a racial issue? Or is there truly a gendered component?[18]

When TXWF began funding research on eviction, beginning in the years preceding the Covid-19 pandemic, they discovered a trend of forced moving and evictions using housing choice vouchers (HVCs) as the factor triggering eviction. Women were the majority of those receiving public support. Through its research, TXWF also understood that housing is the largest expense for most women in Texas. As 2020 unfolded, TXWF discovered the pandemic was accelerating housing-related problems and widespread loss of jobs and income. Dramatic spikes in domestic violence put women in greater housing jeopardy.[19]

One of the most common types of emergencies women worldwide face is access to housing. If you have nowhere to live, you are in a crisis that quickly spirals into more crises, including threats to one's physical safety. For women, especially those with children, this risk spiral of homelessness spins faster and more destructively. Across the globe, access to safe and affordable housing remains one of the greatest barriers to women's wellbeing.

In the fall of 2019, directly before the Covid-19 pandemic struck, TXWF created the Housing Stability Fund and convened its first group of key community stakeholders, a diverse, capable team of leaders in the housing stability sector. This group became a learning community to address complex issues that result in housing instability. Jackson explains, "Where a woman lives determines where her children go to school, how long her commute to work is, and whether she feels safe. Affordable, quality housing is truly an anchor for economic security for Texas women and their families."[20] During the Covid-19 pandemic, the U.S. had national and local eviction moratoriums in effect that protected vulnerable families, but when those protections were eliminated in March 2021, the impact was dramatic and immediate. In Dallas County alone, just one month after the eviction protections were removed, the number of evictions spiked from 44 in 2020 to 855 in 2021.[21]

The Housing Stability Fund awarded its first grant in June 2020 to an agency that had been implementing smart housing stability responses to the Covid-19 pandemic. The Inclusive Communities Project engages in policy advocacy by working with families using government vouchers for housing. In the summer of 2022, a homeowner's association (HOA) in North Texas voted to require every resident who had a HCV in that HOA's area to move out within 30 days. More than 600 residents from 157 households were expected to be displaced by the new, arbitrary leasing rules.[22] The Inclusive Communities Project's initiative, through their Renting Inclusive Communities Project, took immediate action. Working with local attorneys, they could offer legal aid services to every single one of those affected families. Over 90 percent of the HCV recipients living in the HOA were Black. The Department of Justice and the Department of Housing and Urban Development opened cases against the HOA, asserting the rule amounted to a violation of the civil rights of the residents relying on vouchers. The HOA reconsidered their rule, putting it on hold until all the litigation was resolved.

By 2024, TXWF's Housing Stability Fund is projected to invest, through multiyear grants, more than $3.5 million into stable housing for women and families and to provide resources to mitigate the terrible effects of eviction.[23] The statewide advocacy that TXWF funded led to systemic change with the passage of a Tenant Bill of Rights, allowing local communities to prohibit landlords from discriminating against families using HCVs.[24]

## Centering Care During a Crisis

One of the other critical issues that arose due to Covid-19 was a renewed focus on addressing issues of care, given that women were performing between three to six times as much unpaid care as men, and girls were dropping out of school and not returning in some countries due to care responsibilities. Women's funds and the Women's Funding Network increased the focus on advancing decent care work and choice of care for childcare, eldercare and disability care needs as well as responding to care related migration. This included working to place care on the agenda of governments and donors to strengthen care policies, care delivery systems, and intersectional movements for care justice.

The pandemic was also a time when women's and feminist funds looked at their own attitudes and structures to support self-care. Paige Andrew, Chief of Programs, Grantmaking and Operations with FRIDA The Young Feminist Fund, shares what the staff at FRIDA decided during the pandemic:

> It was hard for folks to show up at work and work at 100 percent every day when we were literally living through a pandemic. And not only living through a pandemic but also trying to support grantee partners through a pandemic. The decision was then made that if we're going to be talking about care, if we're going to stand for care, then we need to kind of walk the talk. One way of doing that is to cut back on the work. It's really easy for us, like me as a manager, it's easy for me to tell someone I supervise, hey, maybe you could do a little less this week. But that's not a political commitment; that's not an organizational commitment. We really started as an organization to commit to doing less, to going back to the core work that we do as a fund and letting go of the rest just for a little while to give folks space and time to connect with their communities or to rest, or to care for themselves, or to rethink.[25]

Françoise Moudouthe, CEO, African Women's Development Fund, shares how women's funds are also paying attention to the care needs of women human rights defenders:

> The solidarity, the care, that glue that keeps movements and activists together and makes the movement more than the sum of its parts is critical. There's this initiative that was founded under Theo Sowa and Jessica Horn, which they called the Flourish Retreat. Asking the questions, so, who cares for the defenders? Who defends the defenders? Creating those spaces for healing that are beautiful. Urgent Action Fund does this very well with The Feminist Republik. I think that work is very important. Work around collective care is very important.[26]

Human rights violations, humanitarian emergencies, and climate-related disasters are increasing in frequency. By focusing on the needs of women, girls, and gender-expansive people and resourcing their leadership for strategies and solutions, women's funds work to get the funds where they're most needed—to women at the frontlines of impact and response, including mental health and psychosocial support for first responders.

## Investing in Women's Climate and Environmental Leadership

There is a growing urgency to fund work at the intersection of climate justice and women's economic security. For example, the livelihoods of most African women, especially rural women who are poor, depend on natural resources. Yet modern-day practices in agriculture, fishing, infrastructure projects, mining, and energy have resulted in unprecedented biodiversity loss, habitat degradation, over-exploitation, pollution, and climate change, which have negatively affected the livelihoods of rural women.[27] Recognizing this, the African Women's Development Fund (AWDF) has been resourcing women's groups and initiatives focused on environmental and climate justice, where women within the community participate in the design and planning of the projects. These initiatives address environmental degradation, design sustainable farming practices, create more secure livelihoods, and resource women mobilizing against the destruction of their environment by big corporations, such as mining companies.

According to Rose Buabeng, Programme Officer at AWDF:

> Climate change does not impact everyone equally. Women are disproportionately affected because they are often the ones who work closest to natural resources that are impacted by climate change. There is an urgent need to ensure women at the local level have adequate information, support for their solutions and priorities, rights to natural resources, and a voice at the table where climate and environmental policies are discussed.[28]

One of the AWDF grant partners is the pro-climate, women-led Iseguri Initiative, a grassroots women's environmental group based in the Oti Region of Ghana. With funding from AWDF, Iseguri has supported over 2,000 rural women smallholder farmers to promote sustainable agricultural practices such as water harvesting and irrigation, crop scheduling, cultivation techniques, pesticide and fertilizer use, creation and use of compost, and prevention of post-harvest losses.[29] As a result, they have increased women-led, sustainable agricultural practices, resulting in systemic change and preserving women's jobs throughout the Oti region. Farmers have enjoyed bigger crops of ginger and maize, resulting in greater income and improved nutrition for those living within this rural area.

Buabeng says:

> Grassroots women are leading initiatives to mitigate the impact of climate change on their environment, community, and livelihoods. Community women have led initiatives to stop companies from destroying forests and territories, protect their families from pollution and toxic waste, promote alternative energy, create more sustainable agriculture, and amplify their voices at negotiation tables. Men receive far greater resources for climate-related initiatives because they tend to wage larger-scale, more public efforts. In contrast, community women's advocacy is typically locally based and less visible, making it even more difficult to attract funding and support. Data shows that only 0.01 percent of all worldwide grant dollars support projects addressing climate change and women's rights.[30]

Another movement that has gained important support from women's funds is the Women Forest Defenders in Indonesia. In 2012, Farwiza Farhan was working in Indonesia with the Leuser Ecosystem Management Authority, a government agency tasked with protecting, conserving, and restoring the Leuser Ecosystem. The Leuser Ecosystem is a landscape that spans 2.6 million hectares of relatively intact rainforest. It's the last place on earth where critically endangered wildlife—Sumatran orangutans, rhinos, tigers, and elephants—still roam together in the wild. Aside from its intrinsic beauty and value, it provides clean water, clean air, and protection from natural disasters.

As part of their job to protect this ecosystem, Farwiza and her colleagues were working on a campaign to get law enforcement to uphold the law against a palm oil company that was burning forest. They were gaining traction—and then, suddenly, the government agency they worked for was dismantled. Farwiza said, "We went from being the 'authority' to being the 'outcast.'"

Farwiza and her colleagues loved the Leuser Ecosystem too much to stop, so they created HAkA (which in English means Forest, Nature and Environment of Aceh). HAkA aspired to strengthen protection, conservation, and restoration of the Leuser Ecosystem through grassroots organizing and engaging more women in conservation work.

Then Farwiza met Sumini, from the village of Damaran Baru. Sumini and her community survived a devastating flash flood that destroyed much of her village infrastructure. They knew that forest destruction is closely linked to flash flooding. The community lost their livelihoods and homes and, for a period, had to seek shelter in a refugee camp. In 2020, Farwiza and her HAkA team partnered with Sumini and her village to create a women-led ranger team to protect the forest from illegal logging and encroachment. These women and men then formed Mpu Uteun (forest protector). At first, other community members challenged the women, not believing they could be effective. However, after they achieved success, people changed their attitudes.

Together, they are mobilizing a movement that enables women to protect local rainforests and one of the last intact ecosystems in the world. They are also training grassroots communities to engage in forest monitoring through GPS satellite devices and drone mapping.[31]

Since this time, there's been no more flooding as the forest once again becomes a protective canopy against disasters. Speaking about what they've made possible, Farwiza said, "When women feel empowered to protect the forest, it becomes an infectious spirit for women mobilizing everywhere."[32]

## Funding Those Most Affected to Lead

By letting women and those most affected lead, women's funds often champion the most neglected issues or the riskiest causes affecting women, girls, and gender-expansive people. Women's funds are often the first and, too often, only funder of the most risky and controversial causes. By funding such work, women's funds have helped to shift patriarchal cultures with infusions of funds to those who rarely control capital. And thus, they have also shifted the culture around money itself—enabling women to use it to exert their power collectively as they see fit. Among the many funding practices innovated by women's funds, attracting other funders to the work of the grant partners who champion the risky, controversial issues on their terms has been one of the Global Women's Funding Movement's most exponential funding strategies.

There are only three sex worker-led funds in the world. The Red Umbrella Fund, Third Wave Fund's Sex Worker Giving Circle (SWGC), and the East African Sexual Health and Rights Initiative (UHAI EASHRI). All are feminist funds. They consider themselves to be feminist funds because gender-expansive people are direct beneficiaries of their work. The first global fund to be guided by and for sex workers is the Red Umbrella Fund (RU). RU was started in April 2012 by two international women's funds, Mama Cash and the Astraea Lesbian Foundation for Justice, as an innovative global grantmaking mechanism to confront the legal oppression and social stigma sex workers suffer.

Along with raising funding through its women's fund original partners, RU also established funding avenues for sex work activists to reach more traditional funders while protecting the sex-worker-led approach. They did this by educating the funders on the importance of listening to the workers. Colletaz explains, "Funds like Red Umbrella Fund were created because some traditional funders were interested, but they didn't have the systems to provide core, flexible funding to unregistered groups, particularly criminalized communities." RU made 279 grants to 180 organizations in 68 countries in its first decade.[33]

Annie Hillar, Co-Director, Gender Funders Colab, and former Senior Program Officer of Women's Funds at Mama Cash, says:

> The notion of creating grantmaking mechanism for sex worker rights needed to have not just the participation of sex workers, it actually had to have sex workers in the driver's seat [...] Sex workers are never given that kind of opportunity because they're seen as beneficiaries. They're not considered agents who have power or a voice. They're often victimized or treated in a very paternalistic way by donors.[34]

Mukami Marete, Executive Director of UHAI-EASHRI, Africa's first Indigenous, activist-led and activist-managed fund, says:

> We identify as a feminist fund. We work with structurally silenced people; people for whom the systems and the structures that exist were never built. In a lot of the countries that we work in, the institutions are built on a very patriarchal framework, and that does not allow for body autonomy. Because our communities refuse to fit within that framework, we are labeled deviants, subversives, and transgressors. What that practically means for our communities is pushback from our governments and our families, whether within homes, workplaces, institutions of learning, or even on the streets. It makes it very dangerous just to exist and be who you are.[35]

Third Wave Fund's Sex Worker Giving Circle (SWGC), launched in 2019, was the first sex-worker-led fund housed at a U.S. foundation. It had the dual goal of funding a diverse range of sex-worker-led groups throughout the country and bringing current and former sex workers to the philanthropic decision-making table. The SWGC is inspired by community-led grantmaking at other funds and the long history of sex worker communities caring for each other, especially sex workers of color and trans and gender non-conforming sex workers.

As Christian Giraldo, former Program Officer for the Third Wave Fund's Sex Worker Giving Circle, shares:

> One might expect that this intersectionality would put sex workers on the radar of funders interested in tackling multiple issues. But due to stigma and criminalization, the community is often left to fend for itself. Sex workers are under constant interrogation and constant political assault, which results in fear when speaking to funders. There are many roles that philanthropy can play right now to dismantle and mitigate that dynamic. The Giving Circle has been beating the drum tirelessly about unrestricted, multiyear funding, and making funding easily accessible, with diverse ways of applying—video proposal, one-to-one conversations, metrics on their own terms rather than defined by NGOs.[36]

It's important to recognize the rights of sex workers who have consented to work in the sex industry by choice and who engage in commercial transactions between consenting adults. This is very different from those who have been forcibly exploited or trafficked and for whom many women's funds direct resources to combat human trafficking, forced labor and migration, modern-day slavery, and child soldiers.

## Tackling Sex Trafficking, Locally, Globally

While women's funds often focus on supporting the leadership of local women, girls, and gender-expansive people, often the issues they deal with, like sex trafficking, are global in scope. This was the case with the Women's Foundation of Minnesota when it set out to tackle sex trafficking.

Founded in 1983, the Women's Foundation of Minnesota (WFMN) is the first statewide women's foundation in the United States. WFMN's work with grantee partners and colleagues in the state's criminal justice system informed the fund's efforts to end the sex trafficking of girls in Minnesota, revealing its causes to be deeply rooted in gender and economic injustice. At the same time, the opportunities for prevention exist within a complex, cross-sector field of public agencies, businesses, nonprofit service providers, and the public. WFMN employed a "collective impact framework," recognizing that no sector alone can achieve meaningful progress on complex, systemic social and economic issues. WFMN leveraged its reputation and leadership as a community foundation with statewide influence to identify and convene critical stakeholders.[37]

In 2010, WFMN organized over 100 leaders from all over the state, including donors, elected officials, government agencies, foundations, advocates, corporations, judges, and faith communities, to create a strategic, long-term, multi-sector plan to address child sex trafficking. This resulted in MN Girls Are Not for Sale, an eight-year plan, funded with $8 million, to end the sex trafficking of Minnesota girls and boys through targeted grantmaking, research, public education, and gatherings.

Within a year of the MN Girls Are Not for Sale launch, there was a surge in media coverage on the issue. The Minnesota legislature passed the state's Safe Harbor legislation, which ensures that young people who are sexually exploited are treated as victims and survivors, not criminals. Through the No Wrong Door model, these young people can receive trauma-informed support rather than being treated as juvenile delinquents.[38] When the bill was introduced, the state budget was extremely tight, and the legislature was poised to reject any bill requiring funds to introduce it. WFMN paid the $12,000 fiscal note that enabled the passage of the legislation.[39] This decision to pay the appropriation and focus on lobbying were critical factors in the Safe Harbor's passage. The Women's Foundation of Minnesota noted a "significant shift in language used in media coverage once the MN Girls Are Not for Sale campaign was launched and Safe Harbor was passed. The public awareness and education campaign changed the narrative and resulted in a sea change in how media partners and the public frame the issue. Media coverage began referring to the crime as 'sex trafficking' rather than 'prostitution,' and public perception shifted to viewing children and adults caught in the web of sex trafficking as victims, rather than criminals."[40]

The success of the MN Girls Are Not for Sale campaign and the critical impact it has had on the work to end sex trafficking is undeniable. With cross-sector leaders, the Women's Foundation of Minnesota invested $8 million between 2011 and 2019, changed laws, the narrative, attitudes, and beliefs, published groundbreaking research on sex trafficking, inspired and advocated for federal legislation, developed model protocols for law enforcement, and increased sex trafficking charges and convictions. As a result of efforts funded through the campaign, Minnesota was the first state in the nation to create and fund a statewide comprehensive plan—$47 million to date—to end sex trafficking and sexual exploitation.

Gloria Perez, Executive Director, Women's Foundation of Minnesota says:

> The Women's Foundation has always been focused on system change, to look upstream and think about why women are at risk in our communities. We root everything in research. Investing in listening

within communities and then sharing that research across the state or in whatever community the research is being done is important. That is the power we have as philanthropy. It is about changing that narrative and shining a light on the problem, and then being the backbone to convene groups to say, "This is a systems issue."[41]

Of course, trafficking is not just limited to the sex industry. It also includes forced labor that involves significant violations of labor, public health, and human rights standards worldwide. Falling under the banner of trafficking are different types of trafficking, including sex and child trafficking and forced labor trafficking. Since there is overlap in these different forms, the term "human trafficking" is used to represent the diverse forms of trafficking.[42] Women's funds are supporting work to combat human trafficking in regions as diverse as Latin America, Asia, and the Pacific Islands.

## Investing in Auspicious Conditions

Getting funding to those who are most at risk and on the frontlines of impact so they can devise the solutions and facilitate systemic change is what women's funds do. They move money fast to women's groups, networks, and movements to address immediate needs while ensuring the funds support the long-term approaches needed for transformative change. Ana Oliveira, President and CEO of The New York Women's Foundation, says:

We are not the ones building prosperity for women and families. We are not the ones building; we are the ones investing to create auspicious conditions for those who are building on a daily basis to thrive. Auspicious conditions for movements led by women, for women to grow; auspicious conditions for their visions to flourish.[43]

These auspicious conditions are what contribute to supporting movements to shift power, resources, policies, voice, and norms. This way of working is crucial to achieving the level of systemic change sought by women's funds, as the next chapter shows.

## Notes

1 "Hurricane Katrina," George W. Bush Presidential Library, accessed November 24, 2023, www.georgewbushlibrary.gov/research/topic-guides/hurricane-katrina.

2  "Women, Disasters, and Hurricane Katrina," Institute for Women's Policy Research, Fact Sheet, August 2010, accessed November 24, 2023, https://iwpr. org/wp-content/uploads/2020/09/D492.pdf.

3  "Women and Girls in Disasters," Center for Disaster Philanthropy, accessed November 24, 2023, https://disasterphilanthropy.org/resources/ women-and-girls-in-disasters.

4  Jane Roberts, "National Ms. Foundation among chorus praising Ruby Bright's career," *Daily Memphian*, May 10, 2022, accessed November 24, 2023, https://dailymemphian.com/article/28602/memphis-ruby-bright-honored- ms-foundation.

5  Ruby Bright, interview with Christine Grumm and Laura Risimini, August 18, 2022.

6  Ruby Bright, interview with Christine Grumm and Laura Risimini, August 18, 2022.

7  Hanh Cao Yu, Ph.D., Kelly Johnson, Anna Rubin, and Wally Abrazaldo, "Building Momentum to Sustain Social Change: Evaluation of the Katrina Women's Response Fund, Phase 2 Final Report," Social Policy Research Associates, March 16, 2009, accessed November 24, 2023, https://search. issuelab.org/resources/5860/5860.pdf.

8  "Women," UNHCR, accessed November 24, 2023, www.unhcr.org/ what-we-do/how-we-work/safeguarding-individuals/women.

9  Surina Khan, interview with Christine Grumm and Laura Risimini, October 25, 2022.

10  "Home," Fondo Semillas, accessed November 24, 2023, https://semillas.org. mx/en.

11  "Yolanda Varona decidió transformar el dolor en fuerza y valentía. ¡Conoce su historia!" Fondos Semillas, X Video, accessed May 24, 2024, https://x.com/ fondosemillas/status/1315985724227883008?lang=ar.

12  Alexandra Mendoza, "Deported mom returns to San Diego after more than a decade," *The San Diego Tribune*, June 3, 2022. Accessed November 24, 2023, www.sandiegouniontribune.com/news/immigration/story/2022-06-03/ deported-mom-returns-to-san-diego-after-more-than-a-decade.

13  Alexandra Mendoza, "Deported mom returns to San Diego after more than a decade," *The San Diego Tribune*, June 3, 2022. Accessed November 24, 2023, www.sandiegouniontribune.com/news/immigration/story/2022-06-03/ deported-mom-returns-to-san-diego-after-more-than-a-decade.

14  Alexandra Mendoza, "Deported mom returns to San Diego after more than a decade," *The San Diego Tribune*, June 3, 2022. Accessed November 24, 2023, www.sandiegouniontribune.com/news/immigration/story/2022-06-03/ deported-mom-returns-to-san-diego-after-more-than-a-decade.

15  Jessica Houssian, interview with Christine Grumm and Laura Risimini, November 14, 2022.

16   "Data Driven Gender Equity," The Gender Point, accessed November 24, 2023, https://genderpoint.org.

17   "WFN Names IWPR Exclusive Research Partner for Global Network," Women's Funding Network, September 23, 2021, accessed November 24, 2023, www.womensfundingnetwork.org/2021/09/23/wfn-iwpr-global-partnership.

18   Dena L. Jackson, Ph.D., interview with Laura Risimini, November 28, 2022.

19   "Economic Issues for Women in Texas 2022," Texas Women's Foundation, accessed November 24, 2023, https://txwfecoissues.org/wp-content/uploads/2022/09/TXWF-report-2022.pdf.

20   Dena L. Jackson, Ph.D., interview with Laura Risimini, November 28, 2022.

21   Dena L. Jackson, Ph.D., interview with Laura Risimini, November 28, 2022.

22   Amber Gaudet, "In reversal, Providence HOA to allow Section 8 tenants to finish leases," *Denton Record-Chronicle*, June 29, 2022, Accessed November 24, 2023, https://dentonrc.com/news/providence_village/in-reversal-providence-hoa-to-allow-section-8-tenants-to-finish-leases/article_b5fa7de1-7018-523c-8834-24eb22ae6b98.html.

23   "Economic Issues for Women in Texas 2022," Texas Women's Foundation, accessed November 24, 2023, https://txwfecoissues.org/wp-content/uploads/2022/09/TXWF-report-2022.pdf.

24   "Economic Issues for Women in Texas 2022," Texas Women's Foundation, accessed November 24, 2023, https://txwfecoissues.org/wp-content/uploads/2022/09/TXWF-report-2022.pdf.

25   Paige Andrews, interview Christine Grumm and Laura Risimini, December 5, 2022.

26   Françoise Moudouthe, interview with Christine Grumm, November 9, 2022.

27   Rose Buabeng, "Envisioning a Feminist Earth: African women lead the way," *African Women's Development Fund*, April 22, 2020, accessed November 24, 2023, https://awdf.org/envisioning-a-feminist-earth-african-women-lead-the-way.

28   Rose Buabeng, personal email communication with Laura Risimini, October 12, 2022.

29   Rose Buabeng, "Envisioning a Feminist Earth: African women lead the way," *African Women's Development Fund*, April 22, 2020, accessed November 24, 2023, https://awdf.org/envisioning-a-feminist-earth-african-women-lead-the-way.

30   Rose Buabeng, personal email communication with Laura Risimini, October 12, 2022.

31   Farwiza Farhan, personal email communication with Jane Sloane, October 24, 2023.

32   Farwiza Farhan, Lecture, Lotus Leadership Awards from The Asia Foundation, New York, April 26, 2023.

33   "Grantee-Partners Map," Red Umbrella Fund, accessed November 24, 2023, www.redumbrellafund.org/Grantee-Partners-Map.

34  *Red Umbrella Fund: The Creation of a Collaborative Fund* (Red Umbrella Fund, 2017), accessed November 24, 2023, www.redumbrellafund.org/wp-content/ uploads/2014/07/Red-Umbrella-Fund-The-creation-of-a-Collaborative-Fund.pdf.

35  Kennedy Owiti and Mukami Marete, interview with Laura Risimini, March 2, 2023.

36  Christian Giraldo, interview with Laura Risimini and Hadley Wilhoite, March 1, 2023.

37  "MN Girls Are Not for Sale: A Strategic Campaign to End Sex Trafficking," Women's Foundation of Minnesota, accessed November 24, 2023, www. wfmn.org/mn-girls-are-not-for-sale/?fbclid=IwAR28hRTrf0wU7GcoBO5YV ZOVM10giiiHXd8xvdEwhoi7E1sTPY7SoMUJako.

38  "Safe Harbor/No Wrong Door," Minnesota Department of Human Services, accessed November 24, 2023, https://mn.gov/dhs/partners-and-providers/ program-overviews/child-protection-foster-care-adoption/safe-harbor.

39  "Safe Harbor/No Wrong Door," Minnesota Department of Human Services, accessed November 24, 2023, https://mn.gov/dhs/partners-and-providers/ program-overviews/child-protection-foster-care-adoption/safe-harbor.

40  "MN Girls Are Not for Sale: A Strategic Campaign to End Sex Trafficking," Women's Foundation of Minnesota, accessed November 24, 2023, www. wfmn.org/mn-girls-are-not-for-sale/?fbclid=IwAR28hRTrf0wU7GcoBO5YV ZOVM10giiiHXd8xvdEwhoi7E1sTPY7SoMUJako.

41  Gloria Perez, interview with Laura Risimini, March 10, 2023.

42  Adrianne Haney, "What's the difference? Human trafficking v. sex trafficking," *11alive.com*, March 9, 2017, accessed November 24, 2023, www.11alive. com/article/news/crime/whats-the-difference-human-trafficking-v-sex-trafficking/85-421321351.

43  Ana Oliveira, interview with Laura Risimini, October 28, 2022.

# In It for the Long Haul　　**5**

## Funding Systemic Change Led by Women, Girls, and Gender-Expansive People

### Groundswell

Investing in women's leadership and models of collaborative leadership has been an essential strategy for many women's funds committed to funding systemic change. Women's movements have long been wellsprings of powerful women leaders and have been a reliable funder of these movements. As Gloria Steinem says, "The women's funding movement is an unprecedented event. It is making social change, woman by woman, group by group, neighborhood by neighborhood. And in fact, social change only happens from the bottom up."[1] Gloria Steinem's leadership and advocacy for women-led solutions and trust-based philanthropy exemplify this approach.

### Funding Access to Justice

Women's funds also identify where women's leadership is absent and focus on filling the leadership void. For instance, the Legal Fellowship was established in 2013 by Women's Fund Asia (then named South Asia Women's Fund). The Legal Fellowship was created to address a critical gender gap in the system: the lack of women lawyers in South Asia.[2] The number of female litigators in the primary courts in South Asian countries is alarmingly low. For instance, in Chitrakoot district in Uttar Pradesh, there are only three practicing lawyers out of 600 advocates. The Legal Fellowship, the first in the region, was created to support women lawyers working in

DOI: 10.4324/9781003330455-5

the primary courts and, in doing so, to support a cross-section of women in accessing justice. Tulika Srivastava, former Executive Director of Women's Fund Asia, explains:

> We designed the Legal Fellowship because, in the beginning, there is no one to support women litigants and there is no one to support women who are in difficulties with law. It is essential that there are women lawyers at the very first level. So, we, of course, need financial resources.[3]

Of course, just having women in these roles is not enough. The Legal Fellowship developed a feminist legal praxis that enables lawyers to approach cases with an awareness of discrimination and power imbalances in the legal system to place survivors and claimants at the center of the process. Together with Fellows, the Legal Fellowship developed a feminist code of conduct based on human rights principles, informing the Fellows' approach and ensuring that clients participate in decision making. As well as preparing women for the legal process, Fellows consider their clients' personal safety and emotional wellbeing. They may advise on counseling before taking legal steps or suggest alternative resolutions with gaps in the law. These interventions identify and address critical gaps and needs to support women's access to justice.[4]

In 2013, when it first launched, the Legal Fellowship funded ten lawyers to represent domestic violence and family law cases. It particularly focused on empowering women lawyers from rural, marginalized communities who bring local sensitivity to their roles. Since then, the legal subjects the Fellows have represented have expanded to include discrimination and/or violence based on intersections of caste, class, ethnicity, citizenship, sexual orientation, and gender identity. By 2021, the Legal Fellowship had supported 30 lawyers in five countries: Bangladesh, India, Nepal, Pakistan, and Sri Lanka, and more than a thousand women and gender non-binary persons received legal advice and representation from local feminist lawyers. This all happened with grants totaling US$299,000.[5]

One of the legal Fellows, Tabassum, is based in Hyderabad, India, and joined the fellowship in 2015. Tabassum represents cases of sexual violence, divorce, child support, alimony, and domestic violence. Often, women confront severe intimidation tactics used to pressure them into withdrawing their cases or accepting a settlement out of court. In one domestic violence case, both Tabassum and her client were threatened. Tabassum secured a protection order for her client from the judge. She explains, "The fellowship gave me the skills and expertise to carry out my work independently and courageously. Women's Fund Asia helped me actualize my learning goals through training workshops, where they provided the best and learned trainers."[6]

Since its inception, the Global Women's Funding Movement has worked to shift power, policies, resources, voice, and norms. Shared leadership through collaboration has been the energetic force that has fueled its growth and success. As one Global Women's Funding Movement member said, "I see a lot of work to be done and I can't figure out how to do it unless a lot of people get involved."[7]

## Amplifying Women's Leadership for Systemic Change

The Global Women's Funding Movement has also played a crucial role in amplifying the leadership of women who need a global platform for their bold vision for systemic change. The late Janet Sape was a Papua New Guinean woman who for years had a dream of creating a microbank for women in Papua New Guinea. She was articulate about the reasons why. Two-thirds of women in Papua New Guinea are constantly exposed to domestic violence, and 50% become victims of sexual assault in Papua New Guinea. It has one of the highest rates of violence against women worldwide. For any woman wanting to escape a violent husband in a rural part of Papua New Guinea, it is hard to gain economic independence due to their situation and geographic location.

As Janet said when she started this work:

> More than 80% of PNG women live in rural areas where there's no access to banking or finance. Most of these women work in the informal sector as tailors, farmers, and fisherwomen, where they have no financial security and are very vulnerable. Women can't inherit property and rely on their husband's signatures for security if they want to take out a small loan. That's why I want a microbank for women, to reach the unreachable. We are small people here. We don't have Bill Gates or Oprah Winfrey to champion us. Women have to help each other, especially in an environment where polygamy is increasing, and marriages are shaky. If a woman walks out of a marriage, she's left with nothing. However, if a woman is financially secure, she can buy and own land or a house. She can pay to put food on the table, educate her children, manage her business, and afford health care. Truly, economic independence will be the savior of women in this country.[8]

Janet's proposal to the government was that to be eligible for a loan at this women's bank, women would be required to do compulsory financial literacy training and to have a track record of at least six months of savings. The Global Fund for Women helped Janet get funding for her organization, PNG Women in Business Foundation, to sign up 13,000 women as financial members of this foundation and get over 15,000 women registered in total. However, Janet was still having difficulty convincing the government to sign over a banking license to her organization to establish a bank, even though she had a banking background and a strong infrastructure in place. So, Women's Funding Network board member Jane Sloane nominated Janet for an international WFN Leadership in Equity and Diversity Award (LEAD) Award. Together with the leadership of then WFN Executive Director Michele Ozumba,[9] the Global Fund for Women funded Janet to travel to the U.S. from Papua New Guinea with some of her colleagues to accept the award at the 2014 Women's Funding Network global conference.

When Janet stood up in front of hundreds of women to accept the award, she said:

> You know. We women who have traveled far across the seas to be here tonight. We thought we were alone. We thought that our troubles were our own. Now I see we have all of you women—and men—by our side, you have our backs, which makes all the difference. Thank you for your belief in us.[10]

The Women's Funding Network and Janet's colleagues filmed her receiving the award and beamed the footage to television stations and newspapers in Papua New Guinea. By the time Janet arrived home, she was a rock star. As a result, several weeks later, the Bank of PNG signed over the banking license for the first microbank for women in PNG—one of four in the world at the time. Three years after launching the bank, there were almost 20,000 women customers.

When women are economically secure and free from violence, they are also more able to assume leadership roles and stand for office. With more women in parliament, there will be more opportunities for women to be at the table where decisions are being made. The LEAD award also led to recognition of Janet by others, including APEC Iconic Woman of PNG, Westpac Outstanding Woman, and appointment to the Port Moresby City Commission as a commissioner. That's what happens when you get funds into the hands of women and provide them access to influential forums where they can speak for themselves and be recognized for their vision on a global stage. There is a cascading effect with their leadership and what it inspires other women and girls to believe they can do. This is the power of the Global Women's Funding Movement in amplifying women's transformative leadership and vision to get the funds to where they're needed.

## Investing in Shared Leadership for Systemic Change

Amplifying women's leadership is one strategy and investing in shared leadership for systemic change is another. Indeed, several women's funds, such as FRIDA The Young Feminist Fund, have adopted a co-leadership model while also investing in women's movements that are co-led. zohra moosa, former Co-Executive Director of Mama Cash, shares their decentralized leadership model:

> Co-executive leadership enables us to live our value of sharing power in concrete and specific ways. It breaks with the tradition of the single leader and the idea that one person can and should make the final decisions and hold final responsibility for an organization. This model also builds on our internationalist principles and commitment to embracing more just practices and ways of working.[11]

The convening power of the Global Women's Funding Movement has also been crucial to gaining traction on important issues and leveraging funding and shared leadership. For instance, in 2006, the Women's Funding Network, the Sister Fund, the Atlanta Women's Foundation, the Dallas Women's Foundation, the New York Women's Foundation, the Women's Foundation of Colorado, and the Women's Fund of Western Massachusetts convened a national conversation on Women, Faith, and Philanthropy. The intention was to strengthen partnerships between faith-related organizations and the women's funding movement in recognition of the long history of progressive women of faith in social movements for abolition, women's suffrage, civil rights, and reproductive rights. This convening was also an opportunity to learn from existing work to achieve structural change, such as the New York Women's Foundation's grantmaking to Black churches working on domestic violence. The project was a bold attempt to bring two streams of women's experience together—the women's funding movement and women from faith-related organizations interested in social transformation—and to develop strategies and actions working with women philanthropic and faith leaders.

The world has yet to see the full power of women's collective and collaborative leadership. Women's funds recognize that women's leadership, particularly women's collective leadership, is critical to confronting entrenched systems of oppression and delivering the most seismic and systemic gender justice gains.

## Collaborative Funding for Systemic Change

Collaborative funding has also been an intentional strategy of women's funds to work for systemic change. Collaborative funding is an approach in philanthropy where multiple funders come together to pool their financial resources, expertise, and networks to collectively support a common goal or address a shared issue. It involves coordinated efforts and joint decision making among funders to maximize the impact of their investments. In collaborative funding, funders recognize that by combining their resources and working together, they can achieve greater outcomes than they would individually.

Cynthia Nimmo, former President and CEO of Women's Funding Network, shares:

> As the connecting force of the network, WFN has supported several multi-year collaborations of women's foundations working to reduce poverty and increase women's economic security from Partnership for Women's Prosperity (funded by Walmart Foundation) to the Two-Generation cohort (funded by W.K. Kellogg Foundation, which has been a long term funder of women's funds) and then to the Women's Economic Mobility Hubs (funded by the Bill and Melinda Gates Foundation). In this capacity, WFN is the backbone, acting as the con-venor, the re-grantor, the data collector, and magnifying results to a broader audience. Each of these cohorts has led to policy change in their region.[12]

The Women's Foundation for the State of Arizona successfully trained single mothers in "worthy wage" jobs and is now advocating for the program to be included in the state budget. The Iowa Women's Foundation conducted research, uncovering the significant shortage of affordable and accessible childcare throughout the state. Working across organizations, they created toolkits to transform the childcare arena and were subsequently selected to be on the Governor's Childcare Task Force. And the Chicago Women's Foundation centers on the working poor and has committed to raising the salary of female heads of households in the Englewood neighborhood from an average of $10,000/year to $40,000/year.[13]

This focus on collaborative funding has also been the hallmark of some international women's funds, including Urgent Action Fund. Today, there are four independent Urgent Action Sister Funds: UAF-Africa, UAF-Latin America and the Caribbean, UAF-Asia and Pacific, and Urgent Action Fund for Feminist Activism (formerly UAF for Women's Human Rights), which grants in the Middle East, Europe, the Balkans, the Caucasus, Turkey, Central Asia, Russia, Canada, and the United States. Together, these funds support feminist activism in more than 160 countries and have provided tens of millions of dollars in rapid-response funding to thousands of women and trans and non-binary frontline activists worldwide.

Collaborative, co-equal, and geographically distinct, the Urgent Action Sister Funds are the only global consortium of independent funds with a mission to sustain feminist activism worldwide by providing rapid-response funding to women and trans and non-binary frontline activists. Today, movements such as #MeToo and #Time'sUp and the global push for gender equality reinforce why a rapid-response fund would focus on feminist activists. But when Executive Director Kate Kroeger joined UAF for Feminist Activism, one of the four UAFs, in 2012, funders and advocates frequently questioned its focus.

"There is a very clear resource argument for focusing on women, trans, and non-binary people," Kroeger says, pointing to Human Rights Funders Network (HRFN) data. In 2017, HRFN noted that 18 percent of foundation grants went to women and girls, and less than 2 percent of global funding reached locally led women's rights organizations. The Urgent Action Sister Funds' staff of 100 require more than nimbleness to support a global movement—they rely on their network of supporters working together. "Feminism is about achieving equality for women, trans, and non-binary people, but it's also about challenging power structures," Kroeger says. "Women and LGBTQI people on the front lines of human rights struggles are doing that on a daily basis. We must do the same thing in philanthropy to help them succeed."[14]

## Joining Forces for Exponential Impact

In 2020, in the face of unprecedented threats to women's rights and feminist organizations throughout the world, two women's funds, the Equality Fund and the African Women's Development Fund (AWDF), joined forces to move substantial resources globally to defend and strengthen feminist infrastructure. The global pandemic, coupled with the global rise of authoritarianism, increased climate impact, and conflict, hit women, girls, and gender-expansive people the hardest. Many feminist organizations lost funding for their work while needing to radically adjust their activities, adapt to remote work, and stretch resources to address the deepening impacts of each outbreak in their communities.

In the face of these mounting challenges, feminist activists fought back even harder. The two sister funds, the Equality Fund and AWDF, formed a collaborative funding initiative they named Catalyze and embarked together on attracting money and other resources for feminist groups most in need of support. At the core of the Catalyze collaboration is a deep belief that feminist movements deserve funding that is as bold, flexible, and reliable as they are. Catalyze prioritized funding groups that advance anti-racist, anti-colonial, and intersectional agendas, respond to rights rollbacks, support women, girls, youth, non-binary people, and LGBTQI+ human rights defenders, address violence at multiple levels, and promote economic justice.

"It's an institutional partnership. We are both feminist funds," says Cynthia Eyakuze, Co-VP for Global Programs at the Equality Fund:

> AWDF has existed in this sort of scale. So, we look at AWDF as our big sister. We learn a lot from them. They have a permanent seat on our governing board. They are with us on a kind of investment journey, and they sit on an advisory group. So, it's an institutional partnership. Where Catalyze comes in is the recognition that AWDF, based on the continent, with a very broad reach, is better placed to do the grant making, to identify the kinds of organizations, to be able to accompany them better than the Equality Fund would be at scale. We have a five-year funding commitment to AWDF.[15]

The Catalyze collaboration represented a milestone in the Equality Fund's still young journey as a global women's fund. Established in 2019 with a $300 million grant from the Canadian government, the Equality Fund is a manifestation of all the Global Women's Funding Movement's Feminist Funding principles. The Canadian government's commitment came into being through the encouragement of the Canadian women's fund, Match International, which had spent years educating Canadian government officials on the impact of gender justice on the world. The Equality Fund has since inspired commitments from other governments, including a contribution of £59 million from the UK government.

Catalyze became the Equality Fund's first global feminist funding opportunity and one of the first steps toward achieving its vision of shifting philanthropic power and resources to women's movements. Together, they have funded 101 feminist organizations from over 60 countries, prioritizing those led by Indigenous women, sex workers, youth, and LGBTQI+ communities. In its role, AWDF led a call for proposals across the African continent, ultimately selecting 42 grassroots feminist organizations for funding. The Equality Fund led a call across Asia, the Pacific, Latin America, Eastern Europe, and the Middle East, selecting 30 new grantee partners. Together, the 72 grants allocated totaled $4,365,632.[16] The feminist groups funded by the collaborative comprise a large swath of the global feminist movement infrastructure. The Catalyze grants revitalized these frontline feminist organizations with direct injections of money, allowing them to strengthen, expand their reach, broaden their activity, and focus their vision.

The collaborative process between the Equality Fund and AWDF consecrated democratic philanthropic practices. Funding decisions are shaped by a global panel of advisors from different backgrounds and regions who comprise women's rights and feminist activists, feminist funders, and other feminist allies. Catalyze conducted a consultation process across feminist movements globally with the Association for Women's Rights in Development (AWID). They also designed and launched the Women's Fund Collaborative (now called Fenomenal Fund).[17] In 2020 and 2021, Fenomenal Fund provided resilience grants to women's funds in response to the unprecedented challenges of the Covid-19 pandemic. Forty-three Prospera members applied for the flexible funding to strengthen their leadership, infrastructure, fundraising, communications, resource mobilization capacities, technology, and other efforts each women's fund prioritizes.[18]

"By strengthening the capacity of women's funds to better operate and respond to a rapidly changing world, these funders will be able to better support feminist movements at the forefront of social change," said Emilienne de León, former Executive Director of Prospera International Network of Women's Funds. "[It's] a great opportunity for ensuring a healthy and vibrant ecosystem for funding women's rights and gender justice throughout the world."[19] Speaking about the importance of Prospera, Michelle Reddy, Co-Lead of the Pacific Feminist Fund, says:

> I have my Pacific home of feminists. The Prospera Network is like the home of women's funds. And there's a lot of sharing and giving that's not just financial, but a lot of that, I would say intelligence giving, that's useful.[20]

## Collaborative Funding for Women's Environmental Leadership

Carla López, Executive Director, Central American Women's Fund, shares the power of collective leadership concerning gender and the environment:

> Now, we are in this Global Alliance for Green and Gender Action, a global initiative in collaboration with the environmental movement. From 2016 to 2020, we mobilized, and now, we have €36 million for 2021 to 2025. We are working with 12 women's funds in different countries and regions of the world, especially Africa, Asia, and Latin America. And it's a cross-movement collaboration. As you see, we went from a local alliance, to a regional alliance to a global alliance. An alliance just for women's funds to a cross-movement alliance.[21]

## The Evidence on Collaborative Funding for Systemic Change

Research on collaborative giving conducted by the Bridgespan Group, a global nonprofit that strives to make the world more equitable and just,[22] found that collaborative giving tends to fund in nontraditional and anti-colonialist ways. Their report, "Releasing the Potential of Philanthropic Collaborations," found that "a significant number of collaboratives have charted a course that differs from traditional philanthropy: they tilt toward equity and justice, field and movement building, leaders of color, and, for some, power sharing."[23]

How funds pursue impact is also strikingly different from how institutional philanthropy operates. A third of the respondents said they seek systemic change through "building fields and movements," the most favored approach among collaboratives. The report quotes Tynesha McHarris, co-founder of the Black Feminist Fund, who pinpoints tunnel vision among funders as the cause. "Oftentimes, our movements aren't seen because philanthropy creates silos, and Black feminists can't silo themselves and say, 'racial justice here,' 'gender justice there.' We want to fund movements doing the most transformative, intersectional work but getting the least resources."[24]

The Bridgespan Group report found collaborative funding to be highly effective precisely because it tends to be more inclusive of those who are often not at the decision-making table in philanthropy. "Moreover, collaboratives provide much-needed capacity in areas where donors frequently struggle—sourcing nonprofits they couldn't find alone, supporting leaders with lived experience in the communities they serve, and giving in ways that address systemic challenges."[25]

Collaborations like Catalyze, the Ms. Foundation and Women's Funding Network's Katrina Women's Response Fund, and the Global Alliance for Gender and Climate Action, are examples of the ways women's funds unite and amplify their power and impact gender justice through collaboration. Women's, girls', and trans and non-binary people's leadership is what has built the Global Women's Funding Movement, and, in a virtuous cycle, it is what the Global Women's Funding Movement builds. A core mission of the Global Women's Funding Movement is collaborating to create the infrastructure that supports and amplifies women's leadership.

## Funding Young Women Leading Systemic Change

The National Philanthropic Collaborative of Young Women's Initiatives (The Collaborative) is another women's funds innovation. Its origin story begins in 2014, when the New York City Young Women's Initiative (NYCYWI) was launched as a groundbreaking partnership between the New York Women's Foundation, Girls for Gender Equity and the New York City Council to create a place-based, cross-sector initiative that centers young women of color, amplifies their leadership, and implements their solutions to make progress on racial and gender equity in the city.

In 2018, the NYWF and seven other women's foundations brought this young women's leadership supporting pilot to the White House Council on Women and Girls. Together, they launched the National Philanthropic Collaborative of Young Women's Initiatives with the goal of uniting the philanthropic community and government partners behind an agenda prioritized[26] by young women and girls of color from their localities. By 2023, The Collaborative had grown to 11 U.S. Women's Funds, all united to galvanize resources and ambitiously fund organizations that are led by women of color, serve young women and girls of color, and foster broad systemic change.[27]

## Funds Within Funds Leveraging Systemic Change

Another fund focused on securing systemic change is the Astraea Lesbian Foundation for Justice, established in 1977 as one of the world's first women's funds. At that time, "a small group of indomitable women gathered around a kitchen table in New York City and said, 'If there's going to be a women's movement that prioritizes the needs of lesbians and women of color, we're going to have to fund it ourselves.'"[28] And that's what they did. They began by making small grants to lesbian activists and artists from diverse cultural, racial, and class backgrounds who were organizing locally.

Over the last 45 years, Astraea has been a critical force in building the LGBTQI+ movement worldwide, becoming the first U.S. organization to provide critically needed funding to international LGBTQI+ groups. Astraea invested in critical justice movement infrastructure, including funding the launch of the U.S. Movement Building Initiative to provide significant multiyear support to people of color LGBTQI+-led organizations across the U.S. Today, Astraea is the only philanthropic organization working exclusively to advance LGBTQI+ human rights around the globe.[29] One recent example of Astraea's work to create systemic change is the Intersex Human Rights Fund, the first in the world, which Astraea established in 2015.[30] The Intersex Human Rights Fund demonstrates how women's funds champion marginalized communities, multiply funding for their justice efforts, and leverage systemic change.

Within one year of its founding, Astraea had helped the Intersex Human Rights Fund raise $900,000 from four partner foundations, private donors, and governments for its multiyear grantmaking, capacity building, and philanthropic advocacy efforts. In a notable first, the U.S. Department of State Global Equality Fund recognized intersex human rights by awarding a $250,000 grant over two years to support the fund's convening and movement-building capacity.[31] To address the public blindness to many chronic and physically invasive human rights violations experienced by intersex people, the Intersex Human Rights Fund invested in research and education and released its findings in a report, *We are Real: The Growing Movement Advancing the Human Rights of Intersex People*.[32] "We knew that one of the greatest challenges for funders was a lack of knowledge of intersex people and the movement for intersex human rights," said Sarah Gunther, Astraea's former Director of Programs. Astraea used the report to educate the funding community and demonstrate their commitment to the movement.[33]

The Intersex Human Rights Fund supported the Intersex Justice Project to launch the #EndIntersexSurgery campaign to engage in direct action to ban surgeries on non-consenting young people, including clitoral, vaginal, and testicular surgeries on infants. The project advocates for people to exist freely in the bodies they were born with.[34] In 2020, 34 countries signed a statement at a UN Human Rights Council session condemning "medically unnecessary surgeries" on intersex children as a human rights violation. It was the first time that unnecessary surgeries on minors born with an indeterminate sex had been identified as abuse at the United Nations.[35] The UN's human rights body condemned the surgeries because these irreversible and unnecessary procedures can cause "permanent infertility and lifelong pain, incontinence, loss of sexual sensation, and mental suffering."[36] Despite this, these surgeries remain legal in nearly every country.

## Investing in Disability Reform for Systemic Change

Women's funds recognize that compounding discrimination often severely limits economic opportunity for women and girls, and working intersectionally for systemic change is crucial. Take, for example, women with disabilities in Madagascar, where women are expected to stay at home and not enter the workforce. The laws prohibit women from inheriting wealth, and women are actively excluded from political life. Women with disabilities in Madagascar are profoundly impacted by these strict gender roles. Fela Razafinjato, Founder and President of the Association des Femmes Handicapées de Madagascar (Association of Disabled Women of Madagascar, AFHAM), calls it "double discrimination" by being a woman and having a disability. Women with disabilities are denied the opportunity to support themselves, denied a voice in advocating for their specific needs including accessing health care and employment, and denied the ability to realize their full potential.

When Razafinjato was three years old, she lost the use of her legs to polio. Her parents didn't let this hold her back. Her mother made great efforts to ensure she received the same education as other children her age. Most schools in Madagascar—both private and public—refused to let her attend. Finally, she was admitted to a religious school, but at a terrible toll. She was required to climb long flights of stairs on crutches for years, accompanied by heckling and bullying by her classmates. Still, Razafinjato was able to graduate from business school. She got married and now has two daughters. In 2011, with the help of Mama Cash, one the world's first women's funds, Razafinjato founded AFHAM to promote the rights of women with disabilities in the framework of the fight against poverty. "Women with disabilities stay in the shadows because of prejudice and discrimination. They are afraid to express themselves," Razafinjato says. She continues:

> The challenge is first to change the attitude that women with disabilities have about themselves, and second to change the attitudes of others. There is a huge amount of awareness raising and advocacy to be done. The government has no plan to support women with disabilities.[37]

In Madagascar, most people believe that women with disabilities don't have the skills or the ability to study or work. Razafinjato and her parents faced and overcame many barriers that most women with disabilities cannot overcome; most women with disabilities do not have the opportunity to go to school. This is why AFHAM creates employment opportunities, including a solidarity fund that funds income-generating activities for AFHAM members.

Today, AFHAM has a membership of 600 and operates throughout the country, with activities underway in 19 of Madagascar's 23 administrative regions. Razafinjato explains:

> That's 600 women with disabilities who know their rights. Our members have reclaimed decision-making power over their bodies and their lives. One hundred members have gained financial autonomy, and some are now actively participating in electoral processes. We have enabled many women with disabilities to come out of the shadows and into the light—to shed their invisibility.

## Funding Women's Formal Leadership for Systemic Change

Investing in women's voice and leadership is vital for propelling systemic change. According to Professor Rainbow Murray, an expert on gender politics, representation, and political institutions and a professor of politics at Queen Mary University of London, electing women is the fastest route to gender justice:

> Existing research indicates very clearly that female politicians do indeed look out for other women. In the UK, women MPs have led the way on issues ranging from parental leave to pay and working conditions. In Argentina, women have introduced distinctive perspectives into parliamentary debates on issues such as women's sexual and reproductive health, while in Australia, women have crossed party lines to defend a woman's right to choose. The reverse is also true: there is ample evidence that when women aren't part of the decision-making process, their needs are overlooked, misunderstood, and sometimes even actively suppressed.[38]

Throughout time and throughout the world, it has been women, typically acting collectively, who have consistently come through for women. According to an article in the UK *Guardian* entitled "There's proof: electing women radically improves life for mothers and families," Alexandra

Topping, a senior news reporter focusing on gender and equality, writes under the headline: "When Iceland elected a female president in 1980, it set off a domino effect that turned it into one of the most egalitarian countries":

> In this small nation, there is a near-unquestioned conviction based on decades of evidence that electing women to positions of power benefits women and families ... "There is absolutely no doubt that there is an equivalency between more gender-balanced political representation and better policies for women," says Brynhildur Heiðar, executive manager of the Icelandic Women's Rights Association. "Parental leave, daycare, the gender pay gap—none of these were seen as major issues before women ran for parliament."[39]

Research on women's leadership worldwide reveals important themes that not just women but all of humanity must factor. Not only are women better leaders on behalf of women, but there's also compelling evidence they are better leaders for everyone. Research also shows that women lead in ways that are most needed now, too.

It's important not to lose sight of the greater value of women being elected to parliament—that, globally, they contribute to better decision making on all issues, not just on issues that are seen as women's issues. Having diverse leadership means that issues and opportunities are addressed from diverse experiences and perspectives, including asking different questions and offering different perspectives based on lived experience. Research shows that women in government are more likely to work in more collaborative and bipartisan ways and have a more democratic leadership style.[40]

On the most crucial issues humanity is confronting, like climate change, women leaders also lead better, especially collectively. A study of 130 countries found that those with higher female parliamentary representation are more likely to ratify international environmental treaties.[41] The link between women's leadership and interventions to prevent the worst effects of climate change is so compelling that, since 2000, Rachel's Network, "a community of women at the intersection of environmental advocacy, philanthropy, and leadership," has argued that gender imbalances in government not only prevents equality, but it has significant implications for climate recovery also.[42] Studying 50 years of data, from 1972 to 2022, from the League of Conservation Voters (LCV) on legislators' voting records, Rachel's Network discovered that women Congress members, both in the House and Senate, voted to protect the environment much more often than male Congress members.[43]

Women Congress members were more likely to support legislation on public health, clean air, clean water, renewable energy, and climate action. They were more likely to vote against legislation that would roll back these protections.[44] Women lead more effectively and boldly on climate recovery. This can be detected throughout the world. Research shows that countries with more female representation at the national level are more likely to reduce greenhouse gas emissions, contain air pollution, and conserve biodiversity.[45]

Having more women in elected office leads to better climate health, and it also leads to better public health. Indeed, the more women in power, the fewer deaths in the population, and public health improves too. Edwin Ng and Carles Muntaner, University of Toronto professors, discovered this correlation when researching how male and female politicians in Canada differ from each other. They explain:

> Women work in more collaborative ways. We also found no relationship between women's political leanings in government—whether they belonged to left-wing, centrist or right-wing parties—and mortality rates. Ideological differences among social democratic and fiscally conservative political parties seem less important to mortality rates than increasing the number of women elected to government. This finding supports the idea that women in government tend to work in more collaborative and bipartisan ways than their male counterparts ... Given that women in government can bring about desirable changes in population health, let's figure out how we can genuinely level the political playing field for women.[46]

This phenomenon was confirmed again during the Covid-19 global pandemic. Researchers found that countries ruled by women fared much better through the pandemic and suffered six times fewer Covid-related deaths than countries with governments led by men. Women-led governments were also more likely to flatten the epidemic's curve quickly. The researchers found that women-led governments' approach to the crisis differed because they were more likely to invest in preventative measures.[47]

It takes the force of women's movements to win the scope of victories capable of producing systemic gender justice gains. Women's voting rights, reproductive rights, LGBTQIA+ rights, access to education, legal equality, freedom from violence, and widespread economic independence took tenacious women's movements, some persisting for over a century, to achieve.

The Global Women's Funding Movement has invested in and mentored diverse women leaders globally for half a century. One way they do this is by creating new pipelines of money and resources to invest in women-led initiatives. Indeed, the Global Women's Funding Movement can be considered the greatest financial investment in women's leadership in history and continuing.

## Investing in Women's Advocacy for Systemic Change

Since its founding in 2003, the Solís Policy Institute (SPI) of the Women's Foundation of California has fundamentally shifted California's political landscape by changing who has access to the halls of power. The SPI was founded as an experiential policy advocacy training program advancing racial, economic, and gender justice throughout California. It was built on the belief that "the people closest to the problems and harm should be centered and shaping the solutions to address them."[48] Named in honor of Dr. Beatriz Solís, a passionate advocate of at-risk and disadvantaged communities, the SPI awards year-long fellowships for developing skills, building networks, and amplifying leadership across a dynamic cohort of leaders poised to shape California's policies. SPI Fellows are primarily women of color and gender-expansive people.

Surina Khan, former CEO of the Women's Foundation of California, explains:

> Legislators have told us that SPI has passed more progressive legislation than any other entity in the state, and our potential is limitless. Gender justice advocates are looking at the issues they confront in their communities. Then they're coming up with solutions because they have support not just from the foundation, but we're somebody who can make connections.[49]

Khan continues:

> We just accepted our 20th class for the Policy Institute, now called the Solís Policy Institute. Fifty-one of their bills have been signed into law. There's also increased access to affordable subsidized childcare, renewable energy, and protecting pregnant women in the prison system from being shackled when transported. We now have more than 600 alums connected to thousands of people in their network. It's a true powerhouse because we can and do activate millions of people through that one network alone. We are also part of other coalitions like the Stronger California coalition. I think a collaborative nature is

certainly in our DNA, and I think that's probably true of many other women's foundations across the country and world.[50]

A recent Solís Fellow is Eunisses Hernandez, a young leader who went through the Policy Institute in 2015. With the training and mentorship provided through the Institute, Hernandez led a coalition called the Re-Imagine L.A. County Coalition that reallocated $1 billion that the L.A. County Board of Supervisors had initially allocated to build a new jail facility. L.A. County's Measure J was a groundbreaking initiative generating $1 billion for direct community investment and alternatives to incarceration by reallocating 10 percent of the county budget. Khan explains:

> They describe it as a David and Goliath situation. The Re-Imagine L.A. County Coalition successfully built an inclusive coalition, which included the construction workers union, who initially opposed the Re-Imagine L.A. County Coalition. The construction workers said, "You're trying to take our jobs away." The coalition went and met with them, and they said, "We're not trying to take your jobs away. We come from union families. We want you to build things. We want you to build good things." They won over the construction workers union. Hernandez then ran for office and unseated a very powerful incumbent Democrat. It was time for change, so it's a very inspiring story. She also now sits on our board. This is just one story of all these kinds of different ways that gender justice advocates are looking at the issues that they are confronting in their communities. Then they're coming up with solutions because they have support not just from the foundation, but we're somebody who can make connections.[51]

## The Gate Openers to Wealth

Khan says:

> We're not the gatekeepers to wealth. We're the gate openers. We want to introduce people to donors. For us, in California, I think that we had a convening of our criminal justice alums from the Policy Institute, and one of the people said, "This is the leadership of the criminal justice movement in California, not the women's criminal justice movement in California, but the criminal justice movement in California."[52]

This centering of convening and collaboration is an essential tenet of women's funds. As Felicia Davis Blakley, former President and CEO of the Chicago Foundation for Women, says:

> I do not believe that one person has all the answers to the questions, problems, or the challenges. I feel that solutions are better informed when you have diverse viewpoints at the table. To me, collaboration is the life's blood of change.[53]

## Decolonizing Research for Systemic Change

Also crucial is the work women's funds are doing to decolonize practices and decision making. Bettina Baldeschi, former CEO of the International Women's Development Agency (IWDA) in Australia, says, "In our 2020 strategic plan, we explicitly named our intention to be on a journey to becoming the next best version of ourselves. And what that means is really a commitment to unlearning, to decolonizing, to being explicitly anti-racist."

IWDA commissioned a report on creating equitable south–north partnership research from a Pacific-based researcher, Ofa-Ki-Levuka Guttenbeil-Likiliki, who lives in Tonga. "We were really lucky because we got to be working and doing that learning and unlearning with Ofa [and] to support genuinely locally led decolonizing research," Bettina says. She goes on to say:

> The report goes into a lot of detail about the takeaways, but the few that stood out, using the language of the Pacific, is what is called nurturing the Vā. And the Vā is about the space that is between us. It's relational; it's about shared values and standards. It's about the partnership based on equality, diversity, and inclusion. So, nurturing the Vā is the first principle that we're taking away … Too often, non-feminist organizations think that the relational part is nice to have. At best, they might see it as an important way to shape the tone of the partnership but not the content of the partnership. But Ofa's work demonstrates that this isn't about tone; it's about quality.[54]

Centering the leadership of local women and resourcing them to lead systemic change that is contextual and relational is crucial. Women's funds have been listening, learning, and shifting power and resources, recognizing that much more is needed including consistently interrogating internal beliefs, attitudes and systems as much as external realities.

## Investing in Cross-Movement Coalition Building for Systemic Change

Investing in women's and feminist leadership brings exponential social justice returns. Women's funds know how to identify, support, and amplify the power of women's leadership to advance justice. The Astraea Lesbian Foundation for Justice has worked counter to the norms of traditional philanthropy since its inception over 40 years ago. Its roots are in movements.

J. Bob Alotta, Astraea's second Executive Director from 2011 to 2019, always saw Astraea's role as shifting power and resources from where they intentionally were to where they weren't yet needed to be—grassroots LGBTQI+ movements worldwide. Bob started with an organizational budget of $3 million and grew it to $13 million in 2019.[55] Under Bob's leadership, Astraea expanded global LGBTQI philanthropy through strategic decisions to partner with bilateral governments like the innovative LGBTI Global Development Partnership. This initiative expanded grantmaking in 12 countries and shifted $15.5M to grassroots LGBTQI movement building. With Bob, Astraea also grew its work in the U.S. to combat the criminalization of communities of color.[56]

Brokering shared leadership models and alliance building remains central to Astraea's mission to shift power and resources and by being this change in its structure, work, and revolutionary intent. As the current Executive Director, Joy Chia, says, "We have a critical and transformational role not only in our global feminist and LGBTQI funding ecosystems but also in cross-movement coalition-building."[57]

In speaking about coalition building for women's funds in the Pacific, Michelle Reddy, Co-Lead of the Pacific Feminist Fund, says:

> Viri [Virisila Buadromo, co-lead, Urgent Action Fund for Women's Human Rights Asia and the Pacific] and me—the two of us have been quite instrumental in the women's funds in the region. And it just so happened I was saying we've bloody been amazing. Do you realize it? And she goes, Actually, let's talk about ourselves, and let's congratulate ourselves. And we're like, yes. Cheers. And we're, like, thinking, you know, we really should capture this knowledge and these strategies. And I think a lot of it also comes with loss. We're losing a lot of people in the region from sickness, burnout, and so capturing this knowledge through storytelling, songs, and words is so important.[58]

This work of women's funds in mobilizing and leveraging funds through cross-movement coalition building is a model for how women use their money and power to challenge patriarchy and actively work toward a transformed world. The frame of Women, Money, and Power was to become a mantra for many women's funds as they engaged feminist philanthropists on a journey of coming into their power, individually and as a philanthropic movement for justice.

## Notes

1  Women's Funding Network, "Women's Fund Video Project 12 9 88," YouTube, December 9, 1988, accessed May 17, 2024, www.youtube.com/watch?v=DkuhHxrTTOM.

2  Women's Fund Asia, *A Shared Journey to Justice: The Legal Fellowship* (Women's Fund Asia, May 2022), accessed November 24, 2023, https://womensfundasia.org/assets/research-report/WFA_LegalFellowshipReport_May2022_compressed.pdf.

3  Women's Fund Asia, "SAWF Legal Fellowship," YouTube, February 19, 2018, accessed May 17, 2024, www.youtube.com/watch?v=S3IOUrr5ct4&t=6s.

4  Women's Fund Asia, "SAWF Legal Fellowship," YouTube, February 19, 2018, accessed May 17, 2024, www.youtube.com/watch?v=S3IOUrr5ct4&t=6s.

5  Women's Fund Asia, *A Shared Journey to Justice: The Legal Fellowship* (Women's Fund Asia, May 2022), accessed November 24, 2023, https://womensfundasia.org/assets/research-report/WFA_LegalFellowshipReport_May2022_compressed.pdf.

6  Women's Fund Asia, *A Shared Journey to Justice: The Legal Fellowship* (Women's Fund Asia, May 2022), accessed November 24, 2023, https://womensfundasia.org/assets/research-report/WFA_LegalFellowshipReport_May2022_compressed.pdf.

7  Women's Funding Network, "Women's Fund Video Project 12 9 88," YouTube, December 9, 1988, accessed May 17, 2024, www.youtube.com/watch?v=DkuhHxrTTOM.

8  Sape Janet, speaking at Women's Funding Network Award ceremony, Detroit, Michigan, USA, April 10, 2013, and confirmed in a personal email communication with Jane Sloane, November 4, 2016.

9  Michele Ozumba, personal email communication with Jane Sloane, October 25, 2023.

10  Sape Janet, speaking at Women's Funding Network Award ceremony, Detroit, Michigan, USA, April 10, 2013, and confirmed in a personal email communication with Jane Sloane, November 4, 2016.

11  Mama Cash, "Decolonial feminist leadership ≠ girlbossing! Decolonial feminist leadership demands a break with the #patriarchal & colonial legacy of single "visionary ..." Linked In Post, April 2023, accessed May 17, 2024, www.

linkedin.com/posts/mama-cash_patriarchal-decolonial-feminist-activity-7054749913527500801-p5tO.

12  Cynthia Nimmo, personal email communication with Jane Sloane, October 10, 2023.

13  Cynthia Nimmo, personal email communication with Jane Sloane, October 10, 2023.

14  Michael Seo, "When Rapid Equals Urgent" *Philanthropy News Digest*, October 24, 2018, accessed November 24, 2023, https://philanthropynewsdigest.org/features/ssir-pnd/when-rapid-equals-urgent.

15  Cynthia Eyakuze, interview with Laura Risimini, June 1, 2023.

16  "Equality Fund and AWDF Celebrate Powerful New Community of Grantee Partners," Equality Fund, May 18, 2021, accessed November 24, 2023, https://equalityfund.ca/grantmaking/equality-fund-and-awdf-celebrate-powerful-new-community-of-grantee-partners.

17  Alfonsina Peñaloza, "Seven things the Women's Funds Collaborative taught me about feminist philanthropy," William and Flora Hewlett Foundation, December 16, 2020, accessed November 24, 2023, https://hewlett.org/seven-things-the-womens-funds-collaborative-taught-me-about-feminist-philanthropy.

18  "Weaving the Network," Prospera International Network of Women's Funds (September 20, 2021), accessed November 24, 2023, https://mailchi.mp/prospera-inwf/deepening-our-connection.

19  "Four private foundations announce they will provide at least $20 million in a combined grantmaking initiative to strengthen women's funding organizations around the world," William and Flora Hewlett Foundation, November 20, 2019, accessed November 24, 2023, https://hewlett.org/newsroom/four-private-foundations-announce-grantmaking-initiative-to-strengthen-womens-funding-organizations.

20  Michelle Reddy, interview with Chris Grumm and Laura Risimini, September 26, 2023.

21  Carla Lopez, interview with Chris Grumm and Laura Risimini, November 23, 2022.

22  "About Us," The Bridgespan Group, accessed November 24, 2023, www.bridgespan.org/about-us.

23  Alison Powell and Michael John, "Releasing the Potential of Philanthropic Collaborations," The Bridgespan Group, December 14, 2021, accessed November 24, 2023, www.bridgespan.org/insights/philanthropic-collaborations.

24  Alison Powell and Michael John, "Releasing the Potential of Philanthropic Collaborations," The Bridgespan Group, December 14, 2021, accessed November 24, 2023, www.bridgespan.org/insights/philanthropic-collaborations.

25  Alison Powell and Michael John, "Releasing the Potential of Philanthropic Collaborations," The Bridgespan Group, December 14, 2021, accessed November 24, 2023, www.bridgespan.org/insights/philanthropic-collaborations.

26  "About The Collaborative," National Philanthropic Collaborative of Young Women's Initiatives, accessed November 24, 2023, www.npcywi.org/about.

27  "About The Collaborative," National Philanthropic Collaborative of Young Women's Initiatives, accessed November 24, 2023, www.npcywi.org/about.

28  "About Us: Astraea at 40," Astraea Lesbian Foundation for Justice, accessed November 24, 2023, www.astraeafoundation.org/about-us/astraea-at-40.

29  "Intersex Human Rights Fund," Astraea Lesbian Foundation for Justice, accessed November 24, 2023, http://stag.astraeafoundation.org/apply/intersex-human-rights-fund.

30  "About Us: Astraea at 40," Astraea Lesbian Foundation for Justice, accessed November 24, 2023, www.astraeafoundation.org/about-us/astraea-at-40.

31  Andrew Wallace, "Can a $250,000 Grant Unite a Growing Intersex Movement?" Funders for LGBTQ Issues, November 6, 2016, accessed November 24, 2023, https://lgbtfunders.org/newsposts/can-a-250000-grant-unite-a-growing-intersex-movement.

32  "We are Real: The Growing Movement Advancing the Rights of Intersex People," Astraea Lesbian Foundation for Justice: 2016, accessed November 24, 2023, https://astraeafoundation.org/wearereal.

33  Andrew Wallace, "Can a $250,000 Grant Unite a Growing Intersex Movement?" Funders for LGBTQ Issues, November 6, 2016, accessed November 24, 2023, https://lgbtfunders.org/newsposts/can-a-250000-grant-unite-a-growing-intersex-movement.

34  "Our Mission To #ENDINTERSEXSURGERY," Intersex Justice Project, accessed November 24, 2023, www.intersexjusticeproject.org/about.html.

35  Rachel Savage, "Intersex surgery 'abuses' condemned by 34 states at U.N. rights forum," Thomson Reuters Foundation, October 1, 2020, accessed November 24, 2023, www.reuters.com/article/un-lgbt-health/intersex-surgery-abuses-condemned-by-34-states-at-u-n-rights-forum-idUSL8N2GS5NQ.

36  Kate Sosin, "After years of protest, a top hospital ended intersex surgeries. For activists, it took a deep toll." The 19th News, August 5, 2020, accessed November 24, 2023, https://19thnews.org/2020/08/intersex-youth-surgeries-top-hospital-ended-intersex-activists.

37  "'Into the light': Association des Femmes Handicapées de Madagascar," Mama Cash, accessed May 24, 2024, www.mamacash.org/wp-content/uploads/2022/02/association_des_femmes_handicapees_de_madagascars_story_english.pdf.

38  Rainbow Murray, "Do women represent women?" IPS, February 21, 2018, accessed November 24, 2023, www.ips-journal.eu/in-focus/women-in-politics/do-women-represent-women-2597/.

39  Alexandra Topping, "There's proof: electing women radically improves life for mothers and families," *The Guardian*, December 7, 2017, accessed November

24, 2023, www.theguardian.com/us-news/2017/dec/06/iceland-women-government-better-for-mothers-america-lessons.

40  Edwin Ng and Carles Muntaner, "The more women in government, the healthier a population," The Conversation, January 9, 2019, accessed November 24, 2023, https://theconversation.com/the-more-women-in-government-the-healthier-a-population-107075.

41  Kari Norgaard and Richard York, "Gender Equality and State Environmentalism," *Gender & Society*, Vol. 19, No. 4 (August 2005), 506–522, accessed November 24, 2023, https://doi.org/10.1177/0891243204273612.

42  "When Women Lead: Women's Environmental Voting Records in Congress, 1972–2022," Rachel's Network. Accessed November 24, 2023, https://whenwomenlead.rachelsnetwork.org.

43  "When Women Lead: Women's Environmental Voting Records in Congress, 1972–2022," Rachel's Network. Accessed November 24, 2023, https://whenwomenlead.rachelsnetwork.org.

44  "When Women Lead: Women's Environmental Voting Records in Congress, 1972–2022," Rachel's Network. Accessed November 24, 2023, https://whenwomenlead.rachelsnetwork.org.

45  Luca Coscieme, Lorenzo Fioramonti, and Katherine Trebeck, "Women in power: Countries with female leaders suffer six times fewer Covid deaths and will recover sooner from recession,' openDemocracy, May 26, 2020, accessed November 24, 2023, www.opendemocracy.net/en/can-europe-make-it/women-power-countries-female-leaders-suffer-six-times-fewer-covid-deaths-and-will-recover-sooner-recession.

46  Edwin Ng and Carles Muntaner, "The more women in government, the healthier a population," The Conversation, January 9, 2019, accessed November 24, 2023, https://theconversation.com/the-more-women-in-government-the-healthier-a-population-107075.

47  Luca Coscieme, Lorenzo Fioramonti, and Katherine Trebeck, "Women in power: Countries with female leaders suffer six times fewer Covid deaths and will recover sooner from recession,' openDemocracy, May 26, 2020, accessed November 24, 2023, www.opendemocracy.net/en/can-europe-make-it/women-power-countries-female-leaders-suffer-six-times-fewer-covid-deaths-and-will-recover-sooner-recession.

48  "What We Do: Dr. Beatriz María Solís Policy Institute (SPI)," Women's Foundation California, accessed November 24, 2023, https://womensfoundca.org/what-we-do/training/solis-policy-institute.

49  Surina Khan, interview with Christine Grumm and Laura Risimini, October 25, 2022.

50  Surina Khan, interview with Christine Grumm and Laura Risimini, October 25, 2022.

51 Surina Khan, interview with Christine Grumm and Laura Risimini, October 25, 2022.

52 Surina Khan, interview with Christine Grumm and Laura Risimini, October 25, 2022.

53 Felicia Davis Blakley, interview with Christine Grumm, November 23, 2022.

54 Bettina Baldeschi, interview with Christine Grumm and Laura Risimini, September 7, 2023.

55 "Farewell to J. Bob Alotta!" Astraea Lesbian Foundation for Justice, August 6, 2019, accessed November 24, 2023, www.astraeafoundation.org/stories/farewell-to-j-bob-alotta.

56 "Joy's February 2022 Reflection: Honoring our Black Communities, Celebrating Black LGBTQI Futures," Astraea Lesbian Foundation for Justice, March 2, 2022, accessed November 24, 2023, www.astraeafoundation.org/stories/joys-february-2022-reflection-honoring-our-black-communities-celebrating-black-lgbtqi-futures.

57 "Astraea Lesbian Foundation For Justice Welcomes Joy Chia as New Executive Director," Philanthropy New York, July 20, 2021, accessed November 24, 2023, https://philanthropynewyork.org/news/astraea-lesbian-foundation-justice-welcomes-joy-chia-new-executive-director.

58 Michelle Reddy, interview with Chris Grumm and Laura Risimini, September 26, 2023.

# Women, Money, and Power

**6**

## Coming into Our Own

### Normalizing Conversations on Women, Money, and Power

"Money in this country is power, and if you keep women poor, then they're not much of a threat, and that's just got to change." So, "you take women who have the least access to resources and women who have the greatest access to resources … and we begin to talk about what our needs are, what our experiences are, and there's a sharing that happens that is extremely powerful."[1]

Former President and CEO of Women's Funding Network Cynthia Nimmo says:

> WFN normalized the conversation around women, money and power. We depicted women's foundations as movers and shakers, women donors as important activists, and women professionals as necessary analysts and connectors. With the launch of Women Moving Millions (incubated at WFN), the stigma some women felt about their wealth was erased, and the power of making positive change was spotlighted. Women's foundations were interested in maximizing the power of all funds within their purview, including their endowments. WFN hosted numerous conversations about how and where to invest endowments to demand positive change by companies.[2]

An early project funded by women's funds in the U.S. was the Networking Project for Disabled Women and Girls to help young women with disabilities realize their potential through access to mentors and job opportunities.

DOI: 10.4324/9781003330455-6

When we received funds from a women's foundation, it was a real validation that we were women too, that women's organizations have the vision that women with disabilities are part of the family, the sisterhood. There are many stereotypes that say if you're disabled, you stay at home, you don't go out, you don't lead a regular life. This project shows what women have in common with each other.[3]

One of the young women involved in the project, who secured a job, said, "I like to know that I can be independent, and I can do all I want for me, that I can work for myself. I can earn my own salary. I can make it out there."[4]

The Dallas Women's Foundation was also formed around a commitment to women's economic security, especially around women, money, and power. As one of the founding members recalls:

> A couple of factors informed its formation. One was that it was time for women to pull their chairs up to the table and take responsibility for funding the needs of other women. And the second was that women needed to get into a more honest relationship with money. Women need to know how to make money, obviously, but then they need to know how to manage their money, and they need to know how to give their money. So, the Dallas Women's Foundation came into being.[5]

The foundation was so successful over its 33-year history that it expanded to become the Texas Women's Foundation in 2018, with over $35 million in assets.[6] Speaking about this change, Roslyn Dawson Thompson, Former President and CEO, said:

> As Texas Women's Foundation, our goal is to Transform Texas for Women and Girls by advancing economic security for women, girls, and families across the state, and by ensuring opportunities for them to lead in every sector—from the classroom to the first job, the board room and the halls of government. This matters to every Texan—women and men alike—because our economy and our futures are stronger when Texas women, girls, and families thrive, and our leadership fully reflects our population.[7]

## Practicing Philanthropic Accountability

The Global Women's Funding Movement is the manifestation of how women lead differently with money. Through this worldwide, woman-designed, self-generating, philanthropic apparatus, women can leverage massive social justice victories together. It's women's collective power—channeled through women's funds—that creates a system of "philanthropic accountability." The purpose of women's funds is to fund work that advances gender equality. Such a high level of accountability is missing from most forms of philanthropy. The direction of most private foundations is often informed by a handful of people not part of a larger social justice movement. So they have no real accountability to the issues they champion. Given the feminist funding practice of democratized philanthropy, an engaged philanthropist in a women's fund does not require wealth but simply a dedication to harness the power of money to advance gender equality.

When surveyed, one of the most common goals reported among women's funds is to advance women's philanthropy.[8] The Global Women's Funding Movement donors are rich in diversity by class, age, ability, geography, race, ethnicity, sexual orientation, and income, which is rare in philanthropy. As a result, women's funds have grown stronger, becoming better equipped, more knowledgeable, better resourced, and better positioned to address the level of gender inequality and injustice in communities and globally. In the economic downturn of 2008, for example, when many private foundations were forced to shut down, women's funds experienced a surge in giving.

## Money as a Creative Part of Realizing Rights and Justice

Ellen Sprenger, CEO of Spring Strategies, said of her time as executive director of Mama Cash:

> At the time, in the early 2000s, many WROs [women's rights organizations] were trying to figure out "the money thing." Where was the money, and how could we access more of it? When I became the executive director of Mama Cash, I went through a steep learning curve around resource mobilization. I learned a lot from my American peers, whose way of relating to money and approach to fundraising was quite different from that of my peers in Europe. They helped me see money not as a means to an end but as an integral and creative part of realizing rights and justice. My focus shifted from raising money to establishing relationships with donors and funders around a shared purpose, passion and exchanging ideas, connections, and information. I learned how valuable I was to them as a source of information, inspiration, and connections. This paradigm shift made fundraising much less scary, intimidating, and more interesting. And a whole lot more successful.[9]

The practices of democratized philanthropy are designed to engender a broad base of financial support. Hence, women's funds are not solely reliant on the economic luck and philanthropic predilections of a few. The diversity of women's fund donors results in a philanthropic experience that is unique. When giving to women's funds, donors join a philanthropic movement with women and feminists from all walks of life. The fulfillment of being a vital part of a diverse, effective, and powerful social justice movement makes women's fund donors especially committed to the cause.

## Philanthropic Giving Boosts Wellbeing

Being a donor, in general, is a transformative experience. Giving to a movement and becoming an active part of the solution results in emotional, psychological, physical, and spiritual wellbeing and benefits that are well documented.[10] Lower blood pressure, increased self-esteem, less depression, lower stress levels, longer life, and greater happiness are all part of what happens with giving. Indeed, according to a study by the Women's Philanthropy Institute (WPI) at Indiana University, the more women give to causes, the happier they are. The researchers found that single women who donate more than 2 percent of their income feel more satisfied in life.[11]

Similarly, in households where women have a say in charitable decision making, families are happier than those in households where only men make these decisions or couples make decisions separately. Devra Mesch, former Director of WPI, explains, "This study adds to the understanding that when women drive charitable giving, there is a higher boost in happiness for the entire family."[12]

Given that women built the Global Women's Funding Movement to benefit women and feminist causes, the Global Women's Funding Movement is a uniquely gratifying philanthropic experience for women in particular. Many report that being a part of it has filled deep voids created by being a woman, girl, trans, or non-binary while living within the confines of the patriarchy, even when living with wealth. Linda Calhoun, Women Moving Millions Member and Career Girls founder and CEO, says:

> To see that through being generous of spirit, generous of resources, I can see real change, real impact in the world, and that you don't have to be helpless. You don't have to be a victim. You can make a difference, and you don't have to have all the answers. You don't have to have all the resources, but you can do something and see that what you do and what you give can really help someone; that's the thing that's kept me going.[13]

"All of us want to leave a memorable legacy," says Rose Flenorl, Global Citizenship Manager with FedEx. "And we all want to feel that it's part of our existence on this earth that we made a difference. There's no better way, I think, to make a difference than to invest in women and girls and multiply that investment."[14]

The New York Women's Foundation donor and board member, Abigail Disney believes her work with women's funds filled an inner void left by the misogyny that permeated her childhood. Abigail is the granddaughter of Roy O. Disney, who co-founded the Walt Disney Company with his brother Walt.[15] She was raised in extreme wealth and privilege but grew up with a mother who viewed other women with disdain and suspicion.

Disney says:

> I came from a very anti-feminist home. It wasn't so much that they were overtly anti-feminist as they, well, really, my mother just didn't like women at all. Because my mother's view of it was, you're alone in this. Women can't be trusted. As a wealthy person, you're special; everybody wants to take advantage of you and be suspicious all the time. When you have a mother who doesn't like women, and you're a daughter, you grow up with a twisted sensibility about other women. Really, it was the women's funding movement that returned me to joy. When I got to the women's funding movement, what I learned was I'm just another member of the human race. I'm no different or better or worse than anybody else. That is the good news because it's an invitation to a party I didn't know was happening. Every joyful relationship, every bliss-related moment that I've had has emerged from those powerful relationships that I formed and those endless epiphanies that I lived through that wouldn't have come to me if I hadn't been able to recognize that I'm just another person.[16]

Disney discovered the pervasive impact that occurs when the most affected women lead and began documenting the power of women's collective leadership through her powerful films. She says:

> Privilege makes it hard for a person to be a truly empathic, valuable leader in a social context until she has taken the time and mustered the humility to learn and listen. At The New York Women's Foundation, we were living intersectionality long before we had a word for it because our credibility went to the women who were closest to the problems, the women of color, the queer women, the trans women, and so forth. We were always with those women.[17]

## Paying It Forward

Mona Sinha, Global Executive Director of Equality Now and Former Board Chair of Women Moving Millions, a membership organization for donors who have committed $1 million or more to gender equality, also found that the collective of women donors funding feminist movements was a refreshing antidote to the pervasive sexism she confronted in her childhood. She explains:

> When you asked why I am so determined to create gender equality, I realize that it goes back to childhood. It always does. I grew up in Calcutta, India. I was one of three girls, so I wasn't exactly in that hallowed spot where my birth was celebrated, as male preference is grounded in the culture. My first memory of experiencing gender discrimination was as a five-year-old. My grandfather was a well-known lawyer, and I remember an encounter on a regular Sunday afternoon visit to his home. He was surrounded by his clients, who ruffled my hair and wanted to know what five-year-old me wanted to be when I grew up. I had no idea but, being in their company, I said, "Maybe I want to be a lawyer." They all started laughing. And he said, "Run along. This is not work that women and girls do." It sounded like a reprimand and didn't feel right and always stayed with me. At 18, I decided to lean into being a girl, and I applied to women's colleges in the U.S. I didn't tell my parents because I knew they would not encourage me to leave home. When I got an acceptance telegram from Smith College, my father said he could not pay for it. I think that was a catalyzing moment for me because the yearning to be there was so deep that I knew I had to find Plan B, and quickly. I applied for several scholarships, and an unknown alumna funded me almost 100 percent. That is when I realized that an act of radical generosity was profoundly changing my life. A stranger who did not know me was willing to place a bet on my future. That's when I realized how philanthropy and generosity can be transformative to shaping women's and girls' lives. I think resource mobilization is critical because it has an outsized impact by trickling down to women at the grassroots who could be part of marginalized communities. The women philanthropists exemplified by Women Moving Millions members are risk mitigators because they support young girls of promise to thrive into lives of purpose and economic security. This has an outsized impact on families, communities, and the world. This ecosystem of support can help create a future that's just and equitable. Every funder has a deep personal story. Each

supportive measure I take, whether it's sending money or mentoring hundreds of young women, is because that little five-year-old in me is saying, "I wish I had had you by my side."[18]

## Radical Generosity

As Ana Oliveira, CEO of The New York Women's Foundation, shared with a group of women of color grantees facing the loss of funding from other sources, "We have always been there, we are here now, and we'll be here in the future." For women's funds, accountability to women is built in. The New York Women's Foundation coined the term "radical generosity" to reflect its intentions and hope for the future. Anne Delaney, an artist, activist, philanthropist, and former board chair of The New York Women's Foundation, as well as the founder of the Lambert Foundation and Starry Night Fund, says:

> Radical generosity allows me to ask myself, "What kind of personal commitment do I want to make to help others? How willing am I to accept the status quo without doing something about it, especially when I know that organizations like The New York Women's Foundation change lives?" In New York City, I am one of the people who live with plenty when many around me do not have enough, and that starts to feel untenable. Radical generosity encompasses the question of how much is enough. When making our donations, we tend to wonder if there will be enough left over for ourselves and our family, and we err on the side of being overly cautious. We forget that our lives are immediately richer when we are connected, and the wider that circle of connection, the better. We live in a culture that tells us to hold on to things. But if you have a big boat or house with no one to invite in, then we have missed out on life.[19]

Oliveira explains the reason why many women experience a transformation when they become philanthropists: "It's the love of humanity, an act of creating a world that is bigger than yourself, an expansion of yourself."[20] Supporting feminist activism, disrupting power structures and hierarchies, resisting oppression, and transforming the world by creating new realities *is* a transformative experience. When women philanthropists unite collectively through women's funds, they behave in ways more likely to benefit society as a whole.

The experience of being a donor through women's funds, whether directly or through giving circles, is the experience of being a vital part of the solution. Mary McDaniel, Former Vice-President and Chief Procurement Officer at FedEx Express and a donor to the Women's Foundation for a Greater Memphis, says:

> I think that getting involved with the women's fund helped me to understand that not only do you give to women's funds, but you need to do it consistently. That's actually what the women's fund helped me to grow to, or better understand, or seeded that opportunity inside of me to the point that that's something that I do yearly. I give to the Women's Fund yearly, and I believe my affiliation with the Women's Foundation for a Greater Memphis and the women's funds around the country, whether it's Ms. Foundation or others have allowed me to see how vital this work is and how we must not only speak to it often, but we have to give yearly to support the work that needs to be done.[21]

Kerry Gardner, Co-Chair (with Betty Barka) of the International Women's Development Agency in Australia and a board member of the Global Fund for Women, shares how being part of the Global Women's Funding Movement has influenced her:

> My giving and my husband's giving through our foundation has become much more long-term, untied, trust-based giving in everything we do and our bigger family philanthropy. Now, we adopt almost exclusively long-term, untied, trust-based funding for what we do, and gender and diversity are embedded in all our giving.[22]

## Addressing the Gender Wealth Gap

The Global Women's Funding Movement allows all women to use money to wield power in the radical and revolutionary ways needed to achieve equality. Throughout history, men have gone to great lengths to keep women from money. They have built elaborate legal structures to prevent women from inheriting family wealth and owning property, even if purchased with the income they'd earned. Banks in the United States only recently, and only because they were required by legislation to in 1974,[23] allowed women to apply for credit, and banks today still subject women to higher interest rates. Indeed, women today are less likely to be approved for a loan despite being more likely to make their loan payments. Men and women have also been culturally conditioned to behave differently with their money. Anne

Boden, the Founder of Starling Bank, who commissioned a linguistic study on the ways in which men and women talk about money, explains:

> We uncovered huge discrepancies in how men and women are spoken to about money. 65% of money articles in women's magazines define women as excessive spenders and advise them to limit, restrict, and take better control of shopping "splurges," and they're then encouraged to maximize their economic contributions through forms of thrift like saving small sums, earning small amounts, or finding a means of financial support, like a parent. Or a husband.[24]

Mariko Chang, the author of "Shortchanged," which examines the wealth gap between men and women, explains:

> Girls, as they are growing up, are not socialized to feel that's O.K. for them to have ambition about creating wealth, not the way it is for little boys. They're encouraged to take on roles that let them take care of other people.[25]

Research suggests that men are more likely to seek to derive power and status through philanthropy, such as naming a building by donating to a college, whereas women are more likely to use their wealth to help other people. "Women have not been socialized to brag and have their names on things," said Devra Mesch, formerly of the Women's Philanthropy Institute.[26]

Money *is* power, demonstrated best by patriarchy's hoarding of it. The Global Women's Funding Movement was founded a half-century ago to give women a way to collectively wield their money as a source of great power for all women. It was created and designed to shift power, resources, voice, cultural norms, and policies through women's giving. This has led to a virtuous cycle, creating stronger, more independent women with more wealth who, by investing back in women's rights, are creating the next generation of stronger, even more independent women with even more wealth who must now invest their money in women's rights. Money is power, and women need more of each.

Despite the revolutionary social impact women's movements have had on humanity throughout history, they have been starved of money and resources compared to other social causes. In the United States, funding for women's and girls' organizations represents less than 2 percent of total philanthropic giving. Jacki Zehner, angel investor and women's fund donor, says:

> The money has never been there to fund women. Ever. It's still peanuts. We know this. Women are half the population. We don't have to wait

for men. We need to mobilize women. We know that, on average, women CEOs are more likely to implement higher levels of maternity leave and work life balance, just like female legislators are more likely to pay attention to policies and laws that are more inclusive of women. You have to believe that power in the hands of not all women, but women, will result in different outcomes because they will bring their lived experiences, on average, into their positions of power and influence with help, support, and community.[27]

Many great advancements for women have been won when women of all different income levels have united and invested the money needed to confront the most powerful and entrenched opponents.

## Democratizing Philanthropy Through Giving Circles

Through its feminist values, the Global Women's Funding Movement has innovated and accelerated highly effective and entirely new forms of philanthropy and has worked consistently to attract large numbers of new philanthropists at all income levels. Collaboration is one of women's unique leadership strengths. Women's funds harness it to great effect through giving circles, a crowd-funding mechanism, by growing them rapidly in number and membership.

This collective philanthropic vehicle has origins in Indigenous communities. It's unsurprising, however, that women's funds would embrace and grow this democratic, non-colonial model of philanthropy because that is what women's funds do. According to Adriana Loson-Ceballos, Ph.D., an expert on giving circles and the co-founder of Colmena Consulting:

> In my research, I've found evidence of giving circles among enslaved groups and different Indigenous cultures—for example, it was common practice in Mexico before Cortés … It was popular because in collective giving, the relationships within a community matter. There is dignity in both giving and receiving … Collective giving models are laboratories of democracy.[28]

Elizabeth Barajas-Román, CEO of the Women's Funding Network, shares giving circles (GCs) are one of the most democratic philanthropic methods embraced by women's funds:

> This philanthropic model is democratic, place-based, highly flexible, community-focused, and participant-led. GCs work because they're

an intersectional approach to support the communities hit hardest by the disproportionate impacts of economic hardship, broken social systems, lack of access to health services and information, systemic racism, and institutional violence ... For these reasons, members in our organization, among others, have increasingly embraced GCs for the past 20+ years. One estimate puts just 50 GCs in existence in 1995; today, there are 2,500, and by 2025, it's projected to be up to 3,000.[29]

Typically, each member donates a set amount of money per year, and all the member donations are pooled. The membership considers proposals for philanthropic investments, and together they decide which projects to fund. Usually, no restrictions exist on who and what causes can be funded. Women socialize, learn about being a philanthropist, and act as a collective force for gender justice, a fun, unusual, and powerful experience.[30] Between 2007 and 2017, the number of giving circles tripled. Today, about 70 percent of giving circles are majority women.[31]

Research shows that giving circle members are more likely to give greater amounts, invest their donations strategically, support a wider array of organizations, and volunteer. As giving circles multiply as a powerful form of democratized philanthropy, studies show, they also grow increasingly more diverse. The researchers explain:

> Established giving circle members (those who have been members for at least one year) tend to be older, white, higher income, and married, while newer members (less than one year) tend to be more diverse in terms of age, income, and race (these differences are even more pronounced when comparing new members to 5+ year members). In particular, Latinx participation is more prevalent in newer giving circles.[32]

Newer members are joining giving circles to engage more deeply on a cause or issues they care deeply about.[33]

Thea Sowa, the former CEO of the African Women's Development Fund says:

> [W]hether it's people sharing financial resources to support each other in terms of growth, whether it's people supporting with time or with information or with skills, we grew up with African solidarity and African solidarity giving all around us. And I know there were large chunks of time when we came home; you never knew who would be in the house. You never knew who would be living with you for the next six months, a year, or whatever else because we had a family

that understood that you supported each other. You support your neighbors, and your support in the community. And I think that so many of us understand that and, therefore, understand that African philanthropies have been very often horizontal, not vertical, about solidarity and not charity.[34]

Jessyca Dudley, one of the founders of the South Side Giving Circle housed at the Chicago Foundation for Women, explains the powerful change vehicle giving circles are for communities:

African Americans have a long history of philanthropy in the United States. Whether tithing to the church or supporting their communities through the creation of mutual aid societies, African Americans have always been giving but don't necessarily think of themselves formally as "philanthropists." The South Side Giving Circle is an opportunity to elevate the strong history of philanthropy in Chicago's African American community and demonstrate our collective impact. By engaging with these incredible organizations, we can tell the stories of community-based leadership.[35]

## Giving Circle Case Study: South Side

The South Side Giving Circle (SSGC) is a hyperlocal giving circle that invests in Black women on Chicago's South Side and the south suburbs. Like many giving circles, SSGC works through a women's foundation—in their case, the Chicago Foundation for Women—which mentors and trains each member of SSGC in philanthropic giving. Nicole Robinson, one of seven founders of SSGC, explains:

We come from all walks of life, so some of us work in the nonprofit industry, some of us are in higher education, etc., but the values that we all share is that we are passionate about the success of black women and girls and helping them reach their full potential ... We have a quote from Octavia Butler that says, "All that you touch you change, all that you change changes you, the only lasting truth is change." That's been our mantra.[36]

SSGC started with just over 30 members in 2018, and its membership has doubled. Since it began, they have raised and directed close to $210,000 to Black-woman-led organizations on the South Side.[37] Their grantmaking is aimed at the economic, social, and political power of Black women and girls in the South Side, a section of the city that has historically been under-resourced.[38] SSGC aims to build a network of women that is a force for gender and racial equity within the community. They do this by supporting initiatives that give Black women a voice and grow their political power in the South Side. Members of SSGC engage in the giving circle in various ways. Some invest $500 for those aged 35 and under and $1000 for everyone else, while others also attend meetings and site visits and actively engage with grantees.[39] Together, they choose the organizations that help Black women and girls or that are led by Black women the SSGC will support. Organizations must be located on and serving the South Side of Chicago to be considered for funding and have a stated gender equity angle to their work.[40] All members can nominate potential grantees.[41]

One of SSGC's grantees is Assata's Daughters (AD), which teaches the radical political tradition of Black feminism and how to organize for Black liberation. The original collective created Daughters in 2015 based on their belief that it is the collective obligation of Black people to fight for their freedom. AD provides instruction in the theories, radical strategies, and tactics rooted in the Black queer feminist tradition that helped pioneer the Black liberation movement. AD has also broadened its scope to include showing young men and boys how toxic notions of masculinity and patriarchal systems of injustice impact their interpersonal relationships.

AD uses resistance and civil disobedience in their campaigns to shake things up, directly confronting the systems of power.[42] This includes organizing themselves and their neighbors against gentrification and police violence. AD's goal is to make material improvements in people's lives.[43] "We want to offer the South Side a new narrative about what community can be and how we can leverage our collective resources, ideas, and power to invest in the success of black women and girls," explains Robinson.[44]

## Case Study: The Asian Women's Giving Circle

Collective giving is gaining popularity among younger people, minorities, and especially women. Recent estimates indicate 150,000 donors have given as much as $1.3 billion through giving circles.[45] Women donors rejoice in the unique community brought on by collaborating for gender justice. "These women have become part of my New York City family," says Hali Lee, founder of the Asian Women's Giving Circle, the first and largest giving circle in the U.S. led by Asian American women. "We half-joke that we should find an apartment building in Queens and move in together."[46]

Founded by Lee in 2005, the Asian Women Giving Circle (AWGC) members have combined their funds and secured external funds to raise $1 million and make 100 projects come to life.[47] The all-volunteer group is based in New York City and is rooted in the belief in the transformative power of arts and culture to advance an equitable and just society. Members of the AWGC pool their resources to fund projects led by Asian American women artists and community groups.[48] The group has a minimum $2,500 annual contribution.[49] AWGC is guided by the belief that funding is a form of activism and believes in taking risks. To do so, they invest in emerging and cutting-edge changemakers.

Lee advises:

> It's OK to experiment and adjust your circle's funding focuses ... Your group should also set a goal for how much money to donate in the first year so you can work together to meet this target. But don't panic if you *don't* meet your first funding goal. You should be learning from these missed opportunities. Part of the joy of giving circles is figuring out together how to bounce back.

AWGC holds annual retreats, focusing on solutions to at least one pressing, overarching question. Lee reflects, "The power of giving circles can be encapsulated by one word: community. A few of them [organizations AWGC donates to] have told us various versions of, 'we feel like you're our big sisters cheering on the sidelines.'"[50]

## Innovating New Philanthropic Models

The more people are invested in gender justice, the more likely gender justice will be won. In 1995, Rita Thapa envisioned a women's fund for Nepal. Thapa wanted to help Nepalis by reducing dependence on foreign donors. With Tewa, she introduced the practice of donating regularly for gender equality to both Nepali men and women.[51] Thapa explains:

> Nepal has an ancient traditional culture of giving which is rooted and ingrained in the fabric of Nepali life [whatever one's] religious and cultural background. But philanthropy, as is now understood in the world or practiced mainly in North America and Europe, is not so prevalent, nor is it well understood. It is easy to raise funds to build a temple, a rest house, or even feed those who are hungry. Building a home for abandoned women, people who are elderly, or orphans is more

likely to be understood. But how can one ask for money to support the empowerment of women? The very notion of this question is the fundamental belief that women are powerful.[52]

She says:

> In Nepal, generally, women are "well looked after," "provided for," and respected, so what is the meaning when we say they are not empowered—they are literally worshipped like goddesses! This is veritably what will cross the mind of any possible Nepali donor—men and even women. Besides, "empowering women" through education or income-generating activities is the work of the donor agencies, if not the government. What are the aid agencies doing in the country if not this![53]

With Tewa, Thapa set her sights on transforming that deeply ingrained perception by innovating new fundraising strategies.[54] The program aimed to fundraise locally to help reaffirm that Nepalis themselves could run "sustainable" philanthropic structures in aid-ridden Nepal and avoid the notion of donor dependency. Thapa explains:

> This would also help build communities, make philanthropy more relevant to present times and need, and in the process, help restore human dignity to some extent. The spin-off gains would help educate external donors and NGOs, and if this could be successful, it would provide an inspirational model for feminist initiatives and other development practitioners.[55]

As CEO of the Women's Funding Network, Chris Grumm made her first visit at the end of 2006 to Tewa. During that visit, she was invited to spend the evening with donors and various women leaders from around the country. It was during this event that she heard an amazing story. One evening Rita Thapa gathered her friends together and began by sharing her vision of a women's fund in Nepal. When she finished, they asked her, "Who is going to provide the funds? Where will it come from?" She answered the question by taking off one of her gold bangles and said, "Sisters, we do have these bangles, which belong to us. We can each give a bangle and start from there." It did not take long before she convinced many of her vision and the gold bangle pile started to grow and Tewa was born. After this fundraising story from the local Nepalese women was shared by Rita, the Global Fund for Women came forward and gave the founders their first large grant to help in the building of Tewa. Tewa's membership grew quickly, and they learned over the years how to build their organization, make grants, and construct meeting and revenue space with funding from a continued piling up of gold bangles as well as foundations and donors from the international community.

Thapa says:

> Feminist philanthropy aims at redressing justice across intersectionality. It aims at strengthening the women's movement in its diversity to enable equitable giving and blurring the lines between the donor/ grantee—to be engaged on a path of equitable justice. Ideally, it mandates non-hierarchical, circular structures, grounds itself on feminist values and principles, and ensures ongoing self-reflection and reviews. As the founder of Tewa, I can say that Tewa was founded on those values, and the practice is ongoing so far—I think. If we don't at any time, or we falter, we cannot claim to be a feminist fund.[56]

Tewa also replicated women's fund campaigns that were effective in other countries, including the 88 Days campaign, which starts on December 10 (Human Rights Day) and ends on March 8 (International Women's Day). Tewa learned of this fundraising campaign, which originated from the HER Fund of Hong Kong through its memberships in the Prospera International Network of Women's Funds and the Asian Network for Women's Funds (ANWF). The 88 Days campaign does double duty: raising awareness for women's rights and human rights while mobilizing resources. Tewa, which means "support," had made a special "Thaili" (pouch) for the donors to put their daily small donations for 88 days. This campaign was very successful in its objective to highlight women's rights while demonstrating that even a single rupee a day is a valuable way to support a cause that can make a difference in the lives of rural Nepali women and their families. Tewa used each day to highlight women's rights issues, coupling a powerful awareness campaign with their democratized fundraising efforts.[57]

Patty Chang, CEO and co-founder of Feed the Hunger Fund and Former President and CEO of Women's Foundation of California, reflects on how unique Tewa is in the realm of philanthropy:

> The way that they looked at how do you develop a women's fund from the ground up and the top down, I think really helped them get ahead further, faster. The women with more wealth, married to the rich men putting their gold bracelets on the table to start the organization, to them giving out awards for people who can bring in more

members—even at the 1 rupee, 5-rupee level—they tried to do that building from the ground up, unlike some of our funds that said, hey, $10,000 membership to join.[58]

Community building was key to Tewa's fundraising approach. It is an efficient way of reaching people while inspiring them to invest in change with, literally, change.

## Unleashing the Full Spectrum of Capital

The Global Women's Funding Movement is always examining how money is deployed and exploring new ways it can be raised. Women's funds do this by identifying how women's financial and collaborative power is untapped and can be unleashed. Tuti Scott, founder of Changemaker Strategies, which advises on values-aligned investing, moving money with a gender and racial justice lens, and mobilizing philanthropic dollars for justice,[59] says:

> Women thrive in community, as we know from Women's Philanthropy Institute research. Giving in community gives women a chance to feel validated. They haven't had a lot of spaces where they are validated around their relationship with money or their relationship with giving. It provides them, hopefully, a place where they can see themselves, whether as inheritors, partnered, widowed, or wealth earners. They get to see themselves and learn from one another. I just read from UBS that 60 percent of high-net-worth women defer 100 percent of their investing decisions to their husbands in a heterosexual relationship. Where are we giving spaces and places for women to explore and understand what their full spectrum of capital is doing? That would be my hope for feminist philanthropy. Unless we're talking about the full spectrum of capital, we're not serving the community well. We need to be talking to women about their whole wallet or purse—spending, giving, saving, and investing. We need them to activate all their dollars aligning with their values. Roughly $450 billion is in U.S. philanthropy annually; $70 trillion is in the capital markets. Women and girls are getting 1.6 percent of the $450 billion in U.S. philanthropy. How do we get at least 2 percent of the $70 trillion in the markets moving with a gender and racial lens?[60]

New research shows that progress toward gender equality worldwide is stalled, because of factors including Covid-19 and climate impact and conflict.

UN Women's research claims that "the world is not on track to achieve gender equality by 2030."[61] Current projections, based on the 2022 World Economic Forum Global Gender Gap Report, are that it will take another 132 years to close the gender gap. Knowing gender equality is critical to solving many of our current world crises, there's an even greater moral urgency to rapidly advance gender equality. It is crucial to recognize that overall funding levels for gender equality are severely inadequate and funding must increase exponentially to achieve equality far sooner than projected.[62] This means expanding the reach and influence of women's funds globally.

Michelle Reddy, Co-Lead of Pacific Feminist Fund, shares the story of the creation of the Pacific Feminist Fund:

> The Fiji Women's Fund and Urgent Action Fund [Asia and the Pacific] commissioned this report called "Where is the Money for Women and Girls in the Pacific?" In that report in 2019, key findings came out, and key recommendations were made. One of the recommendations was to set up a Pacific feminist fund because we were finding that less than 1 percent of grant funding coming into the Pacific was going directly to women's organizations and networks. When the findings came out, we didn't share the findings with all potential funders for the Pacific feminist fund. We situated the findings in what is called the Pacific Feminist Forum, which is a forum that occurs every three years and brings together 100 to 150 feminists from across the region. So, in 2019, when the research was completed, we presented those initial findings in that forum and opened the opportunity to get people to ask questions, know, and share concerns. So, in many ways, the ownership and the mandate of the Pacific feminist fund were born within the feminist movement. And so, by the time we formally launched this year, it was again within the third Pacific Feminist Forum. So, to me, I think even the way that we behave and interact is really important.[63]

The Global Women's Funding Movement has boldly created new platforms for feminist organizations, private foundations, and governments. Women's funds and other allies must work together to overcome the inertia and resistance that has made the funding chasm so large. These platforms are intended to bridge the gap between the proven effectiveness of feminist movements and the availability of sustained, flexible, core support to fuel their work at scale. Women's funds' long-standing track record and credibility have enabled them to leverage significant investment from governments, including Canada, the Netherlands, Spain, Australia, the United Kingdom, and the United States.

The Generation Equality Forum (GEF), held in 2021,[64] kickstarted a five-year effort to accelerate significant financial commitments toward global gender equality. The forum, convened by UN Women and co-chaired by the governments of France and Mexico in partnership with civil society and youth, secured $40 billion in funding commitments.[65] At the forum, a small group of governments, led by Canada and the Netherlands, joined with women's funds, including the Global Fund for Women, the Equality Fund, Prospera International Network of Women's Funds, Urgent Action Fund-Africa, Women's Fund Asia, and Fondo Semillas, and women's rights organizations to discuss creating an ongoing alliance devoted to securing more robust funding for feminist movements. The Alliance for Feminist Movements (The Alliance) was their answer. This collaborative multi-stakeholder initiative was announced at the forum and after close consultation with 200 organizations. It was officially launched the following year during the UN General Assembly 2022.[66] The Alliance is dedicated to increasing and improving the quality of resources, securing sustained, flexible, core financial support for feminist movements.[67]

Melinda Wells, Vice President of Strategic Partnerships at the Equality Fund, was at the GEF meeting and remembers:

> There's that feeling, I think, whenever you have a big global initiative like the Generation Equality Forum, there's a lot going on, and what are we going to be left with at the end? What's going to really make the difference? There was the Action Coalition #6, which is focused on strengthening feminist movements. There was a discussion between a number of different stakeholders about how we could make a commitment under that Action Coalition that would lead to something that was sustained, and that brought together people from different stakeholder groups who were committed and dedicated to increasing the funding and support for feminist movements. The question was, how do we design a mechanism beyond the Generation Equality Forum that keeps that mission and focus very clear and tight? We [Equality Fund] were one of the organizations in the design group. Well, I should say that the announcement of the intention to design the Alliance for Feminist Movements was made collaboratively between the Ford Foundation, the Government of Canada, and the Equality Fund. We designed a structure, a membership organization with a very small Secretariat, and a Steering Group designed to manage the governance and direction. The Secretariat right now is hosted by AWID.[68]

The Alliance for Feminist Movements brings together national governments, philanthropic organizations, women's funds, feminist organizations, and international organizations to collectively marshal funding and political support for feminist movements and their critical role in securing women's rights, strengthening democracy, improving economies, and spreading peace. Although not a funding mechanism, The Alliance works to mobilize funding for feminist organizations and movements and experiment with new solutions, launching learning hubs to pilot strategies to raise awareness about the effect of feminist movements on driving positive social change.

The Alliance Steering Committee was structured to have two seats for national governments, three women's funds, three feminist civil society organizations, and one non-voting host member that plays a more administrative role. Together, they focus on exponentially increasing, sustaining, and improving financial and political support for women's rights and feminist organizations and movements. The strength of the Alliance for Feminist Movements comes from bringing together a range of stakeholders to tackle funding and political support issues that are bigger than any single donor–grantee relationship or sector.

A core strategy of women's funds is to ensure the future of gender equality by strengthening women economically. When asked to identify the funding priority areas of their organization, most women's funds chose economic empowerment (61%) and education (50%).[69]

By advancing women's economic empowerment, the Global Women's Funding Movement has grown, building and shifting philanthropic power, directing money toward women's economic security, and winning gender justice victories.

The Prosperity Together project is a powerful example of this commitment to building sustainable capital. Completed in 2020, a coalition of U.S.-based women's funds united to focus collectively on dramatically improving the economic security of low-income women and their families in the U.S. The effort was initiated by a group of six women's funds who committed to working together to invest massive sums to unlock real economic opportunities for women. Over its first year, the coalition grew to 29 organizations. Together, from 2015 to 2020, they invested more than $100 million in strategies within communities to create high-wage job training programs for low-income women, affordable, high-quality childcare, and research to determine best practices and policies that increase economic security for low-income women. [70]

The Iowa Women's Foundation, a Prosperity Together coalition member, funded Women Caring for the Land. This was a training program dedicated to creating more women entrepreneurs in ecological restoration, an emerging sector that focuses on repairing degraded, damaged, or destroyed ecosystems.[71] Bridget Holcomb, executive director of the Women, Food and Agriculture Network in Iowa, notes:

Sometimes conservation work means using chainsaws and fire, and landowners want to hire ecological restorationists to do that work. Looking around, we didn't find a single woman who worked as an ecological restorationist. So, we decided to train them ourselves.[72]

The Washington Area Women's Foundation funded Training Futures, one of the nation's most effective workforce development programs. Training Futures offers a six-month intensive course taught in a simulated office setting and provides trainees with critical skills needed across industries, such as customer service, office administration, tech skills, and records management. The program is highly successful, graduating 90 percent of all participants. Within a year after completing the program, 80 percent are employed with benefits, with an average salary of $12.50 per hour.[73]

## Women Mobilizing Millions

By moving significant amounts of capital into women's economic security, gender justice, and women's movements, women's funds demonstrate the critical role donors serve for the future of gender justice. Indeed, many significant advancements for women were won because women's movements, funded by women of all income levels, emerged to win it. Women of extreme wealth are often discouraged from rocking the power structures in which they are advantageously placed. It takes bravery and autonomy to rattle the halls of power and wealth, especially by someone who is a member of the powerful and wealthy.

Barbara Dobson is a stellar example of a women's fund donor rattling the halls of power. She embodies trust-based philanthropy in giving generously to leaders and funds she believes in and to issues needing funding. Barbara is also fearless—for instance, when she took the stage at the Council on Foundation's Philanthropy's Vision: A Leadership Summit 2008 in Washington, DC, during the recession. The Summit represented the largest convening in the Council's history. Barbara told the hundreds of representatives of philanthropic funds and family funds across the United States who were in the room that it was time to free up the millions in reserve held by philanthropic foundations if they were serious about their commitment to gender and racial justice. Barbara asked them what they were waiting for and spoke as a donor, calling on them to unleash the power of their funds to transform systems and communities.

Another powerful example is the women who dreamed Women Moving Millions (WMM) into being. The idea for WMM was sparked in 2007, when the founders, Helen LaKelly Hunt, Ambassador Swanee Hunt, and Chris

Grumm, catalyzed a major funding initiative to raise the bar on women's giving by asking women to make bold million-dollar commitments to strengthen the capacity of women's funds. Stephanie Clohesy wrote the original documents capturing Helen's and Swanee's thinking for a million-dollar-level giving initiative starting with women's funds. This campaign was launched in partnership with the Women's Funding Network to raise awareness among women about what their giving could make possible through democratized philanthropy.

Jane Sloane, who was at the time Executive Director of the International Women's Funding Network, recalls that moment:

> I remember being at the 2008 WFN global conference where Women Moving Millions was launched, and women's funds with million-dollar donors were invited to the stage. Chris Grumm, President and CEO of the Women's Funding Network, also invited women to become million-dollar donors, stand up, and commit. Women realized they could make that commitment—over whatever number of years they chose—and be part of a rising philanthropic movement for gender justice. It was incredibly powerful being in the room as women rose to make that commitment. It was like a wave of giving across the room, and the energy was electric.[74]

Chris Grumm remembers that the original target for the Women Moving Millions campaign was $100 million over five years; however, the amount raised ended up far more in record time. WMM made history by securing $200 million in commitments from more than 100 donors for over 40 women's funds in under five years.

Recognizing the need to mobilize greater resources for gender justice did not end with this hugely successful campaign. A passionate and committed group of women philanthropists joined to establish it as an organization that catalyzes resources to achieve gender equality. One of the founders, Helen LaKelly Hunt, shares what first inspired her to help pioneer so many pipelines of funding within the Global Women's Funding Movement. These pipelines included several of the earliest women's funds, including The New York Women's Foundation and the Dallas Women's Foundation, as well as some of the largest women donor cultivation efforts like WMM. LaKelly Hunt says:

> What started me on this, I was doing a doctoral dissertation, and I was in a rare book collection area, and I opened a book about the Suffrage Movement. There was a newspaper article, and in it was a letter from

Matilda Joslyn Gage. She worked with Susan B. Anthony and Elizabeth Cady Stanton. She wrote Elizabeth and Susan, and she said, "My dear Elizabeth, I know you and Susan have worked so hard to gain women the right to have a vote in this country, but I've just read this article in the newspaper"; the article was all about how wealthy women fund their husband's alma maters or are funding churches where women are not allowed to speak. Women of wealth were funding this and that, but they didn't fund women's rights. She said, "Why have no women funded women's equality?" Suffrage for women could have been gained way earlier if wealthy women funded it. Only two men were funding the Suffrage Movement, but no women.[75]

Today, Women Moving Millions is a thriving global community with a membership of nearly 400 donors who have committed over $820 million to organizations and initiatives benefiting women and girls. They represent a new era of resources by and for women. In 2020, WMM launched its two-year[76] Give Bold, Get Equal Campaign to mobilize $100 million in new funds for organizations working to advance gender equality by transforming inequitable systems. WMM blew past its timeframe and raised over $110 million in just nine months.[77]

Executive Director Sarah Haacke Byrd says:

> The success of this campaign in such a short time period shows what happens when you combine the power of feminist leadership and community; the impossible becomes possible. We are taking a huge step towards funding gender equality, but the key is momentum. Despite the increased attention to the inequities that impact women and girls worldwide, the funding gap persists.[78]

Haacke Byrd reflects:

> Parity isn't going to be achieved with one board member on one corporate board. To change the structural and systemic inequities for women, you've got to have more funding to support those leaders who know exactly what to do. We call upon every person to join us and give boldly to get equal.[79]

Equity is the mantra of the Global Women's Funding Movement. Guided by feminist funding values, this movement has innovated a highly effective and entirely new form of philanthropy that can leverage massive funding for gender equality, attract large numbers of new philanthropists, and enable women to wield the power of money to use this philanthropic innovation to liberate themselves and others.

Tracy Gary is considered a legend within the women's philanthropy world. Author of *Inspired Philanthropy* and founder of 23 nonprofits,[80] she is a philanthropic and legacy advisor to the Global Women's Funding Movement. She has been a donor activist and movement co-worker for 50 years, since 1973. Gary has witnessed the rare spirit that manifests when women come together to leverage massive resources for gender justice many times over:

> We are bold, sassy, and gaining money, moxie, and momentum. This is not any one person's spark; this is our collective wisdom and a call to ignite the best in each of us. We give time, talent, and treasure, and we still move others to step up in giving circles and investing. Women Moving Millions and hundreds of circles are saving our planet and people by simply honoring and empowering women and girls. Women leading is long overdue. It is time to partner anew and give women and girls a fair shot at cleaning up the mess we are in. The women's funding movement is no small event. It is the counterbalance to a world that has diminished the light of its caring heart.[81]

In 1988, a young Tracy Gary spoke on a Women's Funding Network video about what this commitment to the global women's movement meant:

> We're not just raising money and giving it away; we're raising consciousness, and we're changing people's lives on a personal level … My life has been radically changed by being involved in this work … I feel so passionate about this work that it's an investment every day. I feel like the luckiest person in the world. It feeds my soul.[82]

★★★

The story of the Global Women's Funding Movement is not just a stunning success story. It is a story of courage, creativity, community, and tenacity. With a world in crisis due to increasingly frequent pandemics, climate emergencies, civil wars, and conflicts; with the rise of the strong man, and the closing space for civil society and the commons, there's much to despair about. What offers hope is this bold, sassy, and electric movement mobilizing millions in funds for women-led change that is shifting structures, attitudes, power, resources, and policies for justice.

It was the late Ursula Le Guin who said, "We are volcanoes. When we women offer our experience as our truth, as human truth, all the maps change. There are new mountains."[83]

This force more powerful that is the Global Women's Funding Movement has catalyzed and cascaded resources for fearless feminist movements for justice locally and globally. It has invested in movements to hold ground and gain ground for gender justice and realizing rights. It has trusted women leaders to know the stories and solutions required for radical change and a new world imagined. It has affirmed what Ellen Johnson Sirleaf, Former President of Liberia, has said, "If your dreams do not scare you, they are not big enough."

As the late Wangari Maathai, founder of the Green Belt Movement, and a phenomenal feminist activist for justice, said, "In the course of history, there comes a time when humanity is called to shift to a new level of consciousness, to reach a higher moral ground. A time when we have to shed our fear and give hope to each other. That time is now."[84]

This story is of many women across the globe choosing to give hope to each other, to give to a vision of feminist justice through diverse movements and, in the act of giving, becoming connected to a community that gives soul force to their life. It is the story of a collective dreaming for a new world through the birth and rise of many women's funds. It is the truth telling spoken by the late Maya Angelou that "each time a woman stands up for herself, she stands up for all women."[85] This philanthropic movement represents investment in a vision, yet to be realized, of every woman, every person living free of violence, equitably sharing power and resources, and honoring diversity, Indigenous wisdom, and practices. A world where biodiversity is restored and where poverty and injustice are history. A world where women have full control over their bodies, and where all people have freedom of movement, identity, and expression, and can realize their full potential. A world where there is a culture of giving which kindles joy and radical generosity. For as the writer Angela Davis has said, "I think the importance of doing activist work is precisely because it allows you to give back and to consider yourself not as a single individual who might have achieved whatever, but to be part of an ongoing historical movement."[86]

Katherine Acey, Executive Director Emerita of Astraea Lesbian Foundation for Justice says:

> How do I keep going? I just keep going. Because I believe there's just no other way to be in the world. You can't stop. I think it's important to have joy and to be in the community and have fun, too. My friend Mariame Kaba, who is an activist in anti-prison work, talks about hope in this way. Hope is not an emotion, she says. Sadness, despair, and anger are emotions. Hope is a discipline and if we're going to change the world, then we need to hope. You keep hope and think of it as daily exercise. That's part of what keeps me going, is that hope and belief that we can do better, and we can change the world.[87]

And what will it take to change the world? Lauren Y. Casteel, President and CEO of the Women's Foundation of Colorado, shares her vision:

> My dream is that we become a force and that $50 or even $100 million is not enough. Enough is the minimum. We need to be more than enough. We need to see ourselves as a force, not as a distributor of charity. We're not doling out charity. We are a force for change.[88]

## Notes

1　Women's Funding Network, "Women's Fund Funds Video Project 12 9 88," YouTube, December 9, 1988, 23:17, www.youtube.com/watch?v=DkuhHxr TTOM.

2　Cynthia Nimmo, personal email correspondence Jane Sloane, May 26, 2023.

3　Women's Funding Network, "Women's Fund Funds Video Project 12 9 88," YouTube, December 9, 1988, 23:17, www.youtube.com/watch?v=DkuhHxr TTOM.

4　Women's Funding Network, "Women's Fund Funds Video Project 12 9 88," YouTube, December 9, 1988, 23:17, www.youtube.com/watch?v=DkuhHxr TTOM.

5　Women's Funding Network, "Women's Fund Funds Video Project 12 9 88," YouTube, December 9, 1988, 23:17, www.youtube.com/watch?v=DkuhHxr TTOM.

6　"Dallas Women's Foundation Becomes Texas Women's Foundation," Texas Women's Foundation, accessed on November 24, 2023, https://txwf.org/ dallas-womens-foundation-becomes-texas-womens-foundation.

7　"Dallas Women's Foundation Becomes Texas Women's Foundation," Texas Women's Foundation, accessed on November 24, 2023, https://txwf.org/ dallas-womens-foundation-becomes-texas-womens-foundation.

8　Elizabeth M. Gillespie. *Change Agents: The Goals and Impact of Women's Foundations and Funds*. Indiana University Lilly Family School of Philanthropy, December 2019. Accessed November 24, 2023, https://scholarworks.iupui. edu/server/api/core/bitstreams/c0bcd905-cf4f-4988-8354-c4c0b874f6ba/ content.

9　Ellen Sprenger, "Rethinking funding for women's rights: how to build greater financial resilience and strength in your organization," *Sur—International Journal on Human Rights*, Issue 24, December 2016. Accessed on November 24, 2023, https://sur.conectas.org/en/rethinking-funding-for-womens-rights.

10　"Why Giving Is Good for Your Health," Cleveland Clinic, December 7, 2022, https://health.clevelandclinic.org/why-giving-is-good-for-your-health.

11  Debra Mesch et al. *Women Give 2017*. Indiana University Lilly Family School of Philanthropy: December 2019. Accessed November 24, 2023, https://scholarworks.iupui.edu/handle/1805/14283.

12  Melissa Wylie, "The more women donate, the happier they are," *Bizwomen*, October 18, 2017, accessed November 24, 2023, www.bizjournals.com/bizwomen/news/latest-news/2017/10/the-more-women-donate-the-happier-they-are.html.

13  Linda Calhoun, interview by Laura Risimini, January 13, 2023.

14  Rose Flenorl, interview by Laura Risimini, February 20, 2023.

15  Lois A. Buntz, *Generosity and Gender: Philanthropic Models for Women Donors and the Fund Development Professionals Who Support Them* (Palgrave Macmillan, 2022), 51–53.

16  Abigail Disney, interview by Christine Grumm, April 20, 2023.

17  Abigail Disney, interview by Christine Grumm, April 20, 2023.

18  Mona Sinha, interview by Laura Risimini, January 23, 2023.

19  Sayoni Nyakoon, "An Interview with Anne Delaney, former Board Chair," *The New York Women's Foundation Activist Philanthropist*, Vol. 3, No. 1 (July 13, 2017), 17–19.

20  Lois A. Buntz, *Generosity and Gender: Philanthropic Models for Women Donors and the Fund Development Professionals Who Support Them* (Palgrave Macmillan, 2022), 10.

21  Mary McDaniel, interview with Laura Risimini, December 19, 2022.

22  Kerry Gardner, interview with Christine Grumm and Laura Risimini, September 7, 2023.

23  Erica Sandberg, "The history of women and credit cards," *Bankrate*, March 1, 2023, accessed November 24, 2023, www.bankrate.com/finance/credit-cards/history-of-women-and-credit-cards/#:~:text=In%201974%2C%20the%20Equal%20Credit,card%20in%20their%20own%20name.

24  Anne Boden, "Why We Need To #Makemoneyequal," Starling Bank, March 13, 2018, accessed November 24, 2023, www.starlingbank.com/blog/make-money-equal

25  Susan Chira, "Money Is Power. And Women Need More of Both," *The New York Times*, March 10, 2018, accessed November 24, 2023, www.nytimes.com/2018/03/10/sunday-review/women-money-politics-power.html?te=1&nl=in-her%20words&emc=edit_gn_2019.

26  Susan Chira, "Money Is Power. And Women Need More of Both," *The New York Times*, March 10, 2018, accessed November 24, 2023, www.nytimes.com/2018/03/10/sunday-review/women-money-politics-power.html?te=1&nl=in-her%20words&emc=edit_gn_2019

27  Jacki Zehner, interview with Christine Grumm and Laura Risimini, January 17, 2023.

28 Elizabeth Barajas-Román, "The equitable way forward: giving circles," *Alliance*, May 13, 2023, accessed November 24, 2023, www.alliancemagazine.org/blog/the-equitable-way-forward-giving-circles.

29 Elizabeth Barajas-Román, "The equitable way forward: giving circles," *Alliance*, May 13, 2023, accessed November 24, 2023, www.alliancemagazine.org/blog/the-equitable-way-forward-giving-circles.

30 Lois A. Buntz, *Generosity and Gender: Philanthropic Models for Women Donors and the Fund Development Professionals Who Support Them* (Palgrave Macmillan, 2022), 30–32.

31 "New research shows that giving circles attract increasingly diverse donors," *Indiana University Lilly Family School of Philanthropy*, November 13, 2018, accessed November 24, 2023, https://philanthropy.iupui.edu/news-events/news/_news/2018/new-research-shows-that-giving-circles-attract-increasingly-diverse-donors.html.

32 "New research shows that giving circles attract increasingly diverse donors," *Indiana University Lilly Family School of Philanthropy*, November 13, 201, accessed November 24, 2023, https://philanthropy.iupui.edu/news-events/news/_news/2018/new-research-shows-that-giving-circles-attract-increasingly-diverse-donors.html.

33 "Giving circles," Lilly Family School of Philanthropy IUPUI website, 2023. Last accessed September 15, 2023 https://philanthropy.iupui.edu/institutes/womens-philanthropy-institute/research/giving-circles18.html.

34 Conversations on African Philanthropy, "Theo Sowa | Ep 24 | Conversations on African Philanthropy," YouTube, June 7, 2023, 43:29, accessed on May 20, 2024, www.youtube.com/watch?v=e4m2-EYCGcA&list=PPSV.

35 "Giving Circles: Growing Community By Elevating Black Women + Girls Of Color," Giving Tuesday, July 8 2019, accessed on November 24, 2023, www.givingtuesday.org/blog/giving-circles-growing-community-elevating-black-women-girls-color.

36 Lee Edwards, "Meet the South Side Queenmakers: Philanthropists Team Up to Invest in Black Women and Girls," *Block Club Chicago*, July 25, 2018, accessed on November 24, 2023, https://blockclubchicago.org/2018/07/25/meet-the-south-side-queenmakers-philanthropists-team-up-to-invest-in-black-women-and-girls.

37 "Who We Are—South Side Giving Circle," Chicago Foundation for Women, accessed on November 24, 2023, www.cfw.org/south-side-giving-circle.

38 Whitney Wade, personal email communication with Laura Risimini, December 13, 2022.

39 "Who We Are—South Side Giving Circle," Chicago Foundation for Women, accessed on November 24, 2023, www.cfw.org/south-side-giving-circle.

40 "Giving Circles: Growing Community By Elevating Black Women + Girls Of Color," Giving Tuesday, July 8 2019, accessed on November 24, 2023, www.givingtuesday.org/blog/giving-circles-growing-community-elevating-black-women-girls-color.

41  "What you can do—South Side Giving Circle," Chicago Foundation for Women, accessed on November 24, 2023, www.cfw.org/south-side-giving-circle.

42  "Our Politics," Assata's Daughters, accessed on November 24, 2023, www.assatasdaughters.org/our-politics-2019.

43  "Our Politics," Assata's Daughters, accessed on November 24, 2023, www.assatasdaughters.org/our-politics-2019.

44  "What you can do—South Side Giving Circle," Chicago Foundation for Women, accessed on November 24, 2023, www.cfw.org/south-side-giving-circle.

45  Lini S. Kadaba, "Giving circles, where people pool their money for charity, have quadrupled, especially among women," *The Philadelphia Inquirer*, October 29, 2019, accessed on November 24, 2023, www.inquirer.com/news/giving-circles-project-w-impact100-women-of-vision-philadelphia-20191029.html.

46  Bryan Borzykowski, "When It's Time for Giving, Some People Circle Around," *The New York Times*, November 17, 2018, accessed on November 24, 2023, www.nytimes.com/2018/11/17/business/giving-circles-nonprofits-political-campaigns.html.

47  "Asian Women Giving Circle," Asian Women Giving Circle, accessed on November 24, 2023, https://asianwomengivingcircle.org.

48  "Asian Women Giving Circle," Asian Women Giving Circle, accessed on November 24, 2023, https://asianwomengivingcircle.org.

49  Bryan Borzykowski, "When It's Time for Giving, Some People Circle Around," *The New York Times*, November 17, 2018, accessed on November 24, 2023, www.nytimes.com/2018/11/17/business/giving-circles-nonprofits-political-campaigns.html.

50  Siobhan Neela-Stock, "How to start a giving circle," *Mashable*, December 24, 2019, accessed on November 24, 2023, https://mashable.com/article/how-to-start-a-giving-circle.

51  Rita Thapa, "Tewa—Doing the Impossible: Feminist Action in Nepal The Founder's Story." Sixth Annual Dame Nita Barrow Lecture at Ontario Institute for Studies in Education of the University of Toronto, November 2002, accessed November 24, 2023, https://globalfundcommunityfoundations.org/wp-content/uploads/2011/11/Tewa-Doing-the-Imposssible.pdf, page 1.

52  Rita Thapa, personal email communication with Laura Risimini, September 22, 2022.

53  Rita Thapa, "Tewa—Doing the Impossible: Feminist Action in Nepal The Founder's Story." Sixth Annual Dame Nita Barrow Lecture at Ontario Institute for Studies in Education of the University of Toronto, November 2002, accessed November 24, 2023, https://globalfundcommunityfoundations.org/wp-content/uploads/2011/11/Tewa-Doing-the-Imposssible.pdf, pages 14–15.

54  Rita Thapa, "Tewa—Doing the Impossible: Feminist Action in Nepal The Founder's Story." Sixth Annual Dame Nita Barrow Lecture at Ontario Institute

for Studies in Education of the University of Toronto, November 2002, accessed November 24, 2023, https://globalfundcommunityfoundations.org/wp-content/uploads/2011/11/Tewa-Doing-the-Imposssible.pdf, page 15.

55  Rita Thapa, "Tewa—Doing the Impossible: Feminist Action in Nepal The Founder's Story." Sixth Annual Dame Nita Barrow Lecture at Ontario Institute for Studies in Education of the University of Toronto, November 2002, accessed November 24, 2023, https://globalfundcommunityfoundations.org/wp-content/uploads/2011/11/Tewa-Doing-the-Imposssible.pdf, page 12.

56  Rita Thapa, personal email communication with Laura Risimini, September 22, 2022.

57  "88 Days Campaign," Tewa, accessed November 24, 2023, https://tewa.org.np/88-days-campaign.

58  Patti Chang, interview with Christine Grumm, September 27, 2022.

59  "At the Helm," Changemakers Strategies, accessed November 24, 2023, https://we-are-changemakers.com/about.

60  Tuti Scott, interview with Christine Grumm and Laura Risimini, September 27, 2022.

61  "Goal 5: Achieve gender equality and empower all women and girls," United Nations, accessed November 24, 2023, www.un.org/sustainabledevelopment/gender-equality.

62  "Clarifying Our Purpose, Charting the Way Forward Consultation #2 Survey Results Report Global Alliance for Sustainable Feminist Movements," Global Alliance for Sustainable Feminist Movements. Last accessed September 15, 2023, https://allianceforfeminstmovements.org/wp-content/uploads/2022/07/Global-Alliance-Survey-2-Reprt.pdf.

63  Michelle Reddy, interview with Chris Grumm and Laura Risimini, September 26, 2023.

64  "What is the Generation Equality Forum?" Generation Equality, accessed November 24, 2023, https://forum.generationequality.org/forum.

65  "What is the Generation Equality Forum?" Generation Equality, accessed November 24, 2023, https://forum.generationequality.org/forum.

66  "Gathering Momentum to Accelerate Resourcing of Feminist Movements Globally," Generation Equality Forum, September 9, 2022, accessed November 24, 2023, https://commitments.generationequality.org/Gathering-Momentum-Accelerate-Resourcing-Feminist-Movements-Globally.

67  "Shared Principles and Commitments," Alliance for Feminist Movements, 2022, accessed on November 24, 2023, https://allianceforfeministmovements.org/our-shared-principles-and-commitments.

68  Melinda Wells, interview with Laura Risimini, May 10, 2023.

69  Elizabeth M. Gillespie. *Change Agents: The Goals and Impact of Women's Foundations and Funds.* Indiana University Lilly Family School of Philanthropy,

December 2019. Accessed November 24, 2023, https://scholarworks.iupui.edu/server/api/core/bitstreams/c0bcd905-cf4f-4988-8354-c4c0b874f6ba/content.

70  "Prosperity Together," Women's Funding Network, accessed November 24, 2023, www.womensfundingnetwork.org/what-we-do/strategy-development/prosperity-together.

71  "What is Ecological Restoration?" Society for Ecological Restoration accessed November 24, 2023, https://ser-rrc.org/what-is-ecological-restoration/.

72  "Prosperity Together," Women's Funding Network, accessed November 24, 2023, www.womensfundingnetwork.org/what-we-do/strategy-development/prosperity-together.

73  Jessica Zetzman, "Grantee Partner Spotlight: Northern Virginia Family Service's Training Futures," Washington Area Women's Foundation, July 23, 2015, accessed November 24, 2023, https://thewomensfoundation.org/2015/grantee-partner-spotlight-northern-virginia-family-services-training-futures.

74  Jane Sloane, personal email communication with Christine Grumm, September 22, 2023.

75  Helen Lakelly Hunt, interview with Laura Risimini and Hadley Wilhoite, August 22, 2022.

76  *Women Moving Million: Membership Brochure* (Women Moving Millions, 2022).

77  Steve Neumann, "Serious Money for Women's Rights," University of Minnesota Alumni Association, accessed November 24, 2023, www.minnesotaalumni.org/stories/serious-money-for-women-s-rights.

78  Women Moving Millions, "Women Moving Millions' Give Bold, Get Equal Campaign Exceeds $100 Million in Commitments," PR Newswire, July 2, 2021, accessed November 24, 2023, www.prnewswire.com/news-releases/women-moving-millions-give-bold-get-equal-campaign-exceeds-100-million-in-commitments-301324804.html. .

79  Steve Neumann, "Serious Money for Women's Rights," University of Minnesota Alumni Association, accessed November 24, 2023, www.minnesotaalumni.org/stories/serious-money-for-women-s-rights.

80  Lois A. Buntz, *Generosity and Gender: Philanthropic Models for Women Donors and the Fund Development Professionals Who Support Them* (Palgrave Macmillan, 2022), 38–39.

81  Tracy Gary, personal email correspondence with Helen LaKelly Hunt, January 24, 2023.

82  Women's Funding Network, "Women's Fund Funds Video Project 12 9 88," YouTube, December 9, 1988, 23:17, www.youtube.com/watch?v=DkuhHxrTTOM.

83  "Ursula K. Le Guin," BrainyQuote.com, www.brainyquote.com/quotes/ursula_k_le_guin_150690.

84  Wangari Maathai, Nobel Lecture at Oslo City Hall, Norway, December 2024, accessed November 24, 2023, www.nobelprize.org/prizes/peace/2004/maathai/lecture.

85  "Maya Angelou > Quotes > Quotable Quote," Goodreads.com, www.goodreads.com/quotes/9758677-each-time-a-woman-stands-up-for-herself-she-stands.

86  "41 Best Quotes About Giving Back to Inspire Generosity," Goodgoodgood, accessed May 20, 2004, www.goodgoodgood.co/articles/quotes-for-giving.

87  Katherine Acey, interview with Christine Grumm and Laura Risimini, October 31, 2022.

88  Lauren Y. Casteel, interview with Laura Risimini, September 29, 2022.

# Afterword

## Making a Difference—from Your Neighborhood to the Planet!

We hope this book has excited you about the promise and potential of the Global Women's Funding Movement and that it has left you curious to learn more, and ready to get more involved. Women's funds have so much more to offer each of us in our own communities, regardless of our individual interests and passions. Feminist and women's funds are spread out across the global south, east, and west, and throughout much of the United States and Canada. You will find funds that are highly focused on every aspect of improving and healing the planet and empowering her people. They are all deeply committed to standing up for the causes and ideals that we hold dear, while also advancing the fight on inclusive gender justice.

So, what can you do right now to make a difference on the issues that you care most about? And how can your local, regional, or global women's fund help you feel engaged, hopeful, and part of a community making change? Here are just a few ideas for you to consider:

- **Respect Bodily Integrity**. Are you horrified that, in 2024, women seem to be sliding backwards into having less and less say over their own bodies and the most basic decisions they make about sex, sexuality, pregnancy, and bearing children? After the heroic struggles for abortion rights in the 1960s and 1970s, women and gender-expansive people in the United States and many other parts of the globe are still subjected to unjust laws made to regulate their bodies, gender identities, and sexuality. Your local women's fund cares and supports life-affirming and critical support in the form of abortion services, sex education, contraception, clinics, counseling, legal aid, and policy advocacy.

DOI: 10.4324/9781003330455-7

- **End Gender-Based Violence**. Are you among the one in three women in the world who has experienced some form of sexual or physical harassment, violence, or abuse in their lifetime? Do you know someone who has suffered directly and whose safety, security, and very life has been threatened? If you are looking to make a difference, women's funds are leading the way with grants that strengthen feminist movements to counter violence as a cultural phenomenon, help raise a new generation of boys and men who do not see violence as their only legitimate form of expression, and offer a range of protective and powerful resources to survivors of such abuse.

- **Build Sustainable Economies**. Are you dreaming of a more equitable and just economic future for your city, your region, or your part of the world? Do you wish caregivers had better salaries and that unpaid care work was recognized as being key to all other work? Do you wish young people could study with brilliant feminist economists? Do you wish women had better opportunities for good jobs that could help ensure their independence? Women's funds across the globe are making a range of investments towards a future that is less wasteful, full of purpose, and sustainable.

- **Wage Peace**. Are you feeling a sense of sadness, anger, or anxiety about the ongoing militarized conflicts and wars that are harming so many innocent people? Did you know that many women's funds support groups that build on a long tradition of feminist non-violent resistance by offering peaceful solutions to violent conflict? You can help them invest in women-led efforts to be at the table in peace negotiations, in designing feminist foreign policies, in shifting budget priorities away from weapons and arms purchases to investing in social welfare, health and education.

- **Strengthen Democracy**. Are you saddened or worried about the future of democracy in our country? Or in other parts of the world? Do you wish that you could make investments that could ensure democratic freedoms and protections will survive attacks on institutions and values? A range of feminist funds support groups to expand the rights of all people to live free from discrimination and violence and to have a voice and decision-making power in their own lives and in the economic and political lives of their society. Along with racial, ethnic, and migrant communities, women and gender-expansive individuals have often struggled to be fairly represented in political processes. Women's funds invest in organizations that give communities political power and purpose.

- **Expand Disability Justice**. Do you or someone you love live with a disability? Do you wish that we lived in a world where people with disabilities would be better appreciated for their contributions and celebrated for their many talents? Have you been wondering how you can be part of movements that seek to expand access and opportunities for people with disabilities? Look no further than a women's fund on this list. More and more women's funds are investing in disability rights and disability justice movements and organizations.

- **Educate Generations**. Are you a parent or a teacher? Do you worry about why access to quality education remains elusive for millions of children across the world, including in some of the most privileged and wealthy nations of the globe? If you are passionate about the value of early childhood education, or ensuring that girls stay in schools instead of being married off early, or making sure the future of digital learning includes all our children, you can support a range of women's funds from those doing work in your own state or region, to those ensuring children in Afghanistan, Kenya, or Peru have access to books, opportunities, and good teachers.

- **Forge Climate Solutions**. Are you despairing about the state of our planet? Do you wish we could be more effective in influencing our policy makers or in bringing best practices to bear on the most pressing global crises? Your investments in a women's fund that cares about and supports women-led and feminist responses to climate change, adaptation, and mitigation can be your way of greening your philanthropy. Across the globe and right here in the USA—women and gender-expansive people are leading movements that connect the dots for the communities most adversely affected by climate change and reminding us that the best leaders often emerge from those same communities offering innovation and new solutions to the crisis.

- **Celebrate Art and Artists**. Are you passionate about the arts and want to make sure that a diverse set of voices and individuals get the support they need to brighten our spirits, challenge our imaginations, and document the many ways to look at complex social change issues? Many women's foundations and feminist funds recognize the unsung power of art and artists to make our world more beautiful, more self-reflective, more just, and more free. Make a gift to support a women's fund near you that is in the business of supporting women filmmakers, painters, writers, and musicians.

Many of us hesitate to offer our financial support to causes we care about because we feel our humble resources can't go very far. Yet the story of women's funds that we have shared in these pages constantly reminds us that no contribution is too small or too big. We are all philanthropists. The genius of the model is in its collective power and strength. Many drops of water produce the mighty ocean of feminist transformation. In addition to making your own financial contribution to a women's fund of your choice, you can choose to join a fund as a volunteer—many feminist funds offer opportunities to work side by side with their professional teams for special events and occasions. Since most women's funds are publicly supported charities, they always need some help with fundraising, opening new doors and opportunities to future financial support, and expertise in the areas of marketing, storytelling, and communications. And, finally, you may decide that you would like to offer your services as a member of the governing or advisory board of a women's fund—contact the one that is of most interest to you and ask for an informational interview to learn more about what they are looking for in future board members.

We hope you will be inspired to join this global movement of feminist transformative philanthropy. Here are the women's funds from around the world. We can't wait to make good trouble together!

Authored by Kavita N. Ramdas, Principal, KNR Sisters Consulting and former President and CEO, Global Fund for Women, on behalf of the Co-Authors:

- Ndana Bofu-Tawamba
- Ruby Bright
- Stephanie Clohesy
- Christine Grumm
- Dr. Musimbi Kanyoro
- Helen LaKelly Hunt
- Ana Oliveira
- Laura Risimini
- Jane Sloane
- Jessica Tomlin

## Prospera International Network of Women's Funds

The Prospera International Network of Women's Funds is a global political network of bold, intersectional, diverse, and autonomous women's and feminist funds that nurture transformation by resourcing, supporting, and accompanying movements led by women, girls, trans, intersex, and non-binary people, and collectives primarily in the Global South and East.

To learn more, please visit: **www.prospera-inwf.org**

## *List of Member Funds (listed alphabetically)*

**African Women's Development Fund**
www.awdf.org

**Astraea Lesbian Foundation for Justice**
www.astraeafoundation.org

**AYNI-International Indigenous Women's Fund**
www.fimi-iiwf.org

**Bulgarian Fund for Women**
www.bgfundforwomen.org/en

**Calala Fondo de Mujeres**
www.calala.org

**Doria Feminist Fund**
www.doriafeministfund.org

**Ecumenical Women's Initiative**
www.eiz.hr/en

**Elas Fundo De Investimento Social**
www.fundosocialelas.org

**FemFund Poland**
www.femfund.pl

**Filia Die Frauenstiftung**
www.filia-frauenstiftung.de/en

**Fondo Acción Urgente-América Latina y el Caribe hispanohablante**
www.fondoaccionurgente.org.co

**Fondo Alquimia**
www.fondoalquimia.org

**Fondo Centroamericano de Mujeres**
www.fcmujeres.org

**Fondo de Mujeres Bolivia Apthapi-Jopueti**
www.fondodemujeresbolivia.org.bo

**Fondo de Mujeres del Sur**
www.mujeresdelsur.org

**Fondo Lunaria Mujer**
www.fondolunaria.org

**Fonds Pour Les Femmes Congolaises**
www.ffcrdc.org

**FRIDA The Young Feminist Fund**
www.youngfeministfund.org

**Global Fund for Women**
www.globalfundforwomen.org

**Heart & Hand Fund**
www.heartandhandfund.org

**Her Fund**
www.herfund.org.hk/tc

**Jumuiya Women Fund**
www.jumuiyawomenfund.org

**Korea Foundation for Women**
www.womenfund.or.kr/124

**Mama Cash**
www.mamacash.org

**Mediterranean Women's Fund**
www.medwomensfund.org

**Mones-Mongolian Women's Fund**
www.mones.org.mn

**Pacific Feminist Fund**
www.pacificfeministforum.org

**Reconstruction Women's Fund**
www.rwfund.org/eng

**Semillas—Sociedad Mexicana por Derechos de la Mujer, A.C.**
www.semillas.org.mx

**Slovak-Czech Women's Fund**
www.womensfund.sk/en

**South Asia Women's Foundation India**
www.sawfindia.org

**Taso Foundation**
www.taso.org.ge

**Tewa for Women's Empowerment**
www.tewa.org.np

**The Equality Fund**
www.equalityfund.ca

**Ukrainian Women's Fund**
www.uwf.org.ua/en

**Urgent Action Fund—Africa**
www.uaf-africa.org

**Urgent Action Fund—Asia & Pacific**
www.uafanp.org

**Urgent Action Fund for Feminist Activism**
www.urgentactionfund.org

**VidaAfrolatina**
www.vidaafrolatina.org

**Women's Fund Armenia**
www.womenfundarmenia.org

**Women's Fund Asia**
www.womensfundasia.org

**Women's Fund Fiji**
www.womensfundfiji.org

**Women's Fund in Georgia**
www.womenfundgeorgia.org

**Women's Fund Tanzania - Trust**
https://wftrust.or.tz

**Women First International Fund**
www.womenfirstfund.org

**Women Win**
www.womenwin.org

**XOESE—The Francophone Women's Fund**
www.xoese.org/en/xoese-the-fund-for-francophone-women

## Women's *Funding Network*

The Women's Funding Network is a growing community of more than 120 women's funds, foundations, gender equity funders, allies, and individuals spanning 14 countries. Together, they create a community of practice that creates and evolves intersectional gender-lens approaches to philanthropy, for gender equality and justice across the globe.

To learn more, please visit: **www.wfn.org**

## List of Member Funds (listed alphabetically)

**A Fund for Women of the Madison Community Foundation**
www.madisongives.org/partners/a-fund-for-women

**Arizona Foundation for Women**
www.azfw.org

**Aurora Women and Girls Foundation**
www.aurorafoundation.org

**Australians Investing in Women**
https://aiiw.org.au

**Beekay Foundation**
https://beekayfoundation.com

**Beyond Our Borders**
www.wfco.org/beyond-our-borders

**Boston Women's Fund**
www.bostonwomensfund.org

**Bulgarian Fund for Women**
https://bgfundforwomen.org/en

**Canadian Women's Foundation**
https://canadianwomen.org

**Channel Foundation**
www.channelfoundation.org

**Chicago Foundation for Women**
www.cfw.org

**Collaborate Cleveland**
https://collabcle.org

**Delta Research and Educational Foundation**
www.deltafoundation.net

**Echidna Giving**
https://echidnagiving.org

**Eileen Fisher Foundation**

**Equality Fund**
www.equalityfund.ca

**Fairfield County's Community Foundation's Fund for Women & Girls**
www.fccfoundation.org/fund-for-women-girls

**Fondo Centroamericano de Mujeres—FCAM**
https://fondocentroamericano.org

**Fondo Semillas**
https://semillas.org.mx/en

**Fonds pour les Femmes Congolaises**
www.ffcrdc.org

**Frontline Women's Fund**
https://frontlinewomensfund.org

**Fundación de Mujeres en Puerto Rico**
www.fundacionmujerespuertorico.org

**Fundo Agbara**
https://fundoagbara.org.br

**Gender Justice Fund**
www.genderjusticephilly.org

**Girls Rights Project**
www.girlsrightsproject.com

**Global Fund for Women**
www.globalfundforwomen.org

**Grantmakers for Girls of Color**
www.grantmakersforgirlsofcolor.org

**Groundswell Fund**
https://groundswellfund.org

**I Be Black Girl**
www.ibeblackgirl.com

**Iowa Women's Foundation**
https://iawf.org

**Jeannette Rankin Women's Scholarship Fund**
https://rankinfoundation.org

**Kentucky Foundation for Women**
www.kfw.org

**Maine Women's Fund**
www.mainecf.org/initiatives-impact/maine-women-and-girls

**Metrowest Women's Fund**
www.metrowestwomensfund.com

**Mongolian Women's Fund**
https://mones.org.mn

**Ms. Foundation for Women**
https://forwomen.org

**National Organisation for Women in Sport Physical Activity and Recreation (NOWSPAR)**
www.nowspar.org

**New Hampshire Women's Foundation**
https://nhwomensfoundation.org

**NewMexicoWomen.org**
https://newmexicowomen.org

**Nurturing Wāhine Fund**
www.nurturingwahinefund.org

**Peggy and Jack Baskin Foundation**
https://baskinfoundation.org

**PRBB Foundation**
www.prbbfoundation.org

**Pro Mujer**
https://promujer.org

**Purposeful**
https://wearepurposeful.org

**Return to the Heart Foundation**
https://return2heart.org

**Rise Up**
https://riseuptogether.org

**Rockflower Partners**
www.rockflower.org/partners

**Shadhika**
https://shadhika.org

**Sojourner Foundation**
http://sojournerfoundation.org

**Texas Women's Foundation**
www.txwf.org

**The Ascend Fund**
www.theascendfund.org

**The Asia Foundation**
https://asiafoundation.org

**The Fund for Women and Girls**
www.thefundcc.org

**The New York Women's Foundation**
www.nywf.org

**The Women's Center for Economic Opportunity**
www.womensceo.org

**The Women's Foundation**
https://twfhk.org

**The Women's Foundation of Colorado**
www.wfco.org

**The Women's Fund Miami-Dade**
https://womensfundmiami.org

**The Women's Fund of Central Ohio**
www.womensfundcentralohio.org

**Unitarian Universalist Veatch Program at Shelter Rock**
https://uucsr.org/programs/veatch-program

**Urgent Action Fund for Feminist Activism**
https://urgentactionfund.org

**Valentine Foundation**
www.valentinefoundation.org

**Vermont Women's Fund**
www.vermontwomensfund.org

**Victorian Women's Trust**
www.vwt.org.au

**VidaAfrolatina**
www.vidaafrolatina.org

**WAKE: Women's Alliance for Knowledge Exchange**
www.wakeinternational.org

**Washington Area Women's Foundation**
https://thewomensfoundation.org

**WNY Women's Foundation**
https://wnywomensfoundation.org

**Women International Leaders of Greater Philadelphia**
www.wil-gp.org

**Women's Foundation California**
https://womensfoundca.org

**Women's Foundation for a Greater Memphis**
https://wfgm.org

**Women's Foundation for the State of Arizona**
www.womengiving.org

**Women's Foundation of Alabama**
https://wfalabama.org

**Women's Foundation of Arkansas**
http://womensfoundationarkansas.org

**Women's Foundation of Boston**
https://wfboston.org

**Women's Foundation of Collier County**
https://wfcollier.org

**Women's Foundation of Greater Saint Louis**
www.wfstl.org

**Women's Foundation of Minnesota**
www.wfmn.org

**Women's Foundation of Mississippi**
www.womensfoundationms.org

**Women's Foundation of Montana**
https://wfmontana.org

**Women's Foundation of Oregon**
https://womensfoundationoforegon.org

**Women's Foundation of the South**
http://womensfoundationsouth.org

**Women's Fund for the Fox Valley Region**
www.womensfundfvr.org

**Women's Fund of Central Indiana**
www.womensfund.org

**Women's Fund of East Tennessee**
www.womensfundetn.org

**Women's Fund of Essex County**
www.thewomensfundec.org/what-index

**Women's Fund of Greater Chattanooga**
www.chattanoogawomensfund.org

**Women's Fund of Greater Fort Wayne**
www.womensfundfw.org

**Women's Fund of Greater Milwaukee**
https://womensfundmke.org

**Women's Fund of Hawai'i**
https://womensfundhawaii.org

**Women's Fund of Omaha**
www.omahawomensfund.org

**Women's Fund of Rhode Island**
https://wfri.org

**Women's Fund of the Greater Cincinnati Foundation**
www.gcfdn.org/womensfund

**Women's Fund of Western Massachusetts**
www.mywomensfund.org

**Women's Fund SouthCoast**
https://womensfundsouthcoast.org

**WomenStrong International**
www.womenstrong.org

**Women Win**
www.womenwin.org

**Working for Women**
www.workingforwomen.org

**XOESE—Le Fonds pour Les Femmes Francophones**
https://xoese.org

# Glossary

**#BlackLivesMatter Movement:** In 2013, three radical Black organizers—Alicia Garza, Patrisse Cullors, and Opal Tometi—created a Black-centered political will and movement building project called #BlackLivesMatter. It was in response to the acquittal of Trayvon Martin's murderer, George Zimmerman, in the U.S. The project is now a member-led global network of more than 40 chapters. Its members organize and build local power to intervene in violence inflicted on Black communities by the state and vigilantes.

**Cisgender:** Term that denotes or relates to a person whose sense of personal identity and gender corresponds with the sex assigned to them at birth.

**Domestic Violence:** Acts of violence or abuse against a person living in the same household, typically involving the violent abuse of a spouse or partner.

**Feminist:** An advocate for equal social, political, legal, and economic rights for people of all genders. Feminism is rooted in the acknowledgment of patriarchal power structures.

**Gender:** Social and cultural codes (as opposed to biological sex) used to distinguish between what a society considers "masculine," "feminine," or "other" conduct. Gender is a person's experienced identity, falling anywhere on the binary spectrum of female or male, or beyond that binary. A person's gender is made up of both their internalized gender identity and external gender expression, in the understanding that those two can be the same but can also differ. Gender is a social construct in that, unlike sex, it is a product of society and culture.

**Gender-Based Violence:** Violence directed against a person because of their gender or sex. Gender-based violence can include sexual violence, sexual exploitation, sexual harassment, domestic violence, psychological abuse, harmful traditional practices, economic abuse, and gender-based discriminatory practices.

**Gender Equality:** The state of being equal, especially in status, rights, or opportunities.

**Gender Equity:** The quality of being fair, just, and impartial. Equity recognizes differences in circumstance and privilege and aims for justice and fairness while taking those into account.

**Gender Equality vs Equity:** Equality means each individual or group of people is given the same resources or opportunities. Equity recognizes that each person has different circumstances and allocates the exact resources and opportunities needed to reach an equal outcome. Gender equity is a means to achieve gender equality.

**Gender Expression:** An individual's external appearance and expression of their own gender identity. This may or may not conform to socially defined characteristics traditionally associated with being either masculine or feminine.

**Gender Identity:** A person's internal, deeply felt sense of being a man, woman, non-binary person, or other gender. It does not necessarily correspond to their sex assigned at birth.

**Giving Circle:** A form of participatory philanthropy by a group of individuals with shared values who form a voluntary association to donate their money or time to make a pooled gift.

**Intersectionality:** The interconnected nature of social categorizations such as race, class, and gender as they apply to an individual or group. An intersection of someone's identity can result in overlapping systems of discrimination or disadvantage. The term was first coined by feminist civil-rights scholar and activist Kimberlé Crenshaw in 1989.

**Intersex:** An umbrella term that refers to anyone born with variations in their physical sex characteristics that don't neatly fit into the binary sex categories of male and female.

**Kandakas** Women Sudanese protesters are referred to as "Kandaka," a title given to the Nubian queen of ancient Sudan reflecting a legacy of empowered women who fight for their country and their rights.

**LGBTQI+:** Acronym for lesbian, gay, bisexual, transgender, queer, intersex, and other identities. Used here as an inclusive term for groups and identities sometimes associated together as "sexual and gender minorities."

**#Mahsa Amini:** Mahsa Jina Amini was a young Iranian woman whose arrest in Tehran for standing against mandatory hijab and subsequent death in police custody sparked a wave of protests throughout Iran. Her death sparked widespread protest in Iranian society and acts of solidarity around the world. It also ignited the global Woman, Life, Freedom movement.

**#MeToo Movement:** Founded in 2006 by Tarana Burke to support survivors of sexual violence, particularly young women of color from low-wealth communities, to find pathways to healing. The movement's vision from the beginning has been to address both the dearth of resources for survivors of sexual violence and to build a robust community of advocates and allies. In October 2017, the movement went global as the #MeToo hashtag went viral and survivors across the world came forward about their experiences with sexual assault.

**Misogyny:** Sexual harassment, assault, abuse, hatred, dislike of, or contempt for women and perceived femininity. This ingrained and institutionalized prejudice manifests itself in various forms including but not limited to physical intimidation and abuse, sexual harassment and assault, and social shunning.

**Movement:** A movement is a set of people with a shared experience of injustice, who organize themselves to build their collective power and leadership, and develop a shared agenda for change, which they pursue through collective action, with some continuity over time.

**#NiaUnaMenos:** Spanish for "Not one [woman] less," this is a Latin American fourth-wave grassroots feminist movement, which started in Argentina and has spread across several Latin American countries, that campaigns against gender-based violence. This mass mobilization comes as a response to various systemic issues that proliferate violence against women. In its official website, Ni una menos defines itself as a "collective scream against machista violence." The campaign was started by a collective of Argentine female artists, journalists, and academics, and has grown into "a continental alliance of feminist forces."

**Non-binary:** A person who does not identify exclusively as a man or a woman. Non-binary people may identify as being both a man and a woman, somewhere in between, or as falling completely outside these categories.

**Patriarchy:** The oppressive system in society or government where power is held by cisgender men. The patriarchy is sustained through cultural norms and customs that favor cisgender men and withhold opportunities from other people.

**Racism:** A doctrine or teaching, without scientific support, that does three things: (1) claims to find racial differences in things like character and intelligence; (2) asserts the superiority of one race over another or others; (3) seeks to maintain that dominance through a complex system of beliefs, behaviors, use of language, and policies.

**Sex:** Classification of bodies and people (often at birth) as female, male, or other, based on biological factors such as external sex organs, internal sexual and reproductive organs, hormones, and chromosomes.

**Sex Worker:** An adult who regularly or occasionally receives money or goods in exchange for consensual sexual services.

**Sexual Violence:** Any sexual act, attempt to obtain a sexual act, or other act directed against a person's sexuality using coercion, by any person regardless of their relationship to the victim, in any setting.

**Social Justice:** A process, not an outcome, which (1) seeks fair (re)distribution of resources, opportunities, and responsibilities; (2) challenges the roots of oppression and injustice; (3) empowers all people to exercise self-determination and realize their full potential; and (4) builds social solidarity and community capacity for collaborative action.

**Systemic:** A descriptor for policies, practices, or sets of beliefs that have been established and accepted by the majority as being customary practices throughout a political, social, or economic system.

**Systemic Oppression:** Structurally burdening or placing cruel or unjust barriers on an individual or larger group. This is enacted by those in positions of authority or power, but also extends to all areas of society—in other words, anyone in a position of privilege can contribute to another person or group's oppression in a systematic manner.

**Trafficking:** The recruitment, transportation, transfer, harboring, or receipt of persons by means of the threat, or force, or other forms of coercion, of abduction or fraud, of deception, of the abuse of power or a position of vulnerability, or of the giving or receiving of payments or benefits to achieve the consent of a person having control over another person for the purpose of exploitation. (United Nations Protocol to Prevent, Suppress, and Punish Trafficking in Persons, especially Women and Children.)

**Transgender:** Referring to a person whose gender and personal identity does not correspond with their sex label assigned to them at birth.

**Trans Woman:** Someone who was male assigned at birth who identifies as a woman or on the feminine spectrum.

**Trust-Based Philanthropy:** An approach to giving that addresses the inherent power imbalances between funders, nonprofits, and the communities they serve.

**Women Human Rights Defenders:** Self-identified women and lesbian, bisexual, transgender, queer and intersex people, and others who defend rights and are subject to gender-specific risks and threats due to their human rights work and/or as a direct consequence of their gender identity or sexual orientation.

**Women's Funds and Foundations:** Public nonprofit organizations that are led and governed by people who identify as ciswomen, transwomen, and non-binary people, whose primary purpose is to challenge dominant power structures by moving money, power, and resources to organizations that are led by and advance the leadership and empowerment of marginalized genders, particularly marginalized genders from Black, Indigenous, and communities of color. (Women's Funding Network 2022 Landscape Study of Women's Funds and Foundations)

## Sources

www.hrw.org/report/2023/02/14/why-we-became-activists/violence-against-lesbian-bisexual-and-queer-women-and-non

www.neighborhoodfeminists.com/nf-glossary

https://icma.org/page/glossary-terms-race-equity-and-social-justice

https://creaworld.org/wp-content/uploads/2020/12/All-About-Movements_Web.pdf

www.awid.org/special-focus/women-human-rights-defenders

www.globalfundforwomen.org/movements/me-too

https://blacklivesmatter.com/herstory

https://en.wikipedia.org/wiki/Ni_una_menos

https://en.wikipedia.org/wiki/Mahsa_Amini

www.rstmh.org/news-blog/blog/kandakas-empowerment-and-a-vision-for-the-future-of-healthcare-in-sudan

For Product Safety Concerns and Information please contact our EU
representative  GPSR@taylorandfrancis.com
Taylor & Francis Verlag GmbH, Kaufingerstraße 24, 80331 München, Germany